DON'T
JUST
STAND
THERE!

DON'T
JUST
STAND
THERE!

by INEZ ROBB

DAVID McKAY COMPANY, Inc.

New York

DON'T JUST STAND THERE!

LIBRARY OF CONGRESS CATALOG CARD NUMBER: 62-14179

MANUFACTURED IN THE UNITED STATES OF AMERICA

VAN REES PRESS • NEW YORK

Dedicated to

A warm, gay and loving family of sturdy individualists
who sent me out into the world happy, well-adjusted
and competent to woo and win the only Basic Ingredient
in any woman's life, a Good Husband.

Foreword

FOR YEARS, I have been impressed with the fact that I am among the world's luckiest women—I get paid for my opinions.

Most women have to give theirs away—at home, at the supermarket, the club, the PTA or wherever. But editors, may their wondrous tribe increase, pay for mine. It is incredible. No one is more surprised than I, and pleased, too.

What follows is a range of those opinions, all mine. And paid for!

Acknowledgment

MUCH OF THE MATERIAL in this book originally appeared in the author's columns published from January, 1949, to October, 1953, by International News Service, and from then until the present by Scripps-Howard Newspapers and United Feature Syndicate. The author wishes to express her thanks to both publishers for their kindness in permitting her to use this material.

Contents

Paris of the West
(AND THE HAPPY PAST)

Since the nation soon will be in the throes of celebrating the sixtieth anniversary of powered flight, I would like to pay my respects to the Wright brothers of Kitty Hawk, who got that crate into the air for twelve seconds in 1903.

About twenty years later, they unknowingly got me into the air, too. I owe a good bit to both flights and to the Brothers Wright. In a manner of speaking, they conned me into the newspaper business for good.

The first newspaper story I ever wrote that rated a by-line was a result of my first flight in one of the machines they pioneered. After I saw that by-line, nothing—not even wild editors—could have separated me from the newspaper business.

A first by-line is on a par with a first drink: in either case the victim is doomed, the one to red ink and the other to printer's ink for life— or so they say.

Over thirty years ago (naturally, I was an infant prodigy) I was the combined society editor and proofreader of the *Evening Capital News,* now defunct, in Boise, Idaho. There wasn't sufficient society or proof in Boise to make a full-time job of either and I doubled in brass one summer, waiting for the school bell to ring.

Before it rang, along came the Idaho State Fair and a barnstormer flying what I subsequently learned was known to the aviation world as a flying coffin. He took daring citizens aloft for $5 a flight, a price that made aerial joyriding prohibitive for the society-proofreader.

However, the barnstormer dropped into the *News* office on the opening day of the fair to renew acquaintance with the sports editor.

Both had been members of the Lafayette Escadrille. The barnstormer had come to ask the old comrade-in-wings to go up for a free ride.

"Are you crazy?" countered the sports editor. "I am now a married man with two children and an installment due on the insurance."

The flier asked each man in the office to go for a ride and each disgracefully refused. Finally, no one was left but the society-proofreader.

"Would the little girl like to go?" the aviator asked facetiously. And although I was hurt that he could not see that I was a young lady, I grabbed my coat and hat and was out the door before he could change his mind.

We drove out to the fair grounds in a beat-up jalopy, and I was full of anxiety, all right. I was wearing a bright scarlet coat, and I was scared stiff that Mama and Papa and my aunts and uncles, all at the fair that day, would spot me before I could get into the air and out of their protective clutches.

To make a long story short, we made it. I was strapped into an open-cockpit plane and we roared into the wild blue yonder. The pilot was paid to thrill the crowd with stunts such as loops and fall-leaf dives, I think they were called, and heaven knows what.

You know what? I thought it was wonderful! That's youth for you. I wasn't scared or sick or even nervous. And when it was all over, I thanked the young man, scooted back to the *News* and wrote an account of my adventure. The story had a dreamy lead, even if I do say so over thirty years later—I wrote that the only way a lady could stand on her head with dignity and decorum was in a stunting plane.

Well, sir, the editor slapped a by-line on the story and the rest is history, at least for the Wright brothers, bless them.

🌼   🌼   🌼

Everything's up to date in Boise, and the proud residents of this garden city will thank the rest of the United States to keep that fact firmly in mind.

One of those effete Eastern magazines with a vast circulation some years ago offered this sophisticated community the ultimate insult by referring to it as "an outpost of the old Oregon Trail." The town cried for the blood of Robert de Roos, the author of this slander, and his editors. They would have done well to drop out of sight until the Vigilantes simmered down and dismantled the scaffold.

"Outpost of the old Oregon Trail," my eye—Boise has long been known among connoisseurs of fine living as the Paris of the West. It is a well-known historic fact that the first mess of crepes suzette lighted west of the Mississippi was fired here in the winter of 1861 when an old prospector accidentally dropped a half bottle of brandy into the skillet as he turned his morning flapjacks.

His only comment, which fortunately has been saved for posterity, was "Damndest fire you ever saw; damndest flapjacks I ever et."

This metropolis of 34,481 has as much champagne, servant trouble, traffic headaches, gout, divorce, mortgage money, women's clubs, high-stake bridge, poker and canasta, culture, golf and general low living and high thinking per capita as New York, Boston, San Francisco and New Orleans combined.

An outpost of the old Oregon Trail, indeed—it is true, all right, that a lot of citizens of both sexes still wear Levi's in this region, but they are all custom made. And the general run of ten-gallon hats invariably wear the labels of Cavanagh or Sally Victor.

This is a cosmopolis whose department stores regularly stock the wares of Dior, Mainbocher, Hattie Carnegie, Jane Derby, Ceil Chapman, Mollie Parnis, Ben Zuckerman and Esther Dorothy. The city fathers are all by Brooks Brothers out of *Esquire*.

A heady aroma, a blend of Chanel No. 5 and twelve-year-old Scotch, hangs over any cocktail party. And even tiny children cope gracefully with artichokes, lobster and petits pois.

The last old-timer who mistook caviar for buckshot departed this life suddenly at a New Year's reception in 1873, and was given decent burial.

This is a city with station-wagon and country-club sets, and such a rich, varied and constant social life that after any ten-day visit in my old home town I am forced to retire to New York City to recuperate.

I lead a quiet, nine-o'clock life in New York, browsing among my books and my geraniums. My annual visit to Boise, a city which produces in its homes some of the finest cuisine in the world, affords such intimate acquaintance with the fleshpots and late hours that I flee back to New York to rest up for my next bout with Boise and its urbane citizenry.

Outpost of the old Oregon Trail semicolon Boise is one of the most beautiful towns in America, a gem nestled at the towering foothills of the Sawtooths. The Boise River flows through the city like the Seine through Paris, its banks a continuous park.

An outpost, huh? We got an art museum, a historical museum, the handsomest railroad depot in the U.S.A., one of the biggest airports, and a junior college that imports football players just as any Eastern school.

An outpost, Bob? Kindly step outside and fight like a man semicolon to semicolon.

Some years ago, I flew to Boise in a six-engine panic. My Aunt Nell, who had a firm hand in raising me (children may be reared elsewhere, but they're still raised in Idaho), had fallen on a slippery floor and crushed the ninth vertebra of her small, straight back.

She was a good bit nearer eighty than seventy at the time and the broken back scared the living daylights out of everyone except Aunt Nell.

"I have no intention of dying," she said crossly, "so don't go round acting as if I were!"

Within ten days after the accident, she was able to take a few steps in a brace. And three weeks later, when I left, she was actually able to walk down the porch steps into the yard, although she looked so frail it tore the heart out of one.

"I would rather have one good year on my feet than ten in a wheel chair," she said firmly to the young doctor, who was inclined to be awed by her fortitude.

Later, she liked to muse on the attitude of the young curate who came to call immediately in behalf of the bishop of whose cathedral she had been prop and pillar for years.

"I'm afraid I shocked him," she said demurely. And I'm afraid she did, too.

In his effort to console her, the young cleric said undoubtedly our Heavenly Father knows best; when we are active beyond our years he finds a means of slowing us up.

"Yes," agreed my aunt, "but I do wish He had put on the brakes before I hit the floor."

This report is simply to say that Aunt Nell threw the brace away six months later, and soon was going up and down stairs a half-dozen times a day, weeding her flower garden, baking the most marvelous biscuits in town, presiding over a big house through which guests flowed like water, playing a fast game of bridge, arguing about politics and waiting for her younger son to come home from Korea.

"And then I may visit you, dear," she said to me one day, "but for goodness' sake, don't plan any trips to Grant's Tomb or the United Nations. I want to go to the Stork Club."

The nieces and nephews who have come home to visit Aunt Nell and Aunt Kit over the years have always spent half their time panting in the wake of these two remarkable women, trying to keep up with them mentally and physically.

Only ten years ago, the family finally persuaded Aunt Kit, then seventy-seven, and younger by a year than Aunt Nell, to give up the chairmanship of the Production Committee of the Nampa Red Cross which she held for years. During that time this chapter produced more goods than any chapter of similar size.

It also got her to give up managing the Grace Church dinners, which were her special pride for years. She once said she would lay down her apron if Aunt Nell with her broken back would cease and desist from presiding over the cathedral's annual plum pudding sale, which she headed to my certain knowledge for thirty years.

Of course, one of the biggest problems was to keep Aunt Kit from picking the cherries in her garden, so crammed with flowers it is one of the town sights. Finally, someone hit upon the plea that it wasn't dignified for a woman of her age to be scrambling around in trees, and that did the trick.

In their seventies and eighties they both managed to be chic, modish, gay, witty, savage at canasta and more fun to be with than any other two people I have ever met. They came home from a shopping trip in high fettle one day. They'd bought a maternity dress for one of my cousins, and the salesgirl had shown obvious amazement at the request and had looked at them too carefully.

"My dear, the age of miracles is past," said my Aunt Kit, firmly to the poor girl. "The dress is not for us."

※ ※ ※

"You came through Laramie on the way home, didn't you?" asked Aunt Kit. "But I guess you can't see the old fort from the train windows," she added.

"Well, it wouldn't be like it was when Uncle Will tried to give himself up for murder, anyway," Aunt Nell said. "That was in 1865."

"For heaven's sake, sit down," I said to my two remarkable aunts, "and quit talking in riddles. Whose Uncle Will," I asked, "and what murder?"

My goodness, they said, didn't you ever hear about Uncle Will— your great-uncle—and the time he killed the Union soldier (Grandma didn't name them Kittie Lee and Nellie Virginia for naught!) when he tried to ride across the tablecloth?

Why! It's in two or three books, they said accusingly, as if I had been wasting my time on dime novels.

Uncle Will, they said, was Grandpa Callaway's youngest brother, a dear man but quite vain of his small feet.

My great-grandmother, Cathryn Markham Callaway, at the age of seventy-five developed a determination to visit her two older sons. They were my grandfather and my great-uncle John, who had come to Idaho in the gold rush of 1861. So, with her son Will, and two Negro servants, the indomitable old lady started across the plains by covered wagon from Missouri.

("When your Great-Grandfather Callaway married her in Virginia, he discovered she'd never done a lick of work in her life," Aunt Nell said. "So he bought slaves for her in self-defense. He'd have starved otherwise.")

Most people who came West by covered wagon came to stay, such were the hardships of the journey. But Great-Grandma had come to visit, and after spending the winter with her sons, she headed East again undaunted by her age or the dangers of the trail. Uncle Will and the two servants again accompanied her.

Somewhere in Wyoming not far from Fort Laramie, the little caravan stopped for midday dinner on the return journey. A white cloth had been spread on the ground and the food laid out when a small band of soldiers on scout duty galloped into camp. One of the soldiers, angered probably by the sight of Great-Grandma and her entourage, spurred his horse and galloped for the white cloth.

Great-Uncle Will grabbed his rifle. But the cavalryman, saber swinging, rode on and as he reached the tablecloth, slashed Great-Uncle Will across the face and nearly scooped out one of his eyes.

But even with one eye gone, Great-Uncle Will was a Dead-eye Dick. He killed the soldier with one shot.

The young lieutenant in charge of the scouting party ordered Uncle Will to proceed to Fort Laramie, without guard, and there give himself up for murder. So Great-Grandma, Great-Uncle Will, his head in bandages, and the two servants, trekked to Laramie.

"No one accompanied them, but Uncle Will had given his word to the Union lieutenant," Aunt Kit explained.

The commandant at Fort Laramie showed a surprising lack of interest in Great-Uncle Will when he showed up and insisted on being arrested for murder. He ordered Uncle Will to go on to Fort Kearney, Nebraska, and give himself up at that army post. So the little group, still without guard, set out for Fort Kearney. There Great-Uncle Will again tried to get himself arrested for murder, and again the commandant was not interested. He finally dismissed the case, and told Great-Uncle Will to go away and not bother him any more.

But Great-Grandma and Great-Uncle Will liked the look of Nebraska and stayed there to found the town of Callaway.

But don't think Great-Grandma settled down for good! When she was ninety-eight, she went to California with Great-Uncle Will and his wife. By this time the railroad went part way, and she finished the journey by ship. But she always said there was nothing like the covered wagon!

{♣} {♣} {♣}

In recent years it has been the fashion in fiction to write thousand-page novels about families whose members hate each other like poison.

In these sagas Aunt Lizzie poisons her sister to get Grandma's diamonds and Cousin Curtis destroys his sister's happy home and robs the till on the way out.

"Maybe the reason we are all so happy together is because your grandma had no diamonds," Aunt Nell said in the midst of a family reunion I love to recall.

Whatever the reason, our family has always had a high old time when it gets together. This family gathering wasn't a big one as such things go. But Uncle Frank was there from California. My pretty cousin, Juanita Hedden, was home after two years in Brazil. My cousins Joey and Jack Love and their little boys drove over from Medford, Oregon, and I thumbed my way from New York.

I can't ever remember a time when we didn't love being together. We apparently grew up under the novel impression that families were meant to love each other and have acted on that assumption ever since.

Reunions in this family seem dedicated to two paramount activities: eating and talking.

This is a talented family. Every one of us can and does talk at once and still understands the parties of the second part. That is a big help and timesaver, as we have a great deal of family gossip to exchange. We had, for example, to find out how Uncle Frank was doing with the ponies.

"Brother Frank is like me," said Aunt Nell, seventy-nine. "I have very few vices and I refuse to give them up at my age."

It is hardly fair to say that Aunt Nell took up gambling in her latter years without adding the extenuating circumstances. She drove to California and back that spring to visit her son, Lt. Col. Frank Sinsel, and won the $150 bingo jackpot at the Officers' Club at Fort Ord.

Aunt Nell, the one who had scared us all to death two years before by falling and crushing her ninth vertebra, had been miffed at me when I first got home.

"You wrote recently that I was eighty," she said accusingly, "and I am only seventy-nine. You will discover there's a great difference when you are my age."

"It made me a year older, too," Aunt Kit, a lass of seventy-eight, added. "Everyone in town knows I'm a year younger than Nellie."

After ten days of reunion, the younger members of the family were almost exhausted trying to keep up with this trio, who all remembered being taken to the fort when Indians rampaged through the Boise Valley more than seventy-years ago.

The aunts stuffed us with mounds of fried chicken, cream gravy, corn on the cob, mountain trout, elk steaks, hot rolls, salt-rising bread, huckleberry and lemon pies, cakes and cookies in variety and ice cream to taste.

We all wound up bulging in the wrong spots—and making plans for the next reunion. These fiction fellows ought to get hep to the fact that life can be beautiful for families, too.

I haven't picked up a long-hair publication in the past ten years that hasn't had a polysyllabic piece about geriatrics. The doctors and the scientists have been making a mint of money out of this subject ever since man began to live longer and have less to do.

There has been a good bit of head shaking over what to do with the old folks, particularly if they show fight.

Well, I think the scientists and the medical men might like to take a good look at my favorite case history, my Uncle Frank, and study his solution to this pressing problem. Of course, one thing that may baffle the M.D.'s and the Ph.D's is that Uncle Frank didn't know he was old, although he lived some eighty-three years. And it was confusing, for he looked, acted and thought a good twenty years his own junior.

Uncle Frank's first love, always and forever, was horses. So when it came time for him to solve the problem of how to live with himself and like it in his old age, Uncle Frank up and bought himself a small racing stable. The result was that in his declining years he positively refused to decline—and was a problem to no one, including himself. He was, we all suspected, having the time of his life. "My sunset years may not be exactly gaudy," he used to say, "but they aren't exactly drab either."

Uncle Frank came to town one day from Bay Meadows, a race track not far from San Francisco, to take his visiting niece to luncheon. He could spare the time from the track since none of his three horses were racing that day. And no woman ever had a handsomer escort than this gentleman with his thick white hair, his immaculate linen, his beige slacks and his tailor-made sports jacket.

It was this way, Uncle Frank said: When Aunt Minnie died, he was almost seventy. Their children were grown and had homes and families of their own. And the big cattle ranch in Nevada seemed mighty lonely. He'd been on the state Livestock Commission for years, but it wasn't any fun going to the meetings in Reno without Aunt Minnie.

So he sold out, lock, stock and saddles. And he whacked up the money between three or four banks. Then he bought himself a de luxe trailer and a few race horses.

"Well, everyone said, 'There's no fool like an old fool,' " Uncle

Frank said as we dug into the bourbon and the boeuf à la mode. "They kept saying I wouldn't have a penny left inside of eighteen months.

"But," he said proudly, "I've never touched a penny of the money I banked the day I sold the ranch and the cattle."

He followed the sun through the Southwest and the West, racing his little stable where the sun was warm. The trailer was his home. I never knew a Callaway woman who couldn't cook or a Callaway man who could, but Uncle Frank reversed the field. He took up cooking along with horse racing, and his reputation as a chef among racing people began to equal that of the late Oscar of the Waldorf. He even gave banquets in the trailer.

"Of course, this isn't the first time I've owned race horses," Uncle Frank said. "Before you were born, I kind of inched away from home in my teens and managed to buy a race horse that was famous throughout the West.

"I guess you know that your grandfather Asbill's ranch up in Lake County, California, was right next to Lily Langtry's. Anyway, I saved enough money to buy a colt from the Jersey Lily. It was a colt named Quicksilver that eventually beat almost everything on four legs, before I went into the cattle business myself."

Uncle Frank looked kinda dreamy.

"Yes, sir, there was a woman, the Jersey Lily," he said. "First lady I ever saw ride astride. When she used to ride to town, all the women went indoors and pulled down the blinds. And all the men came outdoors and put down stakes. Fair enough, I always felt."

Anyone in the audience want to ask any questions about geriatrics, horse racing or Lily Langtry?"

🌼   🌼   🌼

When the dog days come I have a private formula (combining the best phases of judo and the blackjack) for dealing with pests who compound the felony by asking, "Hot enough for you?" As the city's midsummer sun beats down, newspapers only add to my adult discomfort when they run those pictures of children frolicking in the Niagara of cold water that gushes from fire hydrants.

When I was growing up in a small Idaho town, hydrants were nonexistent. But we small fry were not without our comforts. First, there was the water wagon, now virtually disappeared from American life. Let's hope a few of these horse-drawn vehicles have wound up in museums.

The water wagon circumnavigated Caldwell twice a day, and its peregrinations were terribly important to children and housewives. Kids followed the white, barrel-shaped wagon as if it were a latter-day Pied Piper. They danced in and out of its gentle waterfall, as the horses jogged along. The kids' bare feet shuffled in the little puddles of water that optimistic city fathers and hopeful housewives believed would settle the midsummer dust.

Alas, Mama was trying to bring me up to be a lady. I was not allowed to run after the water wagon; Mama said it wasn't ladylike. But once virtue faltered and I followed the wagon.

Ah, it was delicious! The cold water sprayed over me and my pinafore in a lovely cascade. I looked like a drowned rat when I got home, and Mama sent me to bed without my supper!

My boy cousins, in their overalls, were allowed to frolic after the wagon. They didn't have to learn to be ladies. The idea that I, too, might have been put in a pair of overalls and allowed to play in the spray never occurred to the grown-up ladies in the family. The idea of a little girl in overalls was unthinkable. (Now you should see their granddaughters! Yet it seems fairly certain they will turn out to be ladies, despite their addiction to blue jeans.)

If children watched for the water wagon, so did their mothers. Like hawks! Good housewives all, they fought the dust all summer long. The ladies wanted that dust settled, laid and disciplined. Woe to the skipper if the wagon missed the matinee performance. If so, indignant housewives phoned the city hall in droves.

Now Caldwell has miles of pavements and a huge municipal swimming pool for its kids, where they all learn to swim. And none of them would recognize a water wagon if one of the old relics came up and bit him. That's progress and as it should be.

But the old water wagon—well, it was fun, too.

The refrigerator is a marvelous invention, but it is no substitute for the family dining table, a forthright sentiment expressed by the ladies of the American Legion Auxiliary and one in which I concur at least 1,000 per cent.

The ladies feel that a lot of juvenile delinquency, one of the nation's most pressing problems, stems from the shocking fact that kids now snatch a meal from the refrigerator, instead of the family table, before dashing off to mug old ladies, rob the corner service station or heist a candy store.

"Children need the love which can best be radiated around the dinner table when the family comes together at the end of the day," say these ladies. Amen, say I.

When I think back on my happy childhood, no part of it is more radiant than the lovely, shining hour at the dining table to which every member of the family, both great and small, looked forward at the end of the day. I have always thanked God that we were either too poor or too unfashionable (and it may have been a combination of both) to eat anywhere but at a common dining board.

In the morning we ate our pancakes or waffles or hot biscuits around a community table in the big, bright kitchen. And in the evening we gathered around the dining-room table, always covered with snowy damask and set with shining silver.

As a child it was the hour I lived for, whether I was home with Mama and Papa, or visiting the aunts and uncles. Papa or one of the uncles sat at the head of the table, and Mama or one of the aunts at the foot, and we kids ranged on each side. And what conversation! It flowed sixteen to the dozen. The grownups were interested in everything: politics, books, bridge, pinochle, the newest Caruso record for the victrola and—in us.

We children soaked up a liberal education at those family dinner tables. We had to. If we wanted to take part in the conversation—and we certainly did—we had to make sense or at least ask questions that made sense. That was a *rule*.

In between the diagnosis of politics and Aunt Kit's grand slam in spades we children were encouraged to tell what had happened in school that day. And if we had been naughty and punished in school we got more of same at home. No adult went to the school to raise Cain because a teacher had disciplined us. That's what teachers were for.

If I may say so who shouldn't, we grew up with excellent table manners, for the simple reason that the adults wouldn't stand for sloppy eating. After I came to New York I was exposed to friends who had never eaten with their parents. Heaven forbid! They ate with nurses or governesses, and without exception their manners were execrable.

As children in Idaho none of us knew we were supposed, psychologically, to hate our parents. We had never heard of a sibling complex.

Refrigerator eating? We had never heard of it, either. And to further augment the arguments of the American Legion Auxiliary for the return of the family dining table, I'll say this: None of us ever turned out to be juvenile delinquents.

ॐ   ॐ   ॐ

When I looked at the poor, burned acres of New Jersey this past summer, brown as if a fire had swept them, I thought nostalgically of Idaho and her irrigated lands.

I was almost grown before I realized that in some parts of the world people actually depend upon rainfall rather than irrigation to provide the essential moisture for farming, lawns, gardens and flowers. We would have endured an almost perpetual drought in the Boise Valley if we had depended on rain. Often rain just didn't happen in the valley from early spring until early winter.

In those days there was something in Idaho known as "dry farming" in regions where no irrigation district or water was available. But this was regarded in the same light as we now view Russian roulette. You really had to be a mite tetched to try it. On the whole, the valley was beautiful and green throughout the growing season. Wherever irrigation watered the arid lands, the desert literally bloomed as a rose.

We lived on the edge of Caldwell, on a two-acre plot, a miniature farm that was part of the original acreage homesteaded by my Grandfather Callaway almost ninety years ago. He had helped form and build the irrigation district that brought life to that part of the valley. As a result, our family had "perpetual water rights." That meant we could "turn on" the water any time we wished, although my father never did.

Thursday night was our night "to use" the water—these old irrigation terms are as firmly fixed in my mind as the Ten Commandments. As he came home from work on Thursday evenings, Papa would stop at the headgate on the main irrigation ditch, open it (pull it out) and the water would flow through the ditch to our place.

By the time we had dinner and the dishes were washed, the lawn and the garden were flooded to a depth of four to six inches. Now Papa took off his shoes, and rolled up his trouser legs, the better to direct the waters in a way that would have made Canute green with envy.

This was the treat I awaited from week to week: I was allowed to strip down to my Ferris waist and panties and romp in the cold water that formed a shallow lake over the lawn. Even Mama—so tall, pretty and dignified—could not resist the lure of the water. Once it was dark, she, too, took off her shoes and stockings, held her skirts ankle high and went wading with Papa and me.

Sometimes Papa "cut off" the water (returned the headgate) at midnight; sometimes he cut it off when he went to work the next morning.

But in the interim, the yard and the garden had been thoroughly saturated. No matter how the sun seared us at midday during the coming week, the garden, lawn and flowers were safe. Ours was a miniature operation compared with the farms in the district. How green was our valley!

Many a time in the years since, when the summer heat of New York has cruelly badgered nearby farmland, I have not longed for the seashore, or mountain lakes or the old swimming hole in Indian Creek or even the suburban swimming pool.

No, I have only to close my eyes, and it is Thursday night again. The cold water from the irrigation ditch is flowing over the lawn and lapping at my ankles. In another ten minutes it will be dusk, and Mama will leave the screen porch to join Papa and me on the lawn.

🏵️ 🏵️ 🏵️

The other day I picked up a New York newspaper and read a headline and story that only a metropolitan editor and gazette would classify as news.

"Garlic Milk Irks Londoners," read the headline. The lead on the story began: "South Londoners complained that the milk they poured in their coffee and tea yesterday was flavored by garlic."

To think that the paper paid cable tolls on that item! Anyone born and raised west of the Hudson River could have told the citified editor that garlic- or onion-flavored milk is standard operating procedure in spring the world around. It isn't news—it's Bossy's spring fling.

Just as certainly as March winds and April showers produce May flowers, just as certainly as a young man's fancy lightly turns to thoughts of, just as surely as the reappearance of the robin and of grass, there is going to be a fortnight in spring when milk takes on the morbid flavor of wild onions and wild garlic. That taste is one of its harbingers.

Within the lifetime of many of us, man has flown faster than sound, extracted the secrets of the atom, sent his own satellites into space and invented electronic brains.

But he has had absolutely no luck at all with some of life's more profound problems, such as teaching old Bossy, when she is first turned out to pasture in the spring, to eschew succulent shoots of wild onion and garlic that dot the "meadow trim with daisies pied."

If anything, milk cows take spring harder even than college students, although, in defense of cows, I have never heard of one involved in a panty raid or a stampede to crowd into a telephone booth. After a long winter of hay and silage, it is useless to expect Bossy to ignore inviting tufts of emerald green onion and garlic.

In all the springs of my childhood, we wrestled in the Boise Valley with milk redolent of garlic or onion the minute the Jersey cow was turned out to pasture. They were delicacies she could not resist, like a woman on a diet confronted by a chocolate bar.

The thick yellow cream that gathered on the milk was contaminated. Papa couldn't abide it on the hot oatmeal. For a fortnight, Mama abandoned making her justly famous opera cream cake with whipped cream filling. None of us had even seen an opera, but we felt it shouldn't be garlic-flavored just the same.

And for a fortnight, until the Jersey settled down to eat the meadow grass, I was let off one of my household chores, the churning. It was the only part of the onion-garlic fiasco I enjoyed. The old wooden churn stood idle (it wasn't until I was almost grown that Mama bought a newfangled glass one with a handle that turned) until the Jersey came to her senses, got off the onion-garlic kick and we could once more enjoy her output.

In the interim, Mama solved the problem in the way her mother had solved it, and in the way I always presumed everyone solved it. Mama fed the Jersey's entire output to the chickens and the pig. Apparently, they had neither taste buds nor taste, and what we humans couldn't abide they consumed with relish.

Later, when the chickens reached the frying pan and the pig the smokehouse, they were uncontaminated by their fortnight of rolling in clover, a fortnight of yellow-rich Jersey milk.

Someday, maybe, man will conquer the common cold and discover a way to keep milk cows out of the wild onions and garlic in spring. But until he does, there really isn't a genuine headline in either.

Ever hung a May basket on a door? This question may expose my ignorance, but I wonder if children in America's small towns still enjoy the excitement of making, decorating and hanging May baskets as they did when I was a moppet?

Since I have lived in New York, I have never seen a May basket. But then it would be difficult for children who ride apartment-house elevators, especially those self-operating monsters, to hang May baskets on an apartment door.

Again, with flowers a luxury item in New York City, where would they get the flowers to fill the top of the baskets, after the bottom had been stuffed with homemade candies, cookies and other goodies?

When I was a child, I had only to step out the back door to gather an armload of apple blossoms, or snowy drifts of pear and cherry blooms and the warm pink of the peach trees. Or I walked across the road in front of the house where multitudes of little May flowers made a dazzling, multi-hued carpet under the gray-green sagebrush.

Flowers were a last-minute addition to the May baskets that had been in process of creation for a fortnight before May first, when we kids traditionally tiptoed around the neighborhood at dusk to leave our May offering on the front porch, push the bell and run as fast as fat legs would take us.

Children saved strawberry and small cardboard boxes from year to year, to use as a base for May baskets.

With colored crepe and tissue papers, dull scissors and enough glue and paste to drive our mothers crazy, we devoted the last two weeks of April to a frenzy of decorating. My, what works of art I felt I had created by April 30!

In the interim, Mama, Grandma and Aunt Nell and Aunt Kit were cajoled into making candies, cookies and little cakes to fill my masterpieces. I had to keep up with the little Jones girls on the right of us.

Well Mama, Grandma and the aunts never let me down, and my May offerings would have done a French *pâtisserie* proud. Only at the last minute, preferably when Papa was looking the other way and unaware of the depredations among his beloved fruit trees, I went out and picked the flowers that crowned these artistic and culinary masterpieces.

Then came the excitement of delivering them, the stealthy ascent of porch steps, hanging the basket on the door knob and praying the homemade handle would hold, and then the most exciting moment of all: the quick job of the doorbell and the hurried scamper off the porch, with heart pounding in rhythm with feet and flailing arms and legs.

What fun it was, when the last basket had been delivered, to go home and discover how many and what treasures had been left on my own doorstep.

Maybe this custom still exists some place. Or maybe it perished with the Age of Innocence. I hope not, but I must be sensible enough to realize that a May basket would offer small competition in a world of space ships, atomic-ray disintegrator guns, debutante dolls (i.e., they can drink) and moppet makeup kits. It would probably be small stuff to small fry of the Soaring Sixties.

❀ ❀ ❀

President Truman looked spruce and proud the day he told the ladies of the Defense Advisory Committee on Women in the Armed Services about his Grandma Young routing a whole band of Indians out in Western Missouri in the Wagon Wheel days.

The story may not have won Mr. Truman any appreciable number of votes, but it's sure and certain that it struck a kindred spark in every household west of the Mississippi.

As a western woman, it used to be a matter of considerable chagrin to me that my grandmothers had left the shootin' irons to the men in the family.

Grandpa Asbill sort of made up for it by owning an Indian reservation in California and Grandpa Callaway enabled me to look folks in the eye by his inclusion in the select group of men in Idaho credited with dispatching to the Happy Hunting Ground the last Indian chieftain to raid the Boise Valley.

By the time I was grown, descendants of three or four other pioneer Idaho families also claimed that it was their grandpa who dispatched the marauding chieftain, known as Bigfoot, for the logical reason that his feet were heap big by any standard.

Unfortunately, Grandpa Callaway died shortly before I was born, so I never heard the thrilling account of Bigfoot's demise first hand. But even when I was growing up in Idaho, Bigfoot was not a man of good repute, even though he had been dead for many years. Old-timers remembered him with a shudder.

I liked President Truman's story of Grandma Young who had red hair and who got sick and tired of the Indians messing around the homestead. Grandma Young lost her temper one day when the Indians seemed menacing and set the dogs, two big shepherds, on them. Well, that's a woman's way: direct action every time.

But Bigfoot was not so obliging. He didn't hang around the settlements—just made forays against them. So Grandpa Callaway and a few other men in the Boise Valley finally set out to track down Bigfoot once and for all. Naturally, we Callaways all think Grandpa was the man who finally turned the trick. And the story in our family has Grandpa, as talented an Indian scout as ever lived, trailing Bigfoot as deftly and silently as his shadow.

Grandpa, by all the signs and portents known to mountain men, was certain that he was not only on Bigfoot's trail but almost on his heels. But when the end came, even Grandpa was surprised—according to the Callaway family legend. Grandpa snaked himself behind a fallen log, one of the dead giants of the forest, so silently that not even his adversary on the other side of the log heard the white man.

When Bigfoot cautiously raised his head for reconnaissance, no one was more surprised than Grandpa, except possibly Bigfoot. Or maybe the Indian never knew what hit him. Because Grandpa, whose reflexes were a caution, never took time to load his gun. He swung it instantly by the barrel, hit Bigfoot with the stock and that was the last of the Indian warrior.

Anyway, that's our family story. Grandpa's rifle with a big notch for Bigfoot is in the Idaho Historical Museum—or it was the last time I visited the place. I hope, for history's sake, that there's a lock of Grandma Young's red hair in the Missouri Museum, too.

When the annual National Antiques Show was held in Madison Square Garden it was not the genuine Chippendale wormholes or the authentic ham-on-rye Sandwich glass that held me spellbound. I was prepared to be enraptured by Duncan Phyfe and Paul Revere, not by three feet of cinnamon-brown plush bear.

But it was the plush bear that enthralled me, and a genuine antique he was, too, fully worthy of consorting with Chippendale and the Adam brothers. For here was the original Teddy bear, made and named in honor of President Teddy Roosevelt, in 1903—the original of all the Teddy bears that have delighted children in every intervening year. Even in the atomic age, some things are eternal and the Teddy bear is one of them. He is as beloved today as he was almost sixty years ago.

When I unexpectedly confronted the original Teddy bear in the Garden, I sat down and had a good sentimental cry on the shoulder of Ben Michtom, whose father made the first Teddy bear. The story of that first cuddly plush bear and what happened subsequently to the Michtoms is another American success story par excellence, and one that brings back some nostalgic memories of my own childhood.

It all came about, Ben said, when the President went bear hunting in Mississippi in 1902. After T.R. killed a bear, he discovered a lone cub near her. The President quickly put up his hand, lest anyone in the group shoot the little bear. With the Presidential party was Clifford Berryman, then the famous cartoonist of the Washington, D.C. *Star*.

Berryman immortalized the Presidential gesture in a cartoon that appeared in the *Star* on November 18, 1902. The late Morris Michtom, father of Ben, owned a tiny toy shop in Brooklyn (the family lived in the rear of the store). The elder Michtom was delighted by the cartoon, which literally swept the country. He got his wife to make up a cuddly little bear, which he sent to the President with a letter asking T.R.'s permission to make and market it as "Teddy's Bear."

President Roosevelt replied, in longhand, that he didn't see how his name could help sell a toy, but he'd be glad to lend it anyway. So Michtom made a few more bear cubs, put them in the window with a picture of T.R. and accidentally founded a family business that today operates a toy factory on Long Island employing 3,000 persons.

Since February, 1903, when the apostrophe was dropped and the Teddy bear became a universal and steady favorite, Ben Michtom estimates that the family firm, The Ideal Toy Corporation, has sold 175,000,000 of these beloved toy animals. The corporation racks up a $35,000,000 business annually, of which the durable Teddy bear accounts for $1,000,000.

Small wonder! What adult, who has grown to maturity since 1903, has not loved a Teddy bear? Of all the toys I owned, Teddy, as he was always called in our home, is the only one I remember right down to his bright, shoe-button eyes. Santa Claus brought him to me the Christmas I was six. He was eighteen inches of soft, golden-brown plush with paws of beige felt. I loved him by day and by night.

After I had carried him every place for years, my sister, Cathryn, inherited him. Her passion for Teddy equaled mine. Finally, he came into the possession of my brother Stephen who cherished Teddy as dearly as had his two sisters. By the time Stephen was three or four, Teddy had begun to look like a picked chicken. The golden-brown plush was threadbare, and he had been hugged until he was limp. Somewhere in the line of succession, Grandma Callaway had replaced Teddy's worn felt paws with scraps of bright red flannel.

It was a long time before I realized that my Teddy had been christened for a man who was President of the United States. I always thought he had been named for my Uncle Ted Hedden, a man who found time to festoon the shrubs and small fruit trees in his garden with lollipops and gumdrops when his small nieces and nephews came to visit.

The sight of that first Teddy bear at Madison Square Garden turned time backward in its flight for me. It brought into sad focus the last time I saw my own bear. My sister, my brother and I were grown, when Papa died. He had a trunk into which, through a lifetime, he had put and guarded such cherished treasures as our report cards, the first childish letters we had written him, Valentines, a May basket, the bookmarks we girls had cross-stitched and the letter opener Stephen had whittled.

In the years since the three of us played with Teddy, we naturally assumed that the little bear had finally gone the way of all old toys. But in the middle layer of Papa's trunk, wrapped in tissue paper and an old silk scarf, was Teddy, worn and battered but treasured by my father to the end.

🌑 🌑 🌑

The biggest fish story in Caldwell, Idaho, is a whopper. It has the added novelty of being true.

When I was in grade school in Caldwell, the pretty girl who lived three blocks up the street from our house liked to fish. This is a common failing in both men and women in a state where trout streams are never very far away, and any fish under twelve inches is regarded as a fingerling.

Since like attracts like, Ruth Miller, our heroine, eventually married a neighbor boy, Glen L. Evans, who was also crazy about fishing. Just for fun one day in 1932 Ruth decided to try her hand at tying a few trout flies for her bridegroom.

The young Evanses came home from their next fishing expedition loaded with trout. Word got around town that fish were mad for Ruth's flies. Friends began asking her to whip up a few of those surefire flies for them.

That was the beginning of a fish-fly factory (try that over on your larynx for size after two sarsaparillas!) that today employs 225 Caldwell citizens and does an annual gross business in excess of a million dollars.

"It began as a hobby," said Ruth as we stood in the middle of the bustling factory. From that slender beginning, Ruth went on to become one of the chief designers of fresh-water fishing tackle in the United States as well as production manager of the factory. Although she retired from both positions five years ago, Ruth is still a director of the company.

Success is where you find it in the U.S.A., and Ruth and Glen found it at home in a town of 15,000 persons. Their factory produces the Glen L. Evans brand tackle, known to fishermen throughout this hemisphere. Furthermore, it is one of the largest plants of its kind in the nation.

Four American Presidents, Calvin Coolidge, Herbert Hoover, Franklin D. Roosevelt and Dwight D. Eisenhower, have used Ruth's flies on fishing expeditions to Get Away From It All in Washington.

It seems a pity that the plastic worms, now made by the factory, were not available for Mr. Coolidge during his years in the White House when his use of the real thing as bait kicked up such a controversy among fly casters.

To the chicken and duck feathers from which Ruth made her first flies have been added peacock feathers from Burma, jungle cock feathers from India, gamecock feathers from Hong Kong, the fuzzy black and white tails of the small impala deer from Africa and other deer tails from Canada. Idaho, one of the last great refuges of wild game in the United States, also supplies 3,000 pairs of wild duck wings annually. During the hunting season little boys whose papas are sure shots receive five cents for each pair of glossy wings they bring to the factory.

All of these exotic ingredients, as well as hackle feathers supplied by the humble Plymouth Rock and Rhode Island Red chicken, are made into the most beautiful and glamorous lures for unsuspecting trout, bass, bullheads, white fish, catfish, carp and a thousand other fresh-water fish.

"Styles in fishing tackle change as much as styles in women's clothes," Ruth explained. "Some fisherman makes a big catch with some fly he has tied at home. Maybe the fish were just biting that day or the man had the luck of a lifetime. But he attributes it to the new fly and before long the neighbors want a fly just like it.

"Sometimes a fisherman sends a sample of his unbeatable lure to the factory. If it passes muster, it is made up in quantity."

Just how affluent fishing society can be is seen in its recent demand for gold and silver lures. Ruth and Glen do a big business in fourteen carat gold spoon-shaped spinners! The perfect gift for the fisherman who has everything, including rich friends. However, standard items continue pretty much unchanged from year to year, Ruth said, as we watched women with incredibly dexterous fingers tie rainbow-hued flies.

"Flies are designed seventy-five per cent to catch fishermen and twenty-five per cent to catch the fish," added Glen, who denies he is a cynic. And by parlaying fish, flies and fishermen, Ruth and Glen have landed a typical American success story in their own front yard.

On Returning to Alma Mater . . .

Some time ago, one of those educational research bureaus sent me a long, nosy questionnaire.

"What," this questionnaire wanted to know among 500 other things, "do you regard as the most lasting benefit of your college education?"

Well, the most lasting benefit of my college days is two friends, Catherine and Bill Van Cleve, of Moberly, Missouri, who invite me to Moberly from time to time to eat my fill of Missouri hickory-smoked country ham. Occasionally the Van Cleves, viewing my life and hard times in New York with compassion, ship me a Missouri country ham just to keep my spirits and my strength up.

Inflation is ruining everything. But neither time, tide nor the government has the power to change the Missouri hickory-smoked country ham. It is still the magnificent, deep, rich mahogany red of yore, flecked here and there with a snowflake of white fat to give it quality and authenticity.

This is a ham with authority; something to put the teeth into and chew: not one of your poor, flabby, modern hams cured with chemicals and commercial processes. The Missouri ham is the product of loving care. When accompanied by its natural companions, red-eye or cream gravy, and a platter of buttermilk biscuits, it is food for the gods.

A man who smokes a Missouri country ham usually learns the art from his father, who, in turn, picked up the knack from his pa.

"That's how it was with me," said Cavella Frazier, who dropped by the Van Cleves at one point to see if the Frazier ham was up to standard. "I learned a lot at the University, but my father taught me about hams."

Mr. Frazier, who has been farming 1,200 acres about six miles from town, used to cure about twenty hams a year—just enough for himself and his friends. To one part of brown sugar and four parts of salt, he added a good pinch of cayenne pepper. This mixture he rubbed with love and patience into each fresh ham. Then he packed the hams in a big wooden box in ample layers of salt, brown sugar and red pepper.

At the end of six weeks, Mr. Frazier unpacked his hams (and bacon, too), rubbed off the extra salt and sugar, and then washed them in lukewarm water.

By then it was March first, and the time was ripe to hang the hams in the smokehouse. There, over a smoldering fire of green hickory wood, Mr. Frazier smoked his pearls without price throughout the whole month of March.

By the end of that time, his ruby jewels were ready for the table, but, he cautioned, they'd be a lot better if they were allowed to hang and cure through the heat of a languid Missouri summer.

How to cook such a ham? Mr. Frazier gave way to his mother, Mrs. Lyda Frazier, in this department. This small, brisk woman has long been a famous cook even in a community of Cordon Bleus.

"Don't soak it, don't pre-cook it," she ordered. "Just take one of Cavella's hams, put it in a brown paper grocery bag and bake it real slow, probably 250 degrees, for seven or eight hours. That bag holds all the flavor in.

"After the ham is cooked, I make a paste of brown sugar, mustard, a little vinegar and right smart of cinnamon and allspice. I put this over the ham and then fasten round slices of pineapple all over it with toothpicks. I put it back in the oven just long enough for the pineapple to brown."

Then Mrs. Frazier made the most famous understatement of the year.

"The result," she said, "is real tasty."

🌺 🌺 🌺

"Because you are married to a mean man who will not take you to night clubs in New York, we have decided to give you a taste of night life in Moberly," said my host, Bill Van Cleve, editor of the Moberly *Monitor-Index,* "at Jerry's Club Plantation."

"It's the El Morocco of our town," said his wife, Catherine. "All I have to do is round up a crowd that's willing to go."

The first two couples she called begged off.

"Get some young people," they advised her.

So my host and hostess scraped up sixteen middle-aged adolescents whose protests they ruthlessly overrode. "Don't be stubborn," I heard Catherine bullying people on the phone, "she's here and we've got to entertain her and besides, we've ordered steaks."

Well, people will go any place today to get a free steak. At 8 P.M., we were all at Jerry's Club Plantation. It sat on the edge of town, a road house with respectability.

Jerry's was a great big place, rather barnlike and bare, with the décor consisting entirely of a chandelier in the center that strongly resembled a neon-lighted doughnut, a small bar in one corner and a juke box capable of playing one hundred separate and distinct records.

Let me ask you right here and now: What have Lester Lanin and Meyer Davis got that a hundred-record juke box hasn't got, except the box has more variety?

My hostess sat me next to Senator Richard J. Chamier, then Democratic Floor Leader of the Missouri State Legislature.

"Don't ask her any cosmic questions, Dick," warned our hostess. "She doesn't know what Russia's going to do any more than you do."

"I thought I was going to get the lowdown," said the senator, a nice, round, bouncy man with a crew cut. He looked at me reproachfully. "Can you dance?"

We got up and approached the juke box.

"You see anything in the titles that sounds old-fashioned, like 'Wabash Blues'?" asked the senator. "That's my speed."

"I can't even read the titles without my glasses," I said. "They are making the print smaller and smaller on juke boxes."

"I guess this machine must be broken," the senator said as he tried to feed nickels into its maw. He simply couldn't make the machine take the nickels, even with main force. "Must be broken," he said hopefully.

"Naw," said a nineteen-year-old who was impatiently waiting for us to get out of the way. "Why don't you be a big spender and try dimes? That's what it takes, Mister."

The senator dug through his pockets in frantic embarrassment for dimes.

"Inflation!" he cried indignantly. "It hits every facet of life!"

So we went back to our table and ate a superb shrimp cocktail, good as anything Pavillon puts out. Then came steaks, the acme of perfection, accompanied by little hot, homemade rolls and a gallon of black, smoking coffee.

By this time the club was jammed with nice, pleasant people having a nice, pleasant time. You couldn't have distinguished them from a crowd at El Morocco except that their manners tended to be better and none was accompanied by a press agent or panda. All the ladies, young or old, were much better dressed than I, and the men, by and large, were sartorial dreamboats.

At 10 P.M., exhausted by such a night out, all we middle-aged adolescents gladly went to the Van Cleve residence to visit. By midnight everyone departed.

As they left, I heard one guest tell mine hostess "Thank heaven, we won't have to do this again until another city hick hits town."

🏵 🏵 🏵

Criminals and old grads should never return to the scenes of their former crimes. Even if they are not apprehended, it is apt to be bad for the morale.

But I wanted to see the University of Missouri, and Catherine Van Cleve agreed to conduct the tour. I explained that I only wanted the fifty-cent tour—just a quick look at the old red campus (because it's red brick, honey, not communist), and the new white campus.

"And then I'd like to drive down fraternity row," I explained. "Since my day, I hear the boys and girls have been building fraternity and sorority houses that combine the best of Buckingham Palace and the Waldorf."

"Yes," said Catherine, "known architecturally as Missouri Buckingham."

"And then I want to stop and see our sorority house," I specified. "I haven't seen the new one and I hear it's colossal."

"Well, you asked for it," said Catherine and off we went.

It was a beautiful day. The red campus looked old and mellow and lovely. The white campus looked big and handsome and efficient.

But it was fraternity row that made me realize what a great, big, important school the University had become in the years since my graduation. We cruised slowly down the old, tree-lined street between rows of improved Versailleses and overblown Petits Trianons.

"I have been hearing rumors that Missouri has the most superduper fraternity houses of 'em all," I said, "and ain't it the truth!"

Pretty soon Catherine drew up and stopped before an overpowering palace.

"You want to come into our little ol' sorority house, or do you want to sit out here and watch the changing of the guard?" she asked.

We both powdered our noses and straightened our hats before starting up the walk. We rang the bell. As the door was opened by a bevy of young, sweet-faced girls, we said in unison "We are old girls . . ." but it was obvious we had said one word too many.

The girls kindly helped us tottering old ladies into the house. We stood in a resplendent foyer off which we glimpsed a magnificent drawing room straight out of the pages of *Town and Country* or a re-run of a Joan Crawford society drama.

The girls started toward the drawing room, a symphony of wall-to-wall carpeting, ultrafashionable putty-colored walls, a concert grand, olive-green upholstery, polished mahogany, flowing draperies, and subdued grandeur.

"Do we take off our shoes?" I asked Catherine.

"After thirty years, home has never been like this," she hissed back.

The girls were charming. They helped Catherine and me upstairs and downstairs and gave us a chance to rest on the landing.

"Would you like to see the sunken garden?" one of the girls asked. "We'll all be sunbathing out there like crazy in another month."

Staggered but game, Catherine and I went to look at the sunken garden, and darned if there isn't one!

Eventually they helped us to the car, guiding our infirm steps, and courteously asked us to return if ever we passed that way again.

"It wasn't the grandeur that killed me," I said as we drove away. "It was the look of incredulity on the face of that redhead when I asked if students still picnicked at Lover's Leap."

"It was tactless of her to ask how you know about the place," Catherine conceded.

"Once in 1946 in Buenos Aires, a man pinched me on the bus," I said wistfully.

"It's as nice a place as any," said Catherine. We drove the rest of the way home in silence.

          💮 💮 💮

Has anyone ever seriously considered the effect of the pinball machine on higher education? Here, indeed, is a fertile field for any ambitious would-be Ph.D. in search of a thesis.

Thoughts of it haunted me after my return to my Alma Mater. It is just possible that with the aid of this modern educational adjunct, the pinball machine, I might have been graduated *summa cum laude* in 1924 instead of *Summa Cum* Get it While the Math Prof Looks the Other Way.

In my college days, even as now, I was never able to add two and two together and get the same answer twice in succession. In those days a student had to depend upon his natural resources, or fingers, for major problems in addition or algebra.

But the modern student, with the pinball machine at his command, can tree Euclid and do his homework simultaneously for the investment of the tenth part of a dollar.

This happy progress in modern education first confronted me when I visited the campus "greasy spoon." At first, it seemed like the same old hangout, only slightly enlarged and not much dirtier and dingier than of yore.

Only gradually did I note the innovations such as the pinball machines, surrounded by earnest students in hot pursuit of higher mathematics.

"You got 600,000. Betcha can't make it 900,000," said a scholarly youth in sweat shirt and gray flannel slacks.

The young Einstein patiently working out his problems on this mechanical brain squared his shoulders, sighted along the hypotenuse and fired. So many lights flashed on and off and there were such cries of awe and admiration that I was given to understand the Phi Beta Kappa of the pinball crowd had made 900,000 and gone on to hit 1,000,000, a singular and stirring performance.

"There's a kid who'll go far," I prophesied to myself and wondered if talent scouts for International Business Machines had yet spotted this young genius. If IBM is interested, he's the blond kid with the crew cut at the pinball machine on the right as you enter.

After all, this is the machine age, and I was not too surprised to discover that the "greasy spoon" had added a juke box since my day. The student juke favorite was a lachrymose young lady who kept sobbing over and over "I won't cry any more."

A prim sign over the soda fountain carries a grim message unknown in my day: the announcement that there is a cover charge when a combo plays (and that means a federal tax, we were reminded). My generation may have had to do geometry the hard way, but at least we tripped the light fantastic without fear of the revenooers.

However, it was another sign over the soda fountain that jarred me loose from my hat and made me realize how time flees.

"Please," read the sign, "do not ask to be served beer unless you are 21 years of age."

In my day it would have read "Please, do not ask for beer unless you wish to be expelled instantly."

Beer was a capital offense in my time, and a student caught with the brew would have been cast into outer darkness. Pinballs and beer. I was born thirty years too soon.

🌸 🌸 🌸

"Everything's up to date in Kansas City" and, for my money, always has been.

I was aware of Kansas City's ultramodernity fully fifteen years before Dick Rodgers and Oscar Hammerstein wrote *Oklahoma!* and included in its score their sincere tribute to the avant-garde leadership of this metropolis.

Kansas City is, in a manner of speaking, the cradle of my own cultural beginning. When I was a student at the University of Missouri, having thumbed my way to that citadel of learning from the fastness of Idaho, I saved my allowance and went to Kansas City to hear Fritz Kreisler play his first concert after World War I.

Maestro Kreisler was the first musician of international repute I had ever heard in the flesh, barring the high school orchestra and the Boise band, although the latter did win the grand championship at the State Fair the year before I was born.

However, the Kreisler concert was only the beginning of my cultural development on that trip to Kansas City. It was the first time I had ever spent a night alone in a hotel and, for the record, I hasten to add that hitherto I had always been accompanied by my mother or grandmother.

The morning after the concert I went to the coffee shop of what is still Kansas City's foremost hotel. I had intended to have a light repast of hot cereal, flannel cakes and ham and eggs, as befits the hour of 9 A.M.

But at the crucial moment a waiter passed me bearing a tray laden with little bitty cakes frosted white, pink, yellow and chocolate. Years later when I saw the Taj Mahal, it was almost as pretty as that tray.

I plucked the waiter's sleeve and asked him what it was he carried and he replied "French pastry." Well, we didn't have that kind of fodder out in Idaho in the old days, and I knew it must be cultural because it was French. So I said I would be obliged to have a few for breakfast. The waiter looked affronted and said "Miss, you don't eat French pastry for breakfast."

"I do," I said with equal firmness and won, and right there began my second encounter with culture in Kansas City. I was in my teens then, but even so it now seems impossible that I was ever young enough to eat French pastry for breakfast and survive.

Now, all these years after, I wish to report that Kansas City is still up to its scuppers in culture and I am still learning.

Perish forbid, but I believe I have discovered the means by which to become an Elsa Maxwell, j.g., if any members of the audience are now planning their seasonal social schedules. Any host or hostess can make with the mostes' if he/she will only invest in an old-fashioned parlor organ and limit his guests to persons in their fricassee rather than their salad days.

My husband and I went to a dinner party recently in a home where an old-fashioned parlor organ is tucked away in the foyer, mainly because our host and hostess collect Americana.

A parlor organ brings out the same sort of sentimental urge that prompted the savant to attend a re-enactment of Lady Godiva's ride through Coventry because nowadays one so seldom sees a white horse.

Parlor organs are at least as scarce as white horses and as apt to prompt an emotional yen for the good old days. There were twelve persons at this dinner party, including our host and hostess, and it turned out that all but two or three of us had (1) played the organ for church or Sunday school in our youth or (2) in the case of three of the gentlemen present, had pumped the organ behind the scenes for the church organist.

One pumper, now a well-known author, J. C. Furnas, said he had got his literary start reading *Dead-eye Dick,* and other paperbacked thrillers, forbidden at home, as he killed time between Sunday hymns.

And a Park Avenue physician remembered only too well that between hymns he had been prone to drop out a low window and race from the church to a corner refreshment stand to take on enough soda pop or ice cream to give him strength to return and pump the next selection.

Unfortunately one Sunday he failed to return in time to pump the Doxology on schedule and his delinquency was unveiled.

Little girls are made of sugar and spice and everything nice. So we ladies when young who played the little church organs in our home towns made up in piety whatever we lacked in talent. But in my case, I fear, no amount of piety could have counterbalanced my tussle with the organ on such occasions as the regular organist went on vacation or was indisposed. It was always a toss-up who would conclude first: the choir or me.

But that other evening it was surprising how much of our old "talents" returned. We spent every moment after dinner around the organ. The gentlemen took turns at pumping and the ladies at the keys, and we went right through the hymnal, mainly from memory.

When we finished off the hymnal we began on Stephen Foster, who sounds wonderful on the organ, too. It was midnight before we knew it. I don't know when I've had so much fun at a party. Everyone else said the same thing.

Anyone have a parlor organ—and happy childhood memories—for sale?

The
                    y
                  l
                l
              a
            e
          R   ∧   Fragile Sex

🏵 🏵 🏵

I am slowly coming to realize that I have been barking up the wrong tree in my selfless fight for a fair break for men.

It is becoming more obvious by the minute that what man really needs isn't a break half so much as sulphur and molasses, cod liver oil and a good iron tonic.

Man is indeed the weaker sex, worse luck, and science and medicine are at last catching up with what philosophy and the late Dr. Kinsey knew all along.

Dr. William G. Leaman Jr., a distinguished Philadelphia physician, agrees with Job, "Man that is born of a woman is of few days, and full of trouble; He cometh forth like a flower and is cut down: He fleeth also as a shadow, and continueth not."

At a medical conference in Oklahoma, Dr. Leaman tossed in the chips. He admitted women have far more bounce to the ounce. We are not only prettier, he said, but smarter, stronger and a better bet for the long haul. Then the good doctor turned the knife in the wound. He said women are much better drivers, too.

In addition, the doctor said, men, when they run around flexing their muscles to prove how big and strong they are, only accomplish one thing—heart attacks.

All in all, it is a mighty gloomy picture Dr. Leaman paints and one in which no woman in her right mind will rejoice. (You want to smash baggage, sister?)

Women are only too well aware as it is that a good man is hard to find, with marriageable women now outnumbering eligible men. So it is doubly disappointing to learn he is even harder to keep in sickness and in what little health he has.

41

Although women predominate numerically in the United States populace, more men than women have died annually in the last few years. This terrible figure reveals that nearly a million men have gone where the woodbine twineth and we girls can't get at 'em.

The fact that the lads, on departure, gallantly leave their worldly wealth to us women in scant consolation. Who, on a January night, was ever able to warm her feet on an annuity?

Government statistics emphasize the depressing fact that a higher percentage of boy than girl babies die in infancy, and that fewer survive adolescence. If man reaches mid-span, he totters along with a degree of health. From there on out, he quickly falls apart at the seams and another rich widow is on the loose.

The dangerous age for men is forty-five to sixty, experts agree. At this point women are just getting their second breath and men are losing their first. In this age bracket, women are preparing to do and dye, and men, alas, to die; women are planning to give up potatoes and desserts and men just to give up; women are pushing all their chips on the table and men are cashing theirs in.

Dr. Leaman says a good wife can help shore up and preserve this doddering wreck for a few more years by getting behind the wheel of the car and driving him to and from work. Saves having a spare car, too.

Somewhere, however, I detect a ripe, fishy odor to all this humility on the part of the boys, including that subtly masculine book by Dr. Ashley Montagu, *The Natural Superiority of Women*. This humble trend could be nothing more than subtle propaganda to get us girls back in the shafts, hewing wood, drawing water and beating the rugs.

For, in addition to Dr. Leaman's catharsis and government statistics, I have also been absorbing notes from the New England *Journal of Medicine*. This periodical says the man who can just sit and do absolutely nothing "may be said to have achieved a new and high level of maturity."

A higher level of maturity for the boys is a noble aspiration, but at whose expense, may I ask?

However, just on the off-chance that men really are more Sinatra than Sandow, a wise wife would do well to be on the safe side and coddle the brute. Obviously it is up to us women to take care of our fragile and respective husbands, if we want them—and not an insurance company—to continue to take care of us. It is our business to—so to speak—stem the tide.

I am going to begin right this minute to take better and more constant care of Mr. R. When he comes home tonight, he will be met at the door by a loving wife with his slippers in her teeth.

An American scientist working on United States manned satellites has seriously suggested before an international space-flight symposium in London that the ideal companions for a two- to three-year journey through the Wild Blue would be two men and a woman.

This suggestion of Professor R. V. Helvey, formerly of Kansas University, is undoubtedly a well-meant attempt to relieve the monogamy of space travel. As the professor so eloquently points out, "the terrible feeling of remoteness and loneliness" will be the greatest problem facing the crew of a space ship.

"These and other biophysical conditions must be taken into account today," is Professor Helvey's delicate explanation of his mixed threesome. And very well put, too.

But if there was ever a proposal designed to sabotage the current United States plans for a manned satellite, it is the innocent professor's. If Uncle Sam should adopt his cozy idea, the seven splendid American astronauts now in training for space travel are, in one woman's opinion, as good as out. Remember, they're all married men. And there isn't a wife alive who is going to wave her husband off into space with another woman—and never mind that second man.

I can just visualize the scene when an astronaut comes home with the glad news that he will not be alone in space.

"Bill and I are not going to go it alone in that satellite," he says, edging into the subject. "The government has decided there ought to be three of us. Remember Elsie Dingblatt in the laboratory—the girl with the buck teeth and the pince-nez and the wen on her chin?"

"Never mind all that malarkey about the buck teeth and the pince-nez and the wen," replies the little woman, beginning to smell a missile mouse. "What has Miss Dingblatt got to do with all this?"

"Well," says the astronaut beginning to wilt at the seams, "the government has decided there ought to be a laboratory technician on the trip and they have chosen Elsie—Miss Dingblatt, that is. She's going along purely in the interests of science and . . ." (That noise you just heard was the roof blowing off.)

And the next thing it knows, the government will be fresh out of astronauts—married ones, anyway. Uncle Sam would have to start all over with bachelors, whom he rejected in the first place in favor of married men since "marriage and stability have a very high correlation."

Or, the government could go a step beyond Professor Helvey and recruit married couples. Just why the professor chose a triangle as his ideal candidates for space travel is hard to fathom, unless he felt it would keep all three in fighting trim.

But, if a satellite is big enough for three, there is no reason it couldn't be enlarged a teeny bit more to accommodate a second woman. Take two married couples along and you may not have quite so much *qui vive,* but—on the other hand—you have a bridge game.

However, if Professor Helvey prevails and a trio is shot aloft, I would like, for the sake of the woman aboard, to repeat the answer of actress Madeleine Carroll to a reporter who once asked her to name the man with whom she would most like to be shipwrecked on a desert island.

With a sophisticated woman's realistic approach to the problem, she tersely replied: "An obstetrician."

From its inception, a great many Americans have taken a dim view of British Socialism on the theory that it is inimical to the Old School Tie and the Finer Things of Life.

It would, we have argued, destroy the Upper Classes and their Wicked Demi-Tasses and tend to reduce to one dull, mean, colorless level all the diverse populace of the Isles.

Furthermore, it was felt that it would put an end to one of Britain's greatest export and dollar commodities: Books of spicy memoirs by the daughters of belted earls (who orter 'ave belted the girls abaht a bit for their own good) and novels of English upper-class manners or romps among the hay. Well, the British are turning out bigger and more aromatic memoirs than ever with gaudier romps in the percale.

And, in addition, word has reached these shores that far from burning the Old School Tie, it has been given a new and enlarged lease on life by the Birtish National Farmers' Union. Furthermore, the 'orny 'anded sons of toil have selected for their official cravat a design that sounds like one of those rahly frightful American ties.

Heretofore, the old school ties of Great Britain have all been stripes on the conservative side. A Rugby man could tell another Rugby man by the critical arrangement of the green, dark blue and light blue stripes in his neckwear.

And a Marlborough Old Boy could tell another Marlborough Old Boy, unless color blind, by the chaste number of red, dark blue and white stripes in his ascot.

But the National Farmers' Union, an up-and-coming bunch, have rejected stripes as an expression of their collective personality and have designed for themselves a tie with forest green background on which is emblazoned in gold, like a Hollywood sunrise, the Union's coat of arms. This is unprecedented, neat and gaudy as Old School Ties go, and a challenge, if you ask me, to Eton, Harrow and Westminster to toss out their old stripes and order up something new, lively and atomic, as befits the new age in which Socialism lives.

An Old Boy from Uppingham isn't going to be content with maroon, blue and white stripes in the future when he could just as easily have a hand-painted tie bedecked with artistes from the Folies Bergères.

As a matter of fact, this innovation on the part of the forward-looking characters in the National Farmers' Union may have its impact on the Old School Tie in America.

For despite all the chitchat, the Old School Tie is not strictly British any more. American clubs and schools adopted it long ago, stripes and all.

You can always tell a Groton man (although you can't tell him much, Uncle Horace used to say) by his cravat of maroon, black and white stripes. And you can always tell a Fly Club guy (Harvard) —although you can't tell him much, either—by his black and gold stripes. By his navy blue and maroon striped ties you can always recognize a Racquet and Tennis man, although there is no guarantee that he will recognize you unless you are wearing similar neckwear. These are indeed the ties that bind.

For one of the nice things about school and club ties is that they so readily separate the sheep from the goats and instantly inform an Old Boy whether he should tip his hat or his mitt. (Conversely, nothing is such hell-on-wheels for an Old Boy as to have to make his own way uncharted at a white-tie party. Gad! It's anarchy!)

Now that the National Farmers' Union has led the way and proved that Every Man can be King these democratic days, I think the United Mine Workers, for instance, ought to adopt a tie, perhaps zig-zag lightning on a background of choler and anthracite.

Anyway, come the revolution, we'll all eat caviar and like it!

Goodness knows, the ornate trend in men's evening wear is enough to make strong men creep. But more alarming still is the general assumption in the men's fashion industry that, without the wheedling and advice of the little woman, the majority of men would look a mess.

This is the dour impression I carried away from a Salute to the Men's Fashion Industry. Of thirty writers who covered this event from a fashion standpoint, the vast majority were women. The ladies who cover women's fashions are now extending their territory to include that relatively new field, men's fashions, heaven help us.

"Where does this leave men?" I asked a brisk young woman, who was running the show.

"It leaves 'em ahead!" she snapped, and then came a torrent of statistics. "Women buy eighty to eighty-seven per cent of all 'furnishings,' that is, socks, belts, garters, shirts, shorts, scarves and sweaters.

"And fifty-one per cent of all men are so incapable of selecting their own clothes that they are accompanied by their wives whenever they make a major purchase like a suit or an overcoat.

"If man's appearance is ever improved, women will be responsible," she continued. "Recently we polled 1,000 women. We simply asked them if their men looked as good as they could or should.

"Sixty-eight per cent of these women not only said 'No,' but wrote long letters that, boiled down, said in effect, 'The Old Man is quite content to be the sartorial bum he's always been.' In other words, the girls have to keep working on them all the time to make them presentable.

"It's a fact," she went on, "that only ten per cent of men have good taste. The other ninety per cent depend upon their women folk to keep them out of the scarecrow class.

"So why shouldn't women write about men's clothing, since they're responsible for most of it?"

At the moment, I was so overwhelmed by a black and gold dinner jacket being modeled on the fashion runway that I couldn't think of a snappy comeback except "Good grief!" The next model, a white dinner jacket, with little golden horses woven through the fabric, drew even stronger words.

The white jacket, modeled by Sugar Ray Robinson, was worn with a ruffled white shirt and black trousers. I suppose they selected Mr.

Robinson for this outfit on the theory he could fight his way out of anything, even a ruffled shirt.

But, men, you see how the wind blows. Are you mice or men? Or a Sugar Ray?

The other big news is that gents who hate their dinner coats can set fire to them at once if they are willing to substitute a black woolen pullover "dinner" sweater with black satin collar.

This innovation was introduced to the haute mode of Paris by Jean Cocteau, member of the French Academy, avant-garde poet, painter, dramatist and movie director, the darling of the French capital for years. He picked it up in Italy; from whom I wouldn't know.

This remarkable garment first burst upon my vision at a private soiree. With the width of a room between us, I was first under the impression that Mr. Cocteau was wearing a black Eisenhower jacket with black satin collar and push-up, bracelet length sleeves.

However, when I met the darling of the French salons a half hour later, it turned out that the garment in question was a black wool sweater with a tightly knit band in the vicinity of the waist and with rather full sleeves ending in tight cuffs.

Cocteau wore the sleeves pushed up between wrist and elbow to show the beautiful white shirts he favors, with full sleeves gathered into wide bands buttoned tightly about the Cocteau wrists. Naturally, there was a black satin collar on the sweater to give it that *soigné* formal note. It was worn with the usual formal black trousers.

I was quite taken with the outfit, which Cocteau considered the ultimate combination of comfort and chic, and forthwith told Monsieur Robb that I would knit him such a sweater with which to confound the drawing rooms of New York.

"Go ahead," he said, with sour visage. "The only thing that gives me hope is that I'll be dead before you ever finish it."

All right. I long have set down as one woman's opinion the inescapable fact that women in short shorts and a brief bra top are no improvement on the landscape. And if the girls incline to be meaty, the result is an over-drape shape, Bra-bra, black sheep—

But as long as I have walked into the lion's cage, let me look right down the occupant's throat and say that men in short shorts and no tops a-tall are not my idea of a Sunday treat, either.

At least women, if they're lucky, have pretty legs. Or so the boys tell me. That's why so many of 'em—men, that is—come home with a crook in the neck on a windy day and the laryngitis where the wolf whistle used to be.

Granted that women have pretty legs, granted—likewise, I'm sure —that men just have legs. If there has ever been a male limb that aroused the beast in women, I have yet to hear the tale, even though I am inclined to think that Sir Laurence Olivier has a mighty tasty and well-turned ankle in doublet and hose.

It beats me why so many of the boys feel they are irresistible in shorts when what sticks from beneath the shorts are not so much legs as shanks. Or, in thousands of instances, just so many broomsticks on which hair tonic, by some miracle, has taken effect.

Long pants, if men would only grasp the fact, were invented mercifully to conceal nature's slipshod work in the limb department, just as skirts, if women were only smart enough to know it, were devised to give my sex a break in the region of the beam.

Long ago I admitted to being a fuddy-dud in my preference for women wearing at least a modicum of clothing in public. But my preference for men in tops—even T-shirts—is based purely on aesthetics. Why a man who resembles a leaky mattress or an invitation to a brush fire thinks he looks irresistible in nothing above the equator is something I don't dig. Even on the beach, he's no bargain—any more than the Big Bertha in the bikini.

In a way, I feel like a heel, writing so tartly about the opposite sex, which has taken centuries to free itself from the hot shackles of conventional clothing in summer. For as long as I can remember, I have felt that the boys must have an invisible hole in the head to swaddle themselves in so many layers of clothing under the burning summer sun.

So here I am, damning them if they do and damning them if they don't. What it all boils down to is an honest desire for the boys to wear comfortable attire, but not to abandon ship entirely. For goodness' sakes, man, don't throw out the baby with the water! Abandon that necktie, if you must, but don't lose your shirt in the process.

Steady, lads. What is indicated is a cool head and a body to match.

🌸 🌸 🌸

There are days when I seem to be getting no place in my ceaseless campaign for equal rights for men. Then there are others when a flood of golden sunshine reveals the goal almost within reach. The sun has been working overtime and the goal seems just around the corner ever since I read that Harvard undergraduates will make their own beds—and lie in them, too. They will make with the dust mops, also.

Only by sharp reductions in room service could the University prevent rents from rising, Harvard announced. Thus homework has become unanimous in the Ivy League, since lads at Yale, Princeton, Dartmouth, Brown, et al., some time before were shaking up the sheets and pushing the dirt under the rug in the interests of economy in education.

The nation as a whole cannot help but rejoice that these students, the country's future leaders, are receiving such thorough indoctrination in domestic science. A smart girl who can get an Ivy Leaguer to the altar in the future can not only look forward to sharing her life with a good provider but with a good housekeeper.

This is bound to make for increasing domestic tranquility in a nation in which the hired girl is all but nonexistent. A bridegroom who has just been graduated *cum laude* in dusting, hanging up his own clothes, bed making and floor waxing is to be sought and cherished above the price of rubies.

College has always been regarded as a preparation for life, but not necessarily for married life until the Ivy League was forced to fire its housekeepers and provide its students with brooms as well as books.

When I was a prom trotter the most appropriate gift for a young man headed for college was a heavy white turtle-neck sweater. Now the lad will settle for a carpet sweeper and a dust cap.

I can already envisage the stirring climax of The Great American Novel, yet unwritten, in which Imogene finally chooses between her two suitors: Bob, graduate of a rich, Midwest State University and member of a fraternity with one footman for every four members, and Joe, the barefoot Harvard boy who faces life with nothing but a degree and a fourth-hand vacuum cleaner.

Spurning the agonies of indecision, Imogene tells Bob to get in his convertible and blow, as she throws her arms around Joe and the vacuum.

"Better a clean hovel," she cries bravely to Bob, "than your Midwest mansion and its cobwebs. I should waste my youth and beauty over a hot mop when Joe has a knack with the vac!"

Well, that's youth for you; that's life! The well-rounded man has always been the aim of college training since the year one. Now, at long last, the goal seems within reach and the term "liberal arts" takes on real meaning. Suppose a man does flunk calculus? If he pulls down an "A" for dusting in the corners and under the bed he certainly can marry the boss's daughter, if not his wife.

Thus does the struggle for equal rights for men slowly inch forward, with the Ivy League in the lead. Dishpan hands today; broom-back tomorrow. What does the future hold? Probably, housemaid's knee.

🏵 🏵 🏵

A good man is hard to find, and no wonder! The sane impulse of any man who reads the women's pages of the daily newspapers even occasionally must be to head pronto for the tall timber. What women, seeking advice, write to the lonely hearts, or the lovelorn or the matrimonial editor is enough to scare the sensitive sex half out of its hat.

The other day I was reading a frightening epistle from a wife who said she loved her husband, BUT—But she just couldn't bear to think of the time, not too far in the future, when he would be retired and consequently around home under foot all day long.

The very idea of her ever-loving around the house, day in, day out, afflicted her with the fantods, declared the American wife, whom I pray is not typical. She predicted that a nervous breakdown was imminent if she had to put up with her spouse from 9 A.M. to 5 P.M. despite the fact his boss and his secretary had borne up for years.

If I, rather than the lovelorn editor, had had the privilege of replying to that letter, I would not have advised this frantic wife to (1) be brave, (2) develop an interest in her husband's hobbies, (3) join a social club for married couples, (4) plan to travel and (5) see the doctor about a good nerve tonic.

I would have told her in plain, strong language to go climb a tree or soak her head, or maybe both. My heart bleeds all right, but for the unsuspecting husband who has been bringing home the bacon for so many years he has forgotten there is any other part of the porker.

Now he is looking forward to a rest well earned, and a time when he can act as if every day were Sunday. And already the Little Woman is acting as if every day were Blue Monday.

Mark my words, the day this man finally retires, he will discover that the wife has just given the rocking chair to the Salvation Army, sent the sofa out to be repaired and mislaid the hammock.

On Cloud Nine as he nears retirement, the poor man is probably fondly recalling the time way back when his young wife used to call him at the office every time the baby cried, asking advice and comfort. He no doubt remembers when she sighed and said how lonely it was in the suburbs—before they could afford to join the country club. And how she wished he were a writer or an artist who could work at home and always be with her, especially during the vernal and autumnal equinoctial seizures of home purification.

He has forgotten that it has been years since financial necessity drove him to mowing the lawn or attending to screens and storm windows. Or that the children and grandchildren now live too far away to keep him out of mischief and from under foot. As the company retirement dinner nears, he little dreams that the Welcome mat at home leads to a rug about to be rudely jerked out from under him.

I am afraid nothing can be done to save him. So my appeal is to the excellent women who edit the women's pages and who are always on the side of right: For heaven's sake girls, keep such letters out of print. Answer them privately, but for the sake of American womanhood, don't publish them.

Girls tell me it is not only much more difficult in these searing times to meet an unattached and eligible man, but that it is almost impossible to break him down and get his promise to love, honor and obey. The boys are cagey, I am informed, and resistance stiffens every day.

Letters such as the above only aggravate the situation. A young man, his fancy stirred up by spring, reads such an epistle and he turns cool, real cool, to any and all attempts to fence him in. It terrifies him to realize that thirty or forty years hence the little woman, instead of welcoming him and his testimonial watch home on a permanent basis, will be wondering what in the world to do with the old bother.

So let us exercise a little feminine pressure on the women's pages or a good man isn't going to be hard to find—it will be utterly impossible.

Look, men, the ladies really aren't trying to displace you. In the mid-twentieth century, the sexes are filled with a sneaky self-pity, each convinced that the other has done him/her wrong. Les girls believe men resent them in nearly every field, and men are certain the opposite sex is engaged in a conspiracy to emasculate them.

The boy authors write as furiously about us as they once wrote about Hitler and the bubonic plague. They and the economic stresses of modern life have pushed millions of us out into the workday world, and how they hate us for it! However, because the boys feel so ever-lastingly put-upon, it is my earnest endeavor from time to time to offer them proof that they are loved, cherished and admired.

Now the women's editors of the nation keep their ears to the ground and their eyes on the stars, which is one reason they are so exhausted at the end of any working day. And these smart and estimable ladies have just been polled about the possibility of a woman Vice-Presidential candidate.

I'll bet a cookie that the boys, huddling in self-protective misery in the club car or on the nineteenth hole, would gloomily have bet their last sou that the women's page editors would vote, to a woman, for a female Vice-Presidential candidate.

I can see the darling lads now, their tears mingling with their martinis, as they long for the good old days when a woman knew her place, a well-worn path between the kitchen and the couch. But our men can take cheer. The women's editors are largely opposed to a Vice-President of their own sex. Seventy-eight per cent said they did not favor the nomination of a woman for the office.

However, it is my feeling that if and when men abdicate their duty, responsibility and place in politics, les girls will be forced to fill the vacuum exactly as they have had had to fill the vacuum left in the home because modern man hasn't wanted to be bothered by many obligations and tasks around that institution that are his by right and tradition.

It is one's woman's opinion that man is, by inheritance and nature, the head of his household in the U.S.A. as elsewhere in the world. He has only to act the part, as did his father and grandfather before him, to leave his womenfolk breathless with admiration.

Take my word for it that a woman really craves a sturdy oak, although she may claim to reject clinging as something best suited to a well-fitted evening gown. But what profit that well-fitted evening gown if the oak has lost its sap?

Let man once more be as Landseer's Monarch of the Glen, the lord of all he surveys in his household. Let him be something more than "a good provider," which has only a materialistic connotation. Let him, at home, be a good provider of moral, spiritual and intellectual as well as financial responsibility. Let him fashion the rectitude and honor of his household with the same pride with which he looks to the security of his business.

Let him once more come to regard the home as something more than an enclave where he gobbles a hasty breakfast, drowses over dinner and sleeps. Let him doff that silly chef's cap and don the mantle of benign authority which, on him, looks a great deal more manly.

The discipline of children has largely been left to women in today's world because Daddy has abdicated the birch rod. Women struggle with tax payments and household accounts, something they never did in my mother's day. They take courses or learn the hard way to repair today's mechanized house because Daddy has also repudiated the monkeywrench.

Well, the lady editors don't want a woman Vice-President. They want what every right thinking woman has wanted from time immemorial—a man worthy of the name.

Men are just darling, and let's have no modest disclaimers on their part. What's more, they are always thinking up the sweetest ways in which to improve my sex and mold it nearer their heart's desire. Now, they'd teach a digger to manage her gold!

The New York State Bankers' Association—all men with money, bless them!—have launched a program or campaign to teach us women the ABCs of money management and of banking. There are more than 1,000 women's clubs and organizations in New York state, and the bankers' association is spreading its educational program through them.

Furthermore, the bankers—goody, goody!—have enlisted other men to help with this missionary endeavor. The ladies are bound to meet some very nice men and—who knows—some of them may even be eligible.

This splendid decision to help my sex understand the intricacies of finance from balanced budgets to blue chips came about in a very interesting way. The bankers discovered that we girls now vote seventy per cent of all corporation stock, are beneficiaries of eighty per cent of all trust funds, spend eighty per cent of all the family income, are the heads of 4½-5 million households or family units and participate as owners or part owners in 500,000 small businesses. (There is no mention of such women as Elizabeth Arden, Helena Rubinstein, and others who head multi-million-dollar organizations.)

Certainly, it is mighty nice of the New York State bankers to undertake to teach financial management to my sex, which seems to have its mitts on most of the nation's money.

But—and honestly I hesitate even to suggest this—is it possible that the bankers are—well, dear me, I don't want to hurt anyone's feelings —trying to educate the wrong sex?

If we women now vote seventy per cent of corporation stock, are empowered to spend eighty per cent of the family income and latch onto eighty per cent of all trust funds, just what is it the bankers hope to teach us? Maybe, how to get the other thirty per cent of corporation stock? How to finagle the other twenty per cent income? How to pry loose the other twenty per cent of trust funds? Honestly, I don't think we girls ought to be pigs! Let the boys have some pocket money, is my motto, or how are they going to pick up the checks? It can't all be done with credit cards.

It is sweet of the bankers to assume that women who head up families, manage businesses and control the major share of the loot need instructions in the fundamentals of banking and money management.

But, and I only venture this suggestion because I love men so much, wouldn't the bankers be doing an even more salutary job if they taught the boys how to hang on to their goods and chattels? Even if he can't take it with him, a man ought to be taught that there's no point in letting it lie around loose where my foxy sex can pounce on it.

If the bankers believe the harsh financial facts of life outlined above —that women own the lion's share—wouldn't it be more logical to teach the boys how to hang on to what they've got, rather than instruct the girls how to separate them from even more?

Man dearly loves to educate women. In the interest of a continuing truce in the battle of the sexes, I think she should always take his guidance with a straight face. Still and all, in this instance I am convinced the bankers are simply setting out to teach their grandmothers how to suck eggs.

Bouquets and Brickbats

Platform of the Conservative Anarchist Party

Heartened by the nationwide response to the Conservative Anarchist Party, whose creation I announced some moons ago, I have been hard at work in a tireless effort to write a platform that will satisfy the intellectual and emotional aspirations of dissidents in both major parties.

As you may remember, the Conservative Anarchists are dedicated not to throwing bombs but to tossing out the duly elected rascals, both Republican and Democratic, who are now cluttering up high public office. You may also recall that the rolls of the new party are open to anyone with a low boiling point and a high regard for plain, old-fashioned honesty.

The first plank in the platform must be a ringing declaration that the new party believes the least government is the best government and is unalterably opposed to the creation of any new federal bureaus as a refuge for incompetent relatives of office holders who might otherwise have to work or starve (i.e., both relatives and office holders).

The second plank must endorse equal rights for men, with full participation in their own pay checks.

The third plank is a bold and challenging endorsement of money, the possession of which in recent years has been taken as ipso facto evidence of crimes and high treason. This plank will firmly state that it is no disgrace to have money and/or property.

Guilt by association with money will be prohibited. No citizen will be branded a pariah and whipped from decent society merely because he has the ambition and talent to earn an honest pile of scratch.

The Conservative Anarchists are against government of the incompetent, by the incompetent and for the incompetent. It will explode the greatest political myth of our time: the so-called common man who doesn't have a cent to his name and believes the government owes him a living.

If elected, the Conservative Anarchists also promise the enactment of a law that will forbid the changing of skirt lengths except at the beginning of each decade. This would effectively abolish the heartbreak, mental anguish and financial squalor now occasioned semi-annually by the designing sadists of the French couture who callously lengthen or shorten skirts every time they turn out a collection.

An able administration with a hep Department of State would have put the Indian sign on this foreign trickery years ago. Let us lift this pall of fear and nervous twitches from American womanhood!

The Conservative Anarchists are opposed 110 per cent to billboards and, if elected, will pass legislation abolishing these eyesores and thus enable the American people to take a good look at this beautiful country in which they live.

The Party also would prohibit the erection of roadside refreshment stands in the form of an ice cream cone, hot dog with mustard, brown, black, red, green, purple, gray, mauve or cerise derby, bean pot, cigar, ark or shoe.

This new party pledges itself to pass a law providing that eighty-nine-cent hamburger contain at least ten per cent of meat by weight. It would change from a social misdemeanor to a felony the act of combing the hair, by man or woman, in a public dining room.

We also advocate making it a criminal act to sell popcorn and chewing gum in movie houses unless (1) the cellophane wrappings are removed in the lobby and (2) each purchaser is equipped with a Maxim silencer. Gum snappers would be summarily executed in the basement.

This is as far as I have gotten with the platform to date. But I am open for suggestions.

Honesty is the Only Policy

I aim to pick a quarrel with an old and time-honored maxim, to wit: Honesty is the best policy.

That has been a high-sounding axiom ever since Cervantes set it down in *Don Quixote*. But it is fallacious, misleading and deceitful, not to say a snare for the feet of the unwary.

Honesty is not the best policy: Honesty is the *only* policy, and the sooner the old saw is amended to this effect, the fewer public officials who will languish in durance vile—perhaps. It is doubtful if even Madison Square Garden could hold all the public figures now convicted or serving time for lying.

If the maxim is eventually amended, I don't want any credit. It should go, posthumously, to Papa. He was the rugged individualist who faced up to Cervantes and the third grade schoolteacher in Caldwell, Idaho, and rewrote the old saw for home consumption.

In those far-off days, they taught penmanship and high moral precepts by making us third graders copy in faltering script such varied truisms as "Sweet mercy is nobility's true badge" and "Poverty is no sin."

So one day when I was dragging my feet at my homework, Papa glanced over my shoulder and saw that I was writing, for the eighty-ninth time "Honesty is the best policy."

Papa insisted that I start all over again and write "Honesty is the *only* policy," and that began his private war with Miss Grant, the third grade teacher. Because Miss Grant fired the paper right back at me and told me to copy the maxim as written: Honesty is the best policy.

That was when Papa marched up to the Lincoln School to confront Miss Grant, and the battle was joined. His argument went something like this:

"I do not want my child taught that honesty is the best policy. I want it pounded into her thick little skull that honesty is the *only* policy.

"If you say that honesty is the best policy, it implies that there are other policies and that there is an element of choice in the matter. But there is no choice. Either you are honest or you aren't. You can't be a 'little bit honest' without being equally dishonest at the same time." In summing up, Papa delivered his *coup de grâce.*

"It's this way, Miss Grant," he said, "there is no such thing as 'a little garlic' or 'a little honesty.' Either you refrain from either or you go whole hog."

Miss Grant stuck by Cervantes, but Papa stuck by honesty, and eventually he wore her down. I was permitted to write "Honesty is the *only* policy." And so was my sister and my brother, when they made third grade.

"If they wind up in jail," Papa told Miss Grant, "it won't be your or my or Cervantes' fault. They'll have done it on their own."

At the risk of sounding not a little stuffy, let me point out that none of us has ever been in jail—although there is yet time. None of Papa's children has ever been caught lying to a grand jury, a congressional committee or a duly constituted court. Or doctoring the books.

It would benefit all to see Papa's reform sweep the country to wit: Honesty is the only policy. While the politicians and public officials are out back writing this truism a hundred times in their copy books, they could very well keep their ball-point pens poised for a hundred-time go at another of Papa's favorite saws: "Tell the truth and shame the devil." Nothing else will.

The Freudian Adenoidian

It does not surprise me at all to read that American adolescents are haunted by worry, twenty-two-carat anxieties and fee-fi-fo-fum fear, as reported to the United States Office of Education by some 1,300 educators across the nation.

Never before in the history of the world have so many been psyched so constantly by such a large assortment of experts and buffs, as American teen-agers. The youngsters are being killed with analysis, both Freudian and adenoidian. It is a truism of any lab that you can only prod a butterfly on a pin just so much before it disintegrates.

But this is only a small part of the burden of worry and anxiety that is making teen-agers old before their time and their brows corrugated with care.

They have problems, all right, and no wonder! Right next door to the anxiety article is juxtaposed a companion piece explaining that the nation's adolescents are conservatively estimated to possess a spending budget of $9.5 billion annually. Wow!

How can young people, with this much swag in their jeans, possibly be happy and carefree? They are probably up to their ears in the Dow Jones theory, Standard and Poor's statistics, and Barron's. Hostages to fortune, indeed!

Remember Laughing Allegra of "The Children's Hour"? ("Between the dark and the daylight, When the night is beginning to lower, Comes a pause in the day's occupations, That is known as the Children's Hour.")

Well, sir, if little Allegra is laughing her head off today, it's probably because she has just made ten points in one of those juicy, gyrating electronic stocks. And she's sick, sick, sick!

So kids don't respect their parents as they did in "the good old days"? How can you expect a lad who has put his spare cash in A.T. & T. to look up to his old man who lost his shirt three years ago in those penny uranium stocks? Youngsters want security, one article points out, and adds "They have thought long and hard about such subjects as financial stability, mortgages and the need to save." (Rather than to shave.)

Oh, don't peg me as one of those old fuddy-duds who think modern youth is rude and off its rocker. My sympathies are with it. When I was an adolescent, my financial worries consisted of a dime every Saturday afternoon after the dusting was finished. This enabled me to enjoy the matinee at the Bijou and either swoon over Blanche Sweet or scream over Harold Lloyd.

I was not forced to select and buy my own clothes, either, as I read is now the custom from kindergarten on. I was relieved of this pressing anxiety my Mama, Grandma and my aunts who made my clothes. I don't ever remember having a store-bought garment until I was old enough to have a full-time job. (I must have been a retarded sad sack, since I didn't know any better than to be happy and well adjusted.)

None of my boy cousins was neurotic over jalopies. They may have been a trifle nuts over bicycles, as I was over roller skates. But they were not bowed down by responsibility for or anxiety over an auto. They didn't have to worry about where their next ten gallons of gas were coming from.

These modern adolescents with $9.5 billion to spend annually earn one-third of that sum, or in excess of $3 billions, which is more than J. P. Morgan made in a lifetime. Kids who have to scrounge up this much hay are already executive-suite cases, jumpy as a yo-yo. And on top of all of this, the wretched strain of going steady! No wonder this is the aspirin age, j.g.

Don't Fence the Seniors In

Ever since I wrote a column questioning the wisdom of putting oldsters on the shelf when they're still full of bounce and beans, my mail has been filled with anguished, indignant and despairing letters from "Senior Citizens" who despise that term as much as I.

The most shocking aspect of this mail is the number of men and women who write that at age forty-five they are "too old" to qualify for jobs, either white or blue collar, in an ever larger segment of American industry. This is especially true for women.

The fact that science has increased the life span amazingly in the past fifty years and that the number of older citizens in our society is rapidly increasing is not nearly as problematic as the undeniable fact that the threshold of "old age" is constantly being lowered.

"Old age," a purely arbitrary boundary, is beginning ever earlier in our society that worships youth and regards the teen-ager as the summit of creation. Forty-five is now the thin edge of old age in our industrial order. It is no longer sixty-five or seventy, as it was in my salad days.

If the letters I receive are any criterion, what older American men and women want more than anything in the world is to be useful. They do not want to be regarded as "finished" or as a "problem" to be pensioned off or, more cruelly, to be swept under the civic rug.

The attempts of social workers or "life engineers" to herd the elders together, willy-nilly, in special reservations is bitterly resented. The best expression of this resentment came to me from Mrs. Jocile Webb Pearson, ninety-one, of Marengo, Iowa, who sent the following poem:

> Hark, from the tombs a doleful sound:
>   Senior citizens, gather 'round—
> Leave your kitchen—music room.
>   Lay down the palette, brush and broom.
> No more clubs or social teas,
>   No more brisk activities,
> Old age is here; you're seven-tee!
>
> No use protest, cry or moan,
>   The fiat's spoken: 'An old folks' home,'
> A shady corner, a rocking chair;
>   We can do our moaning there,
> Where no one hears, and no one cares.

If there is bitter resentment by older men and women over their classification as "Senior Citizens," there is wild despair that they are denied the right to earn more than $1,200 annually (under the age of seventy-two), if they are drawing Social Security payments. I hope devoutly that this silly proviso will be stricken from the law of the land.

Space Monkeys and Mice Stir Hysteria— But What About Men?

Poor old Uncle Sam obviously can't do anything right! Now he is stubbornly going about his space program wrong-end-to. What he should do, and at once, is shoot a whole series of men into space to make absolutely certain that it will be safe and comfortable for more mice, monkeys, cats and dogs to follow suit. Instead, in complete disregard of all humane sensitivities, Uncle Sam callously sent animals into space first to prove such a journey feasible for man.

The above is the gist of a storm of letters deponent has received ever since the government first sent an animal aloft.

The writers have all protested the cruelty and awful inhumanity of sending mouse or monkey into space, but not one word, not one single word, about the possible cruelty or awful inhumanity of hurling exceptionally brilliant and fine young men into space.

These letters protesting science's "senseless torture of helpless animals" (and this phrase runs through all the letters like a threnody) are simply variations on the outraged correspondence that came my way after the Russians shot Laika into the air. I was exhorted to do something—preferably to go out in space and rescue the Soviet dog.

At the time, I could not help feeling that there would have been nary a protest from the self-nominated animal lovers if the Russians had put a child into orbit, or if the United States substituted infants for mice in our space probes.

In short, I would like to hear "Indignant Dog Lover," "Outraged Cat Fancier" and "Angry Friend of Monkeys" express at least a bit of concern over the fate of the men, either American or Russian, who have been and will be catapulted ever more frequently into space within the next few years.

I am fed up with that portion of the public that regards all scientists as sadists who get their kicks out of torturing animals. From the letters I have received on this general subject over a twenty-year period, one would conclude, if he didn't have horse sense—and here I bow to the animal kingdom—that all medical and scientific experiments involving animals are performed for the bestial pleasure of the experimenters.

That is hysterical nonsense written by hysterics. I am repelled by the writers' complete lack of concern for their fellow man whose very life has hinged on controlled laboratory tests with mice and monkeys, cats and dogs—and will in the future.

It is these hysterics, not the scientists, who are without humanity. I have had letters crying out against the use of monkeys in the making of the Salk vaccine in the war on polio and against the use of mice in attempts to find the cause and cure of cancer, man's dreadful scourge.

It is repellent to read accusations against the medical profession, sworn to cherish life, charging it with gleefully torturing animals. And now it is equally abhorrent to receive furious letters that level these same charges against other branches of science.

If any writer has proof that an animal, any animal, is being senselessly "tortured" for the personal pleasure of scientists, it is his duty not to write to me but to run to the nearest police station. In this animal-loving nation, there are at least as many stern laws to protect animals as children from cruelty.

And, in the meantime, may I ask the correspondents who are wringing their hands over the lot of mouse or monkey shot into space, to give even five minutes' thought to the fate of the lonely men who follow them into orbit?

Wrap It Up!

Nothing in this age of specialization has really surprised me since the greeting card industry came to full flower.

For a long time I felt the heights had been scaled by the missive dedicated "To my ex-wife on her birthday anniversary."

But even this was topped recently in the case of a Scotch terrier with whom I am on speaking terms. This dog underwent a tonsillectomy, an operation that I understand is rare indeed even among dogs of distinction.

However, the greeting card industry proved equal to the occasion. My friend was gratified to receive a standard convalescent card bedecked with a likeness of his own breed and bearing the legend "Hope you are recovering both your bark and bite."

There is now a gift-wrapping paper and ribbon designed for every possible gift and for every conceivable occasion under this uncertain sun—including the possibility that your pet elephant may eventually undergo an appendectomy and some well-wisher desires to gift-wrap for Jumbo a bushel of delicious goobers.

At Christmas, the United States of America sweeps into its furnaces and trash baskets a whopping fortune in gift wrappings, mayhap as much as $25,000,000 worth, possibly twice as much. One of the manufacturing authorities in this field has found it hard even to guess how much the nation spends for gift wrappings in the holiday season. But it is a pretty penny, indeed.

And as for what it spends for wrapping up wedding, engagement, anniversary, Valentine, Mother's Day, Father's Day, birthday, graduation, congratulatory, Easter, Thanksgiving, Halloween, shower, Bon Voyage, Homecoming, convalescent, Sadie Hawkins Day and Labor Day gifts, not to mention those in honor of National Apple Week, no man knoweth.

My informant is the man with the appropriate paper and the right ribbon for each and every occasion, not excepting Ground Hog Day. The only thing that amazes him about the convalescent card for my chum, the Scottie, is that the beef bone accompanying the card was not wrapped and tied in the "Scottie" ensemble.

"Of course, the ribbon with the Scottie woven in it also bears the legend 'Do not open until Christmas' and this may explain the oversight," the gentleman mused, and methought he made a mental note to run off some of that Scottie ribbon minus the Christmas warning.

"Thirty years ago, everyone wrapped gift packages in white tissue paper. The only variation was red or green ribbon at Christmastime, white for weddings, pink for engagement presents and maybe blue for babies," he enlarged.

"But wrapping a package in white tissue paper today would be like driving a Model-T, or even a Stanley Steamer."

Naturally, his Valentine's Day ribbon and papers are red, with entwined hearts pierced by an arrow and bearing the motto (not original) "To my Valentine." The wedding ribbons and papers are a mélange of lover's knots, lilies of the valley and wedding bells. The Easter offerings are awash with bunnies, Easter lilies, eggs and "Happy Easter." Soon he and his associates will be busy dreaming up something grandiose for Father's Day.

"What about a ribbon with the legend 'Hello, Sucker!' " I suggested.

He looked pained. "We aim to make everyone happy," he said.

Stacked Cards

Everything is instanter these days, from coffee to lather to sympathy. Or, for that matter, birthday greetings, best wishes, condolences or thank-you's for gifts, parties or a weekend in the country.

Greeting card manufacturers have banished forever the cruel ordeal of communicating with friends or loved ones by means of handwritten notes or smoke signals.

Of all this, even I, who live in a hollow tree deep in the forest, am well aware. Despite all the years of typewriter pounding, I can still write by hand, and legibly. So I am not apt to frequent card shops except the little one in our neighborhood where I buy pencils, refills and ball points, carbon paper, typewriter ribbons and stationery. Even so, it's been a long time since I peered at the cards.

But a few days ago I went around to the shop to buy cards. I have a cousin who will be in the hospital for a month. I hoped a clutch of gay greetings, one a day, might break the monotony of hospital life.

Well, the long and short of it is that I left the card shop with nothing more substantial than my blushes. Somehow, sometime while my back has been turned to the greeting card racks, they have been filled with scatological stuff.

There was no choice between cards whose floral motifs and pinched prose suggested that the recipient was probably not long for this world and just plain dirty postcards suggesting he is too much with it. These greeting card manufacturers don't mess around with double and triple entendres. They have advanced beyond dissimulation to mighty plain speaking wherein a spade is, at best, a shovel. Among the hottest items are cards enclosing eight to twelve pages of dirty and dull jokes that would even depress old Joe Miller on his healthiest days.

Fifteen or twenty years ago one used to hear about, or even know, persons who made a tidy sum annually by supplying greeting card manufacturers with elevated and so-called poetry for various occasions. Now, apparently, they're paying the boys to pick the stuff up out of the gutter.

The present sick, sick, sick trend is obviously a giant step beyond the "drop dead" greetings that suddenly took over the card business five or six years ago. Many of them were pretty far out and some on the ghastly side. They belonged to the Instant Insult school. But where the drop-dead school lacked taste, the present school lacks decency.

The current trend in greeting cards is, presumably, the backwash of the filth on the news counters, the magazine racks, the paperbacks and the stag-night movie and theater stuff that nowadays is performed for mixed audiences.

The police and the proper authorities all over the country wring their hands, make loud outcry and do nothing. The word "censorship" —even in reference to the most flagrant abuses—throws them into a paralytic state. Public taste and public morals are pegged to the lowest common denominator.

A Dog's Life for Sure

If the Society for the Prevention of Cruelty to Animals doesn't get cracking at once, a dog's life will soon be unbearable. It's bad enough for people to put on the dog, but for dogs to be forced to put on people is too much.

Once upon a time and not too long ago, there was a firm belief around the world that nature had equipped dogs with exactly what they required in the way of covering. If a dog belonged to a long-haired breed, it was permissible to clip his coat for summer comfort. But that was as far as any humanitarian with respect for man's best friend would have dreamed of going.

Now I am not one of those pessimists who believes that the world is going to hell in a hand basket, but I am becoming fearful that a decadent portion of it is headed in that direction in a dog basket, or perhaps I should say a clothesbasket.

Since World War II more and more beauty salons for dogs have opened, all with a sideline of clothes for the poor animal.

But I did not take the dog-dressers seriously until recently when one of the oldest and most conservative department stores on Fifth Avenue opened up a boutique of custom-made togs for dogs, featuring everything from dog pajamas at $15 a pair to mink coats at $110 and up.

At the opening of this dressy dog department, it quickly became apparent that mother-and-daughter outfits have been succeeded by mother-and-dog look-alikes. The well-dressed woman and her dog wear matching outfits, and, reading from left to right, the canine is the one with the hang-dog look walking on all fours—in shoes yet!

Since pink in any shade is always a fashionable color for spring, Rover, heaven help him, will wear it and like it even unto a metallic-woven cocktail jacket. Once upon a time only mad dogs and Englishmen went out in the noonday sun, but I should think that any dog would be mad—furious!—that had to go out to cocktails in a pink metallic jacket.

Any dog forced to wear a cocktail jacket deserves a double martini on the house and a mickey for his master. Once upon a time, one expected chorus girls, movie starlets, debutantes and other publicity seekers to press for attention with a dog wearing a rhinestone collar. And one of the most time-honored ways of attracting news photographers during Fifth Avenue's Easter parade is to be accompanied by a humiliated hound wearing a silly hat.

But it is only in recent years that Lassie and her like have been forced to submit to wardrobes. When my cousins and I were children, we were not even allowed to subject any family pet to doll clothes. This was regarded as cruel and unusual punishment for any self-respecting cat or dog. Fig leaves were strictly for homo sapiens.

A Bellyful of Broadway

I am willing to bet six, two and even that every legitimate show and motion picture presented on Broadway this season will be a problem play. And with one typewriter tied behind me, I can case the problem.

The problem this season, as last season and the season before that, will be to hear what goes on behind the footlights.

The customer who antes up two bucks to see a first-run Broadway movie or $9.90 for an orchestra seat to a show does so at his own peril. There is no statute on the books or in the theater code to protect him from the pest who goes to the theater to eat and talk.

Every year, any number of authorities write scholarly pieces, amounting to obituaries, on the demise of the theater. They suggest it can be saved only by better actors, better plays, better theaters and more and better angels.

Nonsense! The theater can be saved by something far more simple, namely, better manners. The genius who will eventually apply the pulmotor to the theater is at present some unsung Gaylord Hauser who will put an audience on a diet and keep it there until it is too weak to talk simultaneously with the cast.

Popcorn, not television, is the dagger pointing at the heart—or anyway liver and lights—of the movies. I was driven out of the movie theater by popcorn and cellophane long before teevee came to curdle an otherwise happy home.

When the talking pictures opened up snack bars in the lobby they were simply imitating the lemming. And when they started wrapping the popcorn, chewing gum, sandwiches, taffy apples, cotton candy, hot dogs, dill pickles, herrings and pretzels in cellophane, they couldn't have invalided the industry more quickly with a sawed-off shotgun.

I can take my movies straight, so I went on the wagon when they started serving them with a napkin and a relish tray. For every patron the Hollywood cosmic planners have lured into the movies with popcorn, they have driven 100 screaming out into the night.

The movies are dying, all right, and of overeating.

As for the legitimate theater, it may or may not be on the ropes. But it will certainly be on the floor for the count unless theater managers from here on out are willing either to gag or kill the customers who are wired for sound. I favor the latter alternative as being more salutary and lasting.

The number of persons who come to the theater merely to talk, whose conversational flow is stimulated beyond control by the mere sight of a backdrop, has grown in geometric ratio in the past ten years. The paying customer who comes to listen to the actors, to con what is transpiring on the stage, is today a minority whose position is comparable to an opposition party in the U.S.S.R.

I barely escaped alive the other evening when I went to the Ballet Theater, a joyous evening of magnificent dancing and music—I guess. The trio in front of me put its respective heads together throughout the performance. And even though the heads were obviously empty, they were also opaque.

Not only was I unable to see but likewise to hear. This gallant trio, undeterred by the noise made by a thoughtless orchestra, bravely talked over and above it. When, hopeful of getting a fraction of my money's worth, I politely asked the group to pipe down, I was set upon and denounced in ringing tones.

Apart from minor bruises and confusion, I escaped without injury. However, it has taught me a lesson my mother tried to impart when I was young: Never interrupt a conversation!

The movies have been eaten out of house and home, and the theater, alas, is being talked to death, and not by itself.

Easy Does It

If ever a nation needed a good, stiff temperance lecture and a sensible, widespread temperance organization with a practical program, it's the United States of America.

This nation now boasts 5,015,000 heavy drinkers, including chronic lushes and semi-sots who are no bargain in the Rumpus Room, much less any other place. The populace also numbers 70,000,000 social drinkers, according to the National Council on Alcoholism. It should be—but probably won't be—a sobering fact that alcoholism ranks among the quartet of major health threats in this country. It is bracketed with cancer, mental illness and heart disease.

The statistics are appalling. One out of every thirteen men aged twenty or over is an alcoholic. Three out of four alcoholics are between the ages of thirty-five and fifty-five. There are at least 1,650,000 problem drinkers in industry.

These facts and figures are going to be seized upon with shrieks of mingled joy and disaster by all the prohibition organizations in the nation. These bigots and busybodies will be around thumping their tubs once more, screaming for prohibition with a capital "P" and pressuring politicians. Prohibitionists will blithely ignore the fact that this was a temperate nation until they foisted the Eighteenth Amendment, alcoholism and gangsterism on it at one and the same time.

There are no temperance organizations of nationwide importance today that are really effective from coast to coast. What the nation is faced with, instead, is warped, intolerant old biddies in both skirts and pants who plug for prohibition despite the obvious evils it fastened on the United States in the twenties and thirties.

We need intelligent men and women to carry the temperance message up and down the land, in schools, churches and homes. Temperance, says *Webster's New Collegiate Dictionary,* is "habitual moderation in the indulgence of the appetites and passions; moderation—one of the cardinal virtues. Self-control; calmness."

Instead, the country is faced with a band of prohibitionists to whom temperance, in the sense of moderation in outlook, understanding and speech is completely foreign.

Such zealots will not face up to the fact that with the repeal of prohibition, the gangsters produced by the Eighteenth Amendment began muscling into politics, narcotics and so-called legitimate businesses. It will take the United States a century to recover from the stench of prohibition, if it ever does.

Prohibition made drinking "smart." It made it fashionable, and it made it widespread. It made it all but compulsory. The nation is suffering from that combination today.

This nation drinks too much. But a new crop of Carrie Nations is not the answer. A genuine temperance movement is what the country could use.

There is a faint ray of light in the East. It is possible that economic necessities may boost some of the populace on the temperance wagon. With the tendencies of states to increase taxes on liquor, the cost of a spree may begin to sober up some of the boys and girls.

It has been the experience of such states as Rhode Island, Texas, Virginia and Colorado that a stiff raise in the excise tax on liquor is accompanied by a drop both in consumption and in excise revenue. Since Rhode Island, in 1951, hiked the excise tax, sales of liquor in that state have continued to lag behind the national average. In Colorado, where the excise tax was boosted 12.5 per cent in 1959, consumption dropped 7.9 per cent the following year.

Distillers and importers of liquors are always hard at work to keep the tax bite from going up and to cut it, if possible. However, I firmly believe in all the taxes the traffic will bear. It is my conviction that anyone who can afford to drink the cup that cheers can jolly well afford to pay the tax.

The World Just Isn't Big Enough to Hold Pigeons and People

Wars and rumors of war continue to rock the globe. But one world-wide conflict, as universal as freedom vs. communism, is largely overlooked. That is the continuing struggle for supremacy between people and pigeons.

Unless nations forget their differences and unite in this struggle, pigeons are apt to win and abolish people before the H-bombs do. As any city dweller is aware, pigeons are gaining on us all the time, getting bolder and brassier by the minute. And messier, too.

Nothing is sacred to these feathered louts, with their greedy, beady eyes and their beatnik swagger. When Robert Moses tried to run Will Shakespeare out of New York's Central Park public opinion stopped him cold. But what pigeons, who never read a Gallup poll, have done and continue to do to Will's statue in the same territory would make even Mr. Moses blush.

Pigeons are the Jukes of the bird world, and foul-up is their middle name. They have no respect for statues, public buildings or pedestrians. Cities throughout the world have spent billions in various attempts to rid their environs of pigeons in the name of sanitation and safety. But nothing short of a double-barreled shotgun or equalizer puts man on a par with pigeons.

All my pigeon pique came to the surface one day when I cut through Bryant Park, a lovely, leafy bower, on the way to Broadway to pick up a pair of theater tickets. That is, I started to cut through Bryant Park. But I hastily retreated. Pigeons are in full control there. And if the saturation aerial bombardments were not amply alarming, the birds are now sufficiently strong and organized to push people off the park sidewalks.

In the park, people were running from pigeons, both on the hoof and on the wing. But what really shook me was the sight of foolish people feeding the enemy. They stood in the park, scattering handfuls of peanuts and bread crumbs to sneering, strutting pigeons who have boasted that they will bury us (people).

There ought to be a law that makes pigeon-feeding a crime. The necessity of making pigeon-feeding a hanging offense was emphasized when I reached Broadway and the statue of Father Duffy, World War I hero. What pigeons have done to Father Duffy doesn't bear repeating.

People have never yet been able to best pigeons. The only way to win is to send the whole squalid tribe into extinction.

When St. Paul's Cathedral repaired its wartime damage, it installed at great expense anti-pigeon doo-dads to keep the dirty birds off copings and spires. Well, it keeps the pigeons off copings and spires, all right. But the Okies of the feathered world have simply set up housekeeping on the great flight of stairs leading up to St. Paul's. When I was in London last, I had to kick the birds out of the way to get into church.

Pigeons have passed their usefulness in either war or peace. It is now either people or pigeons to the death. The world isn't big enough for both.

All Sheets in the Wind

It is the fractious habit of all Americans who live west of the Hudson to denounce New York City as the Sodom and Gomorrah of the modern world and to paint its citizens as sinful voluptuaries already in hock to Beelzebub.

If this canard makes life more tolerable to fellow citizens beyond the Hudson, well and good. But it is a base libel without support in fact or principle.

The truth is that New Yorkers are a mousy, inhibited lot who would be scandalized by the regular Saturday night goings-on in any country club west of the Palisades.

By and large, New Yorkers are industrious, home-loving citizens who are devoted to their children and their television and who don't see the inside of a night club from one year's end to another.

The fiction that they are always drunk and disorderly is just that: fiction.

I have given a considerable amount of thought to this legend over the years as I have tramped up and down, back and forth across these United States. And I have come to the conclusion that New York is an oasis of sober rectitude and high moral purpose in the broad land.

For instance, drinking is a social custom in New York, at least in my mob. But west of the Hudson it seems to be a steady habit. Understand, I'm not criticizing; I'm simply pointing out the differences in local customs. Or maybe the sun just reaches the yardarm more quickly in other communities.

I believe a steady diet of double martinis would make the average New Yorker stiff as a goat, particularly at high noon. But I encountered communities out thataway where the double martini is regarded as nothing more than a midmorning eye-opener.

On one or two occasions I was looked upon as a nervous Nellie because I was skeptical that a pailful of double martinis and a Swiss-on-rye constituted the best luncheon foundation for an afternoon behind the steering wheel.

The double Manhattan, known in my circle as the kiss of death, is another dietary staple beyond the Hudson. However, it was explained to me that the big, economy-size Manhattan is really a money-saving operation for the drinker.

Like the single Manhattan, the double-M requires the service of only one cherry. Naturally, the vacuum caused by the absence of the second cherry must be filled with life-giving whisky, and the buyer get a bargain. In hangovers, too, I presume.

As I say, the double martini and the double Manhattan may exist in New York, but not in my social circle. Neither does the boilermaker, a by-product of nuclear fission to which I was introduced on my latest trip.

This consisted of a water glass half filled with bourbon and served with a bottle of beer. The object was to chase A with B, and live to tell the tale. My hostess, the dean of women in a secondary school, then proceeded to tamp down both with a half glass of brandy. This seemed a stunning tour de force, both gastronomically and educationally.

These dosages would fell in rows such New Yorkers as I know. But I have returned home convinced that the American stomach is an all-purpose, lead-lined organ, impervious to such incandescent mixes as the coconut grenade, equal parts of coconut milk, gin and pernod.

On the whole, we New Yorkers are staid sobersides, cautious and conservative in our drinking, and much maligned in our habits. A resident of the Bowery may take his canned heat straight, but fancy him tempting fate with a banana cow!

Go for Abstract Art?
Better Have Your Blood Pressure Checked!

"Live and learn," says the old saw. And isn't it the truth? At long last I have discovered the basic reason there is so little rapport between me and the real-gone Abstract school of art.

The reason is Simon-simple: I have had low blood pressure all my life. This discovery is a great source of relief, as I had feared there was some flaw in my makeup that prevented my appreciation of the finer things of life.

However, as I was browsing through a magazine, I came upon a piece about Dr. Elie Bontzolakis, sixty-one, of Paris, a general practitioner who has had as patients over the years some seventy producers of abstract art.

It is the doctor's observation that the higher the blood pressure in his artist-patient, the greater the tendency to abstractionism. As it is, Dr. Bontzolakis simply equates emotional disturbances and high blood pressure with abstract painting.

Two thirds of the abstract painters whom he has treated, the Paris doctor dismisses as poseurs or artistic quacks who turn out abstract canvases because of (1) lack of talent, (2) laziness and (3) both the snob appeal and ready money currently surrounding abstractionism.

That leaves a third of the abstract painters who are "passionately sincere," in the doctor's opinion, and equally sick, sick, sick. This third suffers from anxiety and nervous tension, high blood pressure, irrational fears, chronic delirium and schizophrenia. They itch, too, which the doctor attributes to an allergy with an emotional basis.

Among the doctor's case histories is the artist who suffered from extremely high blood pressure and all its classic symptoms. And man, were his canvases wild! But, through medication and therapy, the doctor got the artist's blood pressure down to normal, and what do you know? He gave up abstractionism for expressionism in art. He and his art became normal as blueberry pie.

So a few years passed in which the doctor did not see this reformed artist. Then the artist returned, blood pressure higher'n a kite. And guess what? He was on the abstractionist sauce again and his art was in the weird ward once more.

If the latter-day Picasso has failed to send you any place but out of the room, Dr. Bontzolakis has the explanation. The contemporary Picasso is "obviously arteriosclerotic" and jumping with hypertension.

Dr. Bontzolakis' shrewd observations are going to enable a lot of us who don't dig abstractionism to hold up our respective heads once more in intellectual circles. To be able to trace my malaise to blood pressure has given me a new lease on artistic life. Can I help it if my blood pressure is low and I like Winslow Homer?

Today's Wedding Guest Provides Hope Chest

During half of one year I received at ten-day intervals rush bulletins from a press agent who insists that today's bride, unlike those of thirty years ago, rushes into matrimony without the aid and comfort of a hope chest.

Apparently he believes that no girl in my era could possibly have snared a husband without a baited hope chest. (Ha! He should see what I caught without a hope chest, or—at one time—much hope.)

His argument is that today's bride doesn't want to be stuck with a lot of dopey old stuff, fashionable today but dated tomorrow. Suppose plaid sheets suddenly supersede striped ones?

Or suppose that bath towels with horizontal instead of vertical stripes suddenly become the rage? A girl can't be too cautious. Or so his argument runs. (And it does have some validity. There is a great big box at the top of the Robb linen closet filled with heavy linen damask tablecloths, in all size, that haven't been out of the blue tissue paper in years.)

Anyway, today's bride wants her linen closet free and unencumbered. Thus she can rush out and buy the latest, when she scents a trend for table mats of coconut fibers, hand woven and painted by tribal artists.

Wel-l-l-l, I only buy part of this argument. Times have changed all right from the days when, with or without a hope chest, Big Daddy was expected to supply each of his daughters with enough household linens, silver, china and assorted household goods to last at least a decade.

The bride's father today still faces bankruptcy unless he can persuade the kids to elope. But he should thank his lucky stars that he is off the hook for a lot of items with which his counterpart was stuck in my day.

The bride of today no longer bothers with a hope chest, because somehow, in the last few decades, the onus for supplying its contents has slipped from her shoulders and those of Big Daddy to the wedding guests.

The first thing a girl does, after nailing a prospective bridegroom to the mast, is to rush downtown to all the better (meaning expensive) stores, and select the most costly silver, bone china, crystal and monogrammed linen patterns in the precinct.

Then she and the merchants quickly spread the glad tidings that the bride-to-be has made her selections. All you, the guest and friend-of-the-family, need do is pony up the cash for a half-dozen sterling silver salad forks, or a dozen service plates, or crystal goblets far better than anything you, the guest, have ever been able to afford or far better than the blushing bride-to-be has ever had at home. (She is blushing because she is committing this highway act without a mask.)

Anyway, what Papa and the hope chest used to provide is now provided by the hapless guest, who didn't expect to spend so much on a gift, but can't afford not to keep up with the Joneses, who are scraping to keep up with the Browns.

Oh, the gift without the giver is bare, but the wedding giver in a really active June is likely to be plucked pretty bare himself.

Music to Scalp By

The daily mail is a sometime pleasure, rather like a Chinese sweet-and-sour sauce. Or half balm, half mustard plaster.

To be hailed as a vocal leader of "lost causes" is gratifying only until I realize that I haven't been winning all my jousts. Still, a resident of St. Louis asks me not to lower my lance.

"Please, keep after piped-in music. New horrors are being plotted against the captive audiences in restaurants, airplanes, bus terminals, supermarkets, banks, stores and any place where the public gathers.

"Now my wife has just read that a patent has been granted an inventor—probably Public Enemy No. 9—who has 'perfected' a system for piping music into individual hair dryers.

"My wife says that this is the end. She says the day she has to listen to piped-in music under the dryer is the day she stops going to beauty shops and begins putting up her hair in pin curls at home.

"We have been married sixteen years, and I have always willingly paid the beauty shop bills, even if it meant hamburger an extra night a week. This is because I can't stand the sight of a woman with her hair screwed up in little knobs held by bobby pins.

"Please, Mrs. Robb, save my marriage. Start a crusade against music piped into hair dryers. The men of America will bless you for it."

Here is a fight I shall gladly lead—win, lose or draw.

Ever since Mark Antony demanded the lend-lease of the ears of his friends, Romans and countrymen, there has been a desperate conspiracy against mankind's eardrums. In our time, the din has reached such a horrid pitch that man can't even hear himself think, which is doubtless one of the prime reasons twentieth-century man is in such a bind.

The mid-twentieth century can be boiled down and compressed into one universal question: "What's that again?" No man can be expected to hear anything, no matter how priceless the pearls, on the first bounce.

The industrial revolution started the racket, the automobile augmented it and radio and television compounded it, but it remained for the loudspeaker and public address system to elevate as the luckiest man in the world the individual with the tin ear.

The average citizen is defenseless against the assault on his eardrums. He can hardly find a restaurant, no matter how good or bad, where he isn't forced to listen to piped-in music. Try to find one where you can get ham and eggs, peace and quiet and a chance to compose the soul!

We live in the age of abundance, when man can bless himself with everything but silence. It must not be tolerated because it's free.

I have been driven out of half a dozen five-and-dimes in New York because the hard sell has been substituted for silence. The voice of Big Sister, directing the hapless customer to bargains at this or that counter, fills the store. There is no escape from it, short of picking up one's marbles and shopping elsewhere.

But the handwriting is plainly on the wall. Once in Memphis I went into a big department store, only to find it echoing to the irritating, all-pervading voice of a local Big Sister insidiously, incessantly crooning bargains available throughout the emporium. I took my trade elsewhere.

However, it's obvious there will come a time when I cannot take my custom elsewhere, because every store will be filled with the voice of Big Sister. Then—and I warn the nation's merchandising princes— the mail order catalog will come into its own again.

Today, silence is almost un-American. Nature abhors a vacuum. Commerce abhors silence and fills it with the juke box. We are cursed by the fact that we shall have music or a commercial wherever we go.

Silence is golden but, alas, this country went off the gold standard long ago.

Pay As You Go

My cohorts among the cosmic columnists continue their campaigns for world peace, the good neighbor policy, nuclear supremacy and stabilization of the dollar. And good luck to one and all, say I. However, at this point I must admit that I am more than a mite discouraged that they are certain to achieve their mighty goals before I even get a half-Nelson on my more modest aims. These include such humble but obviously impossible objectives as suppression of billboards, abolition of slacks on women and clean public rest rooms.

The billboard lobby, one of the most powerful in the land, continues to deface our beautiful country. More women than ever are wedged into slacks. And as for clean rest rooms! Well! I wish the powerful public health services and the impressive medical associations would take their eyes off the stars and their noble, far-off goals long enough to take a good, hard look at the situation just down the hall in the so-called public rest rooms.

Let these two groups take a little time off to battle for sanitary rest rooms, a problem more urgent, more widespread and more crucial to general public health than a lot of the long-term projects now absorbing their time and money.

This probably dates me, but I can remember a day when rest rooms were both clean and free, including soap and towels.

However, in recent years, we have become accustomed in everything to pay as we go. First it took a nickel to unlock the automatic door affixed to the rest room. But those days are gone forever, too. Among the various things a nickel won't buy any longer is a rest room. The standard charge these days is a dime, which is inflation with a vengeance.

But my beef is not that it now costs more, but that the customer doesn't get anything for his money. The public rest room used to be a form of public service. Now, in too many instances, it's a racket.

Recently I visited the rest room in one of New York's two great railway stations. I found row after row of pay toilets, at ten cents each. They were not one whit cleaner than the two or three free toilets hidden in the back of the room. As usual, the customer got nothing for his money.

When I wished to wash my hands at the station a sign notified me that there was a charge for use of a cloth towel. I looked around for a paper towel. There was a dispenser for paper towels, all right. But on it was hung a crudely lettered sign "Out of Order." The sign was smudged, fly-specked and eligible for an old age pension. It was only too obvious that the paper-towel dispenser had been "out of order" for eons and probably by the design of whoever benefited from the cloth towel concession.

The point is that the station situation isn't really unusual. And while I am all for world peace and stabilization of the dollar, I would also like to get the rest room situation cleaned up once and for all.

Just Drop a Miltown in the Martini

Further to complicate the problem of cocktail parties, the scourge of civilization, comes—of all things—higher mathematics! Dr. William R. MacLean, professor of electrical engineering at the Polytechnic Institute of Brooklyn, has worked out a complicated equation that will tell a host or hostess "the safe number of well-mannered guests that can be invited to a quiet cocktail party."

In the first place, there are two contradictions in terms in that one quote alone. Well-mannered persons simply do not go to cocktail parties. Oh, they may be well mannered when they start out to such a party, but their manners inevitably undergo a subtle sea change en route to the binge.

Methinks the professor was cloistered too long in the groves of Academe. It is axiomatic that no well-mannered person could possibly survive at a cocktail party, where the law of the jungle has always prevailed. In such gatherings, it's an eye for an eye, a claw for a claw and a clout for a cocktail.

In the second place, has anyone ever attended a quiet cocktail party? If such a gathering doesn't sound like a boiler factory at high noon, it isn't a success.

Even the New York police recognize that fact. There is the ancient story of the distraught couple who phoned the police to send an officer at once to quiet the raucous cocktail party going on in the apartment just overhead. The officer arrived at the party, but he only added new blood. The party grew more decibel-er than ever.

Within the hour, the couple, still more harassed, called the police station once more and asked further help. "Sorry," said the desk sergeant, "but we can only spare one officer to a party."

Dr. MacLean's complicated equation to achieve a quiet cocktail party included the dimensions of the room where the party is to be held, its sound-absorption co-efficient, mean free-path of a sound ray in said room, the talking-to-noise ratio, the number of persons conversing in each group and the distance the talkers are from the listeners.

This leads me to believe that Dr. MacLean's acquaintance with cocktail parties was as purely theoretical as his equation. The only mean free-path that counts at a cocktail party is the path to the bar, always over an obstacle course. And conversation, Dr. MacLean? Listeners? There is no conversation at a cocktail party. Talkers, yes. Shouters, yes. But listeners? No! The listener is the missing link who stayed home with a good book.

Saddle Sores

I have a whole new crop of corns. And they are not on my feet. This new set was acquired from attending a brace of public dinners. There ought to be a law. There ought to be several laws. But the most crying need of the moment is a law prohibiting testimonial dinners, period.

I was about to suggest a law prohibiting public dinners with more than two speakers orating for a combined period in excess of twenty minutes. But on second thought, I think it is best to abolish this sort of general nuisance altogether. Halfway measures will never scotch this peril.

At the first of the two testimonial dinners or talkathons, I listened to ten speakers drone through two hours and fifty minutes of misspent oratory. At the end of that period, I was numb in more spots than one and laboring under the impression that I had grown to the chair in the interim. This proved untrue, however. With a little coaxing and shoving, a little pulling and hauling, I was eventually able to move. But it was a good three days before my circulation returned to normal.

At the second talkathon, my ears were bent by seven lesser Demosthenes for a grand total of two hours and ten minutes, by which time I had more saddle sores than a tenderfoot on a dude ranch.

In each instance some 2,000 persons had paid fifty dollars a plate to crowd into a ballroom, eat a modern version of an old-fashioned seventy-five-cent blue-plate special and see a testimonial plaque or scroll presented to a relatively innocent man of whom everyone thought well until the oratory began. But it is hard to love anyone, no matter how noble his character, when the second hour of oratory in praise of his virtues fades and the third begins.

At the climax, when the plaque or scroll is finally presented to the guy, everyone in the audience is looking at him with dull, pain-glazed, bloodshot eyes and thinking why didn't they mail it to this little jerk in the first place and save all the wear and tear. The talkathon defeats the testimonial.

Everyone staggers off, vowing never to attend another testimonial dinner. But it is like swearing off sarsaparilla. Apparently it is habit forming, for testimonial dinners are not only a nightly feature of life in New York but in every American city, large and small.

Let a man work fifty years for the same firm, let him sell a million dollars worth of insurance in twelve months, let him stop a runaway horse, let him drive a bus for twenty-five years without more than half killing anyone or let the creep leap off the Empire State with a parachute, and somebody organizes a testimonial dinner in his behalf. And a whole new set of corns is born.

At one of my two dinners, the chief ornaments at the speakers' table were former President Herbert Hoover and Bernard M. Baruch. I looked at these two elder statesmen and marveled at the number of public and testimonial dinners they had been forced to undergo in their lifetimes.

The dinners, if laid end to end, would call for a year's output of the world's sodium bicarbonate mines and the oratory would spread somnolence a foot deep across the United States and Lower California.

However, it seems to me that Mr. Baruch was better equipped to endure testimonial dinners than the former President. I noticed that Mr. Baruch arranged his handsome features in a look of lively and intelligent interest as the oratory began and then quietly turned off his hearing aid.

The Civil Defense Lie

Since the end of World War II, the American people have been fed nothing but nonsense—bilge—about civil defense.

From its very beginning, civil defense has been a pitiful mockery, not because honest men have not tried with limited means, but because of the failure of three administrations to look the grim facts of atomic war in the face, to discuss publicly its catastrophic effects and to deal honestly with the populace and the problem.

The accelerated effort to get the American people to build haphazard shelters in their back yards is both futile and deceitful. There may be tiny communities in which the family breadwinner, the school child and the mother, maybe a voluntary worker in a hospital or shopper at the supermarket, can—in the brief time following an alert that means nuclear war—manage to get to the family shelter.

But the United States is an overwhelmingly urban nation, although legally we do much to deny and thwart this incontrovertible fact. In how many American cities of even 30,000 to 50,000 people, with traffic in the hysterical snarl such an alert would cause, would the father or the school child ever get home to the shelter of that back-yard molehill?

With fifteen to thirty minutes leeway at the most—it's according to which scientist you read—how will any working man and woman, how will any child, be able to reach that back-yard shelter, in the average American community? If, by grace of God, the alert comes at night, the family with a home shelter may make it.

But otherwise, it is a snare and a delusion, and I am outraged that my government will foist such a myth on its people. Will the government tell me just where in New York, as an apartment dweller, I am supposed to build a family shelter?

No aspect of the present drive to get Americans to build back-yard shelters is so cruel or deceitful as the unspoken assumption that every member of a family, thus "protected," will be able to reach home base. The assumption of "togetherness" in this shelter program is a lie.

How, in the name of truth and mercy, will the man who works in any fairly large city and lives in its suburbs ever get home after the alert sounds? We Americans are not so stupid as to believe that, once the alert goes off, the school bus will deliver our children in front of the household shelter before the world is irrevocably split by nuclear fission.

We have been told repeatedly that it will cost too many billions to erect shelters to save civilians. Then what is to save the nation? This is the richest country in the world, rich beyond the dreams of the avarice of man in any century, yet we are not rich enough to build shelters to save the people of the nation who mean its very survival!

For shame that we refuse to face reality, that we dupe ourselves with a back-yard shelter program and that we are unwilling to raise the taxes that would produce a meaningful national effort, undertaken by the federal government. The Army, the Navy, the Air Force and the Marine Corps are not matters of individual initiative but of the most minute federal planning. Only similar planning at the federal level can save the civilian populace.

This do-it-yourself, every-man-for-himself shelter program now being urged on the nation is fallacious and falls apart completely in our urban civilization. It will not work even for the man with a gun to fend off his neighbor's child in the fatal moment of decision.

Let us have at this time a little reality and hard sense about civil defense. The federal government can no more pass the buck to the private citizen in this massive enterprise than the government can depend upon the private, unorganized initiative of the citizen to form its armed forces.

The Will to Live, and the Will to Die

An old woman of eighty-nine who longed to return to Sicily to live out the rest of her days and to die in her native land got her dear wish after all. Thanks to the generosity of a New York philanthropist, who wished to remain anonymous, and a travel agency which bought her ticket home, Mrs. Nicolina Castagna returned to Sicily. She even had a little money in her pocket, sent by kind persons who were touched by her plight when I reported it.

Mrs. Castagna is the tiny, shriveled woman who ran afoul of New Jersey justice and the Middlesex County Welfare Department. Neither the courts of New Brunswick, where she lived in squalor, nor the

Welfare Department, which paid her a monthly average of $66 on which to exist for thirteen years, could believe that out of this pittance she could save enough for a ticket to Sicily and $3,500 to support her after she reached there. When Mrs. Castagna was "apprehended" on the strength of anonymous phone calls, police discovered in her squalid room a ticket to Sicily and the $3,500. She was within hours of sailing when the insistent anonymous informer sent police hurrying to her wretched home.

Neither the judge nor the Welfare Department placed credence in Mrs. Castagna's story that for years she had lived on a diet of bread and onions, and denied herself every comfort, to scrape together money for a boat trip and a nest egg that would prevent her being a burden to kinsfolk there.

After the death of her blind husband in 1948, Mrs. Castagna was wholly alone. It was then that she began the long, pinch-penny bread-and-onion regime that would take her home to die among the few relatives still living. About her state of semi-starvation the Welfare Department obviously did nothing. It was only when her little hoard was uncovered that it rushed indignantly into court.

You may play the horses, shoot dice or live in the bingo parlors on relief but, obviously, it is against the moral order to save! Anyway, Mrs. Castagna's ticket and her money were taken away from her by the courts and the funds returned to the indignant Welfare Department. It was then that the telephone began to ring. Immediately, the Sessa Travel Agency of Brooklyn called to say it would provide passage for Mrs. Castagna. And so it did. She sailed aboard the S.S. *Queen Frederica*.

Then came a call from a gentleman who begged anonymity, but who offered to replace Mrs. Castagna's confiscated money. And so he did. A letter of credit from his bank for $3,500 went forward in Mrs. Castagna's name to a bank in Sicily. In addition, kind readers sent their contributions ranging from a dollar to a check for $50.

Mrs. Castagna wept when she heard the news that her dream was to be realized. But she had never really lost faith, for the little old lady had never unpacked her shabby bags. And her faith was justified, for at last she headed for home and, let us hope, final years of peace and happiness.

"And the Greatest of These"

People are simply the greatest; hence, this hymn in praise of. Because of people scattered all over the United States, Dr. Gordon S. Seagrave, the Burma Surgeon of fact and legend, was showered with money and gifts in kind that added up to more than $100,000.

For the first time since Dr. Seagrave began his ministering to the Burmese forty years ago, his hospital in Namhkam, a malarial region, has screens. It wasn't easy to get the screening to Namhkam, which is remote even by jet standards, but people saw that it arrived. Within two weeks after I wrote about the hospital's needs and Dr. Seagrave's continuing work in Burma, with emphasis on the need for screening, it was on its long way to Namhkam. At the time I wrote that column, I added, as a real afterthought, that any reader who wanted to help the hospital could send a check to the American Medical Center for Burma, 3 Penn Center Plaza, Philadelphia, Pa. I am ashamed to admit that I feared the hat-passing wouldn't raise a cent.

But checks ranging up to $100 began flowing into headquarters. In the end, those checks added up to $7,634.25, a sum that enabled Dr. Seagrave to provide such necessities as real hospital beds and mobile stretchers, of which the institution was in great need. Immediately the big drug companies, which have always helped Dr. Seagrave, got busy and dispatched an extra $100,000 in medications to him. That fine organization, CARE, spurred by the word that Dr. Seagrave longed for a new ambulance, sent just what the doctor ordered: a jeep-ambulance geared to Burma's rough roads. As an added starter, CARE also dispatched twenty-five expensive midwifery kits to the hospital, another item badly needed.

Next came two letters that stunned the Philadelphia headquarters. A generous Southern woman wrote that she would assume the cost of screening the hospital buildings. In the next mail came a letter from the Screen Manufacturers Association offering to provide enough aluminum and fibrous glass insect screening, just what the hospital needed, for all the buildings in the hospital group. The latter offer was accepted.

One of the most heart-warming letters received, plus a check for $10, came from a young doctor in Brooklyn whose sentiments were typical of so many written by contributors:

"The story of Dr. Seagrave's struggle to maintain his hospital on a pittance has troubled me ever since I read about it. In this shrinking world, nothing is more apparent than that we are all our brother's keeper, no matter where he lives.

"The kind of service Dr. Seagrave is giving the Burmese will do more good for the United States than all the money the government can give the country. I am not opposed to foreign aid, but I believe that aid from one man to another is far more readily understood and appreciated.

"A hospital shouldn't be a propaganda instrument, but it can't help but be in the hands of a dedicated man like Seagrave. I am amazed by the fact that he can treat 5,000 in-patients and 10,000 out-patients a year on a budget of $75,000. He must be a magician as well as a doctor."

Dr. Seagrave is not only a magician and a doctor, but a good man who lives without rest or comfort. In 1962, during the fortieth anniversary of his service to the Burmese, Dr. Seagrave has received a salary of only $90 a month. Part of that pittance is always plowed back into necessities for the two hundred and fifty-bed hospital, plus fifty floor pads that are always occupied. But understanding people at least gave him the "luxury" of screening, drugs, the longed-for ambulance and cash to buy some of the necessities that eternally outrace the money available to him.

In Praise of People

There has been a lot of loose talk for centuries to the effect that man's best friend is (1) the dog and/or (2) the horse.

But when the squeeze is on and the chips are down, man's best friend is people: just plain, ordinary, everyday people. And I would like to present some evidence because, generally speaking, people have been taking an awful beating of late.

People have kind of hit bottom recently and public opinion has been more or less against them, with no one willing to say a good word for the next fellow and everyone trying to hang one on his neighbor.

The air is full of man's inhumanity and iniquities to man. These are the times that try men's souls, and snapping, snarling and back-biting are the order of the day. Man is preoccupied with war, ax murders, public larceny, organized crime, political skullduggery and the cussedness of his kind. The general moral and ethical tone has, to put the best face on it, been discouraging.

All in all, people seem at their lowest ebb and it doesn't surprise me to find more and more individuals buying a framed copy of that old curmudgeon cartooned by William Steig and captioned "People Are No Damn Good." I was saving money to buy a copy myself at one point.

Yet at that time my family and I became the recipients of so much plain, unadorned kindness from people, the vast majority of them strangers, that I would like to write a little testimony to people while there is yet time.

My mother was suddenly, dreadfully injured in an auto accident near Woodland, California. The moment the word arrived, there began for my brother in Fort Myers, Virginia, my sister in Tulsa and myself in New York the desperate race for air reservations West on the crowded Easter weekend.

But just plain people began being wonderful. People got the tickets for us and people dispatched us on the fastest planes. And people met us in San Francisco to drive us to Woodland where other people had taken Mother to the Woodland Clinic Hospital, known as The Little Mayo of the West.

There, in a strange town where none of us knew a soul, people made us welcome, and tried to make us comfortable.

The people who owned the hotel, where we first stayed, joined with Mrs. Roy Ratekin, who then ran the Red Cross, to find us rooms directly across from the hospital where we could be closer to Mother.

People at the hospital, whether doctors or nurses or Julia, who scrubbed the floors, surrounded my mother and her children with warmth, sympathy and the deep kindness that sometimes works the miracle where medicine and great professional skill cannot.

And finally, when the doctor said that Mother could be moved East near one of her children, we were overwhelmed with the greatest kindness of all. For our mother would never again be able to sit up or walk, and the problem of transportation for an old lady so gravely injured boiled down to a sleeper plane, the doctor said.

But there were no sleeper planes from Sacramento or San Francisco to Tulsa, where our mother could receive the care she needed in the great Catholic hospital there, St. John's. We simply did not know what to do: We could not leave our mother alone and yet there seemed no possible means to take her with us.

And then people went into action. People we scarcely knew, but who had heard of Mother's plight and our dilemma, came to our rescue. People found some other people, whom we did not know and had never seen, who loaned us a private airplane, equipped with a couch, to take Mother to Tulsa. And the donor—a so-called soulless corporation—would not accept a penny in payment!

It was the miracle we had prayed for. God heard our prayers, but it was His people who made the miracle possible. As long as we live, we shall never cease being grateful to people, all kinds of people, mostly strangers, who turned themselves inside out to be helpful.

People—I don't know what we would have done without them in those six weeks.

The Killer We Tolerate

The newspapers said she was a quiet little spinster: the woman who was the millionth victim of the senseless automobile carnage in this nation.

A quiet, cautious little woman, they described her, who would walk out of her way to cross the street at a traffic light, for its added protection.

But scant good her caution did the quiet little spinster, whose final, brief distinction is that she was the millionth person killed in this country by an automobile, the millionth victim of a monster more cruel and insatiable than Moloch or Minotaur.

A brief distinction, indeed: Who remembers her name today when we are well on the way toward the second million!

For a fortnight, my desk was covered with handouts and press releases from a dozen different safety organizations, asking for cooperation in a nationwide drive to entreat Americans to stop killing each other on the highways.

I wish I could believe that what I wrote had had the slightest effect on a populace that shrinks in horror from the carnage of war but shrugs off—with indifference, as far as anyone can tell—the vaster carnage of the highway.

Like the little spinster, my mother was quiet and gentle, too, a woman incapable of violence, but she was killed by violence on the highway. She had lived to a good age, seventy-nine, in peace and quiet, and at the end of that life of tranquility and calm, she was fatally injured in a hideous automobile accident.

Perhaps "murdered" is the better word for what happened to my mother: It was an accident without rhyme or reason—one of those senseless disasters that clutter our highways with dead and dying, with the wreckage of lives as well as of cars. And which, for some self-destroying reason, we as a nation dismiss without a second thought. The killed are transmuted into statistics, nothing more.

My mother was riding in an automobile which was hit broadside by a speeding car in California on Good Friday. The driver of the car in which Mother was a passenger was killed instantly. His wife was so frightfully injured that she will be an invalid the rest of her life.

Mama—she never wanted us children to call her anything else—was nearer dead than alive when she was taken to the Woodland Clinic at Woodland, California. She was blood-soaked and her clothing had to be cut from her battered body.

It isn't nice to read about, is it? It wasn't nice for her two daughters or her son to hear or to see, either. Mama was always so pretty; age never really affected her lovely skin and her big blue eyes. And her snow-white hair only seemed like a silver crown to us.

But by the time we reached her, the silver hair had been shaved away from her face and there were twenty stitches in her scalp, and her pretty face—well, glasses cut when they are shattered.

New drugs—the miracle ones—kept Mama alive for fourteen weeks after the accident. That is, they kept the body alive. Mama never regained consciousness. Our only consolation was the fact that she never suffered and, as far as we could reconstruct the accident, never knew what struck her down—so that even for a split second, we hope, she never shrank in terror from the impending crash, never knew fear at the end of a long and happy life.

This is the first time I have been able to write about Mama since she died, or discuss the accident.

I can't quite explain how, but I feel I owed it to the quiet, gentle little spinster who was the millionth victim. Mama, so quiet and gentle, was one of the million, one of the final thousands to make that hideous, horrible, appalling total.

I would like to think that the story of the little spinster and of Mama might spare some of the second million. I long to think so, but I do not have much hope.

Every Girl Should Have a Husband—
Preferably Her Own

Experts claim the whole American scene has been dramatically transformed in the past thirty years by the auto, movies, radio and television. But the church supper and the cook-food sales are immutable. Both offer continuing evidence that despite the can opener and frozen foods, the American woman is still a splendid cook.

There are no statistics on how much money church women raise annually by wrestling with pots and pans. The ladies may be no financial wizards. But their devotion and cooking have supported American churches ever since the Founding Mothers landed.

It makes no difference whether the church is in New York City, Three Forks, Montana, Flemington, New Jersey, or Caldwell, Boise or Nampa, Idaho, if what it needs is money—and what church doesn't?—the ladies are in there pitching over the range. They, bless them, are the true Hot Stove League.

I began mulling over this aspect of American life because of a gift made to the Chester Hill Methodist Church of Mount Vernon, New York, where my sister-in-law and her friends have cooked for years. The ladies of the Chester Hill Church set a fine table. I try never to miss their dinner in connection with the annual church fair around Christmas time. Other church dinners are held there throughout the year.

The cooking has never been any real problem for women willing to give of their time and energy. The real headache was always the mountainous stack of dishes to be washed and wiped after such dinners. It killed the ladies to do it after a hard day over the church stove. Yet it took too much of the profits to hire dishwashers at a dollar and a half an hour.

However, the problem was finally solved. Miss Olga Hingsburg, a member of the church, gave it $1,000 for an electric dishwasher and then an additional check to pay for its installation. This was not the easy gift of a rich woman. For thirty-five years, Miss Hingsburg taught school, a woman devoted to her profession and to her church.

Churches, whether they need them or not, are forever the beneficiaries of stained glass windows, carillons, art, organs, choir screens and altars. But this is the first instance, to my knowledge, of the loving gift of an electric dishwasher to a church because, obviously, it was one of the essentials most needed for the greater glory of God.

"I'm just a practical person," Miss Hingsburg explained when she was asked about her unique gift. "I thought the church needed it."

There are no donors' name plates on dishwashers. Or on electric refrigerators, either. For it developed that the dishwasher was not the only practical gift the schoolteacher had made to God. She endowed the Congregational Church of Bridgewater, Connecticut, where she lives in the summer, with the needed refrigerator.

As Administrative Assistant in Charge of Guidance in the Tilden High School, Brooklyn, Miss Hingsburg, now retired, did her best to give youngsters a good start in life. But her interest did not end with American children. For years, this schoolteacher supported a Dutch foster child, a little girl whose father was killed in World War II.

Miss Hingsburg's dishwasher, her refrigerator and her orphan, no less than multitudes of American women cooking to support their God, are inspiring evidence of a vibrant, living religious faith that women never let waver in this land. This generation has only picked up the apron where it was dropped by their mothers, grandmothers and great-grandmothers, who accepted it from devout women who came before.

One year in four comes a gladsome time when every man, woman and child who can intimidate an editor rushes into print with predictions of things to come during Leap Year.

Just to keep the record straight, I shall be happy to oblige with some sure-fire predictions of my own. There will be innumerable—and libelous—pieces printed in newspapers and magazines, indicating that this is the only annum in which some girls can get a man. All such pieces will hint that the year will be no more than 366 Sadie Hawkins Days, with men relentlessly run to earth by rapacious females.

As every right-thinking woman knows, this is simply an old and despicable canard, calculated to scare men to death and make them more gun-shy and wary than ever. And, goodness knows, things are difficult enough as it is without putting the sly creatures on further guard.

Everyone in his right mind knows that girls do not chase men. It is a very unladylike thing to do even in extremis, or Leap Year. Nothing, but nothing, is so distressing as girls chasing men unless it is men not chasing girls. And, of course, that is the most distressing thing of all.

Furthermore, man likes to believe he is the pursuer. There is no reason to disillusion him one year in four by creating the impression that there is an open season on him. When women chase men it merely gives them a reputation for being bold, forward hussies up to no good. (Or, again, smart, shrewd operators up to no good but their own.)

It is my honest advice to any girl to let a man always do the pursuing, even if she has to get behind and push. And now we come to a vital point: How to bait the trap. You can't get a man with a gun—or a missile. I believe Mama knew best. The old ways, tried and true since Adam, still get results. If a modern girl wants to fancy up the old rules here and there with a little modern schmaltz, okay. But she discards them at her own peril.

Such simple admonitions as "the way to a man's heart is through his stomach" are as immutable as the fact that the square of the hypotenuse is equal to the sum of the square of the two sides of a right-angle triangle. (But, ladies, please do not get mixed up in any other kind of triangles. Every girl should have a husband, but preferably her own.)

So, feed the brute, and if a girl is smart, he need never know it was one of those frozen dinners she just heated up in the oven.

Naturally, there are bound to be intellectuals in both sexes. The law of averages attends to that. And they deserve nothing more richly than each other. Doubtless, there is a Phi Beta Kappa mating call. And it must get some response as I frequently see Phi Beta Kappas of both sexes wearing wedding rings. But the old rule of thumb for young unmarried ladies still holds good: Never be seen in public with a copy of *The Atlantic Monthly*.

In summation, I would like to point out that man's atavistic distrust of the brainy female has been more brilliantly stated by Eugene O'Neill than by any other writer. In his neglected play *Marco Millions,* he causes Marco Polo to speak one of the most profound lines in all literature, to wit, "Who wants a great thinker around the house?"

True, Marco was a Venetian Babbitt. But there are a lot more Babbitts on the loose than O'Neills.

Man still likes his women reasonably helpless. He wants to believe that he is not only the intellectual but the physical superior. There is no earthly reason for women to change tires, balance checkbooks or wrestle with suitcases as long as such simple satisfactions feed the male ego. Let him mix the martinis and take the cork out of the wine bottle as long as it makes him happy.

The ultramodern young, unmarried woman may snort at these simple, old-fashioned rules. But that may be the reason she is unmarried. Her mother was married, I hope, and her grandmother before that. And they didn't snort; they applied!

Only one other word of advice: Avoid as you would the plague all those lengthy questionnaires in newspapers and magazines entitled "Should I Marry?," "Am I Emotionally Mature?," "Will I Make a Good Wife?" and/or 'Should I Wed Fred?"

That way lies emotional chaos. I only read these questionnaires now for my own amazement. One so-called marriage counselor recently asked critically, "Do you sometimes compliment a person even though it is not deserved?"

Ha! is my briefest comment to that. If a girl does not compliment a person—and you know whom—even though it is not deserved, she is going to be out at first. That is a rule so elemental that girl babes in their cradles know it. And if a girl does not compliment a person, once she gets him to the altar, she is going to be out at home plate!

Men are the sensitive, emotional sex, verging on hysteria, and a girl must be prepared to tell a man at least once daily that she loves him. She must compliment him on his clothes. And tell him how handsome he is every time he gets a haircut, even though the simultaneous passage of time and hair sometimes makes the cut difficult to detect.

Well, as I said in the beginning, nothing distresses me more than the implication that Leap Year is, for women, merely a catch-as-catch-can season. Further than that, I can only say Happy Leap Year, good hunting and fire when ready, Miss Gridley.

If men are increasingly altar-shy, statistics have made them so. Leap Year is not so much a concession to but a necessity for my sex since the broadcasting of actuarial tables demonstrating that a husband is prone to depart this vale in advance of his wife.

For a woman to seize this thesis and embroider on it is nothing less than treason to her kind. Yet I have at hand the woman's page of a large Midwestern newspaper that features an article calculated to scare the daylights out of any man and send him careening to the nearest monastery.

"Any wife whose husband has passed forty-five had better sit down with him some night and find out what he has provided for her to live on after he is dead," says the forthright lady editor in one of the bluntest lead sentences it has ever been my misfortune to encounter.

However, this is merely the windup. She then swiftly outlines a six-point program to keep the wolf away from the door of the impending widow and it's a daisy (the program, that is).

First, says the pragmatic lady, "convince your husband that he probably will die before you do.

"Men being men, it won't be easy," she tosses in gratuitously, "but it is a statistical fact that most husbands die before their wives."

Once a woman has convinced her ever-lovin' that time's a wasting and he is not long for this world—and if he has not yet fainted dead as a mackerel—the wife is advised to "get out of your head the idea that $10,000 is money."

If he is still listening the little woman should now show him up for the tin-horn piker he is in these inflationary times.

Why, $10,000 is "just about enough to make an unhappy trap for a widow," the editor declares. "If she invests it, she'll do well to get $35 a month. If she spends it to live on, it'll probably carry her just about far enough to make her incapacitated to get a job." (By this time, the author apparently assumes our poor widow would be weakened to the point of rickets after living on her budget diet.)

Furthermore, says this writer, it will take a surprising hunk of that $10,000 merely to bury the brute.

So, after a wife has checked up on her husband's pension possibilities, his insurance and his social security status, she should take another long look at this fading flower and decide whether she will sell the house, once he has gone to his reward, rent it or move in with her children (I can already hear the kids barring the door).

Finally, the lady editor advises the forward-looking wife to cultivate a lot of women friends to stand by her in her hour of bereavement and to take up "church, painting, writing, pets, handicraft or perhaps charity" to occupy her time once good old George has given up the ghost.

I think it was wise, indeed, of the editor to advise her future widows to cultivate women friends. It seems unlikely to me that any woman would be able to cultivate a man friend in that Midwest city for some time to come.

It becomes harder and harder to latch onto a good man, and no wonder. Men are, in hard fact, the thin-skinned sex, and women seem determined to scare them to death long before their allotted time.

Many of them never will see three score and ten, and probably glad of it.

On the other hand, unless the gloom-and-doom content of my mail eases off rapidly, it could make a photo finish of my husband's and my own farewell to this mortal coil.

It is a well-known fact in the publishing world that books run in cycles. Ideas are in the air and highly contagious, as witness the decade of live-and-like-it tomes to which the reading public has been exposed.

But the Pollyanna cycle is running its course, apparently, and is to be followed by a Cassandra cycle. In less than a month a number of books, all intent on preparing me for widowhood, have reached my desk.

Now I am not superstitious, but I am a little Irish. Even the first volume dedicated to helping me adjust to widowhood seemed superfluous. In fact, in something bordering on panic, I rushed into the living room, thrust a thermometer into the mouth of my husband, clamped my fingers on his pulse and begged him to speak to me.

"How can I, with this damn thing in my mouth?" he sputtered over the thermometer.

Three days later, when the second book arrived, dealing with the social, financial, personal and emotional problems of widowhood, I began nagging Add to see the family doctor and have a complete physical examination. I entreated him to look both ways when crossing the street, to drive carefully and lie down for thirty minutes before dinner.

"Jimmy Walker said no one was ever ruined by a book," my husband reminded me.

I tried putting on a bold front, but I began slipping vitamins into his coffee and a tonic for tired hemoglobin into his Scotch and soda.

It made me feel better, even though Add said it was a crying shame a man couldn't get a cup of decent coffee in his own home and bootleggers must be back in the game, cutting the Scotch again.

However, my peace of mind was short-lived. Two more books, exhorting me to deal logically with widowhood, arrived by the same mail, and I found myself hysterically wondering if I had a decent black dress to my name. Or if I could ever bake a loaf of bread like Mama used to make. One of the widows in my growing library on the subject of widowhood baked herself back to normal life through the homemade loaf.

"What are you bawling about?" demanded the head of the house.

"Because I can't make bread," I sobbed. "And I'll never, never learn to get along without you. What shall I do?"

He made several pungent suggestions, ending in a ukase that he would, in the future, open all books arriving at the house.

I've been feeling a lot better since then. But Add is looking quite peaked. The last book he opened, under the new house rule, is titled, *Your Family Without You,* which the dust jacket boosts as "The best way to plan and arrange your affairs to assure the maximum income for your wife and children."

Now we are both reaching for a sedative instead of a sweet.

June is usually bustin' out all over with sweet girl graduates and advice hurled in their direction. The commencement addresses to which they have to listen is the price they pay for a diploma.

The price was pretty high at the Tobé-Coburn School the day the pretty girl graduates had to listen to me before they could latch onto a sheepskin.

I don't know what the school, which prepares its students for commercial careers in the hard-bitten fashion world, or the graduates, expected. But my advice was to get married if they could and work if they would.

No career for women has yet been invented that can hold a candle to matrimony; no happiness comparable to that to be found with a husband and a home.

But for a variety of twentieth-century reasons, many women must draw a bead on both prospective husband and probable employer. Through emancipation of the fair sex, this century has bestowed a unique privilege on modern woman: it has freed us to dance attendance not on one man but two—husband and employer.

For a less sturdy sex than mine, this could add up to double jeopardy. But more and more women are successfully and happily combining marriage and a business career by the simple expedient of a little juggling here, a bit of sleight-of-hand there, the use of a few old mirrors and a twenty-four-hour day.

There is no question about what makes Annie run if she is doing her best to please both husband and employer! She is the target of the new double standard that requires her to maintain a home just like mother used to make and to run her job as efficiently as that maiden lady in the file room who, alas, lives for her work.

The married woman who also works at a career—any job that pays more than $50 per week—must have the tact of a diplomat, the wisdom of the ages and the stamina of a horse to keep both the men in her life content and satisfied.

For, when all is said and done, it is men, not women, who need tender, loving care. We are living in an age of transition. Out of it may eventually come some kind of equal partnership of the sexes. But in the interim, we live in a world in which it is man's custom, right and privilege to be the head of his household, no matter how much bacon the little woman brings home every payday.

There may be a great day ahead for brunettes when gentlemen will not prefer blondes. But I doubt if there will ever come a day when they do not prefer a vine that clings.

It is far better, I warned the young ladies, to have a happy husband in the house than a stag at bay. Because a stag at bay in the home may soon turn out to be a wolf howling on another doorstep.

{❦} {❦} {❦}

The more we alarmed Americans pry into the causes of juvenile delinquency, the more we suspect parental delinquency as the villain in the woodpile.

But I feel there is one increasingly popular theory that won't hold water—the easy out of blaming the working wife and mother for the whole fiasco. Idle wives and mothers, maybe. Neglectful and indulgent mothers, yes. But working mothers, per se, no.

My generation seems to feel that the working mother is a recent invention, probably of the devil. But the widow who has had to support a family is as old as time. So is the wife suddenly responsible for the livelihood of a household that includes an invalid husband.

Through the ages, such women have produced many of the world's finest. In the twentieth century, there is Mrs. Lillian Gilbreth, distinguished consulting engineer and real heroine of *Cheaper by the Dozen*. After the death of her husband, Mrs. Gilbreth managed to feed, clothe and educate her brood of twelve children. None developed into problem cases.

When I was a child in Caldwell, Idaho, I went to school with two boys and a girl whose widowed mother washed and ironed seven days a week. There were no pensions or social security in those days.

Her boys had paper routes, cut lawns and did odd jobs to help out. The daughter worked after school and on Saturdays as a household helper. Problems? Nonsense! They all grew up to be a credit to Mrs. Jones and the community.

Recently I met a distinguished editor who told me that his mother, now in her eighties, is still living in the university town to which she moved with her five young children after the death of her clergyman husband.

She had just enough money to pay two months' rent on a house and to advertise for boarders and roomers. Her son remembers that she worked from dawn till long past dusk. But she managed to put each of her brood through the university.

"We didn't have time to be juvenile delinquents," this editor said. "We all had to pitch in and help."

Only a short time ago I received an invitation to attend a medical school graduation from a boy with whose mother I went to school. Elsa was widowed when he was a baby and his two sisters were under seven. She has taught school ever since to support her children, who are solid young citizens.

The evidence will not support the theory that the working mother is, ipso facto, a delinquent mother. The woman who through economic necessity works to support her children probably spends at least as much time with them as does the bridge-playing mother at the country club.

Perhaps it isn't the amount of time a mother spends with her children that counts so much as how she spends it.

The literature spawned by The Greater New York Safety Council, Inc. in the laudable interest of Safety First, Last and Always, has brightened many a dull day for me. Especially memorable was the *aide mémoire* issued some Junes ago warning any bridegroom against hefting his bride over the doorstep lest he sustain permanent injury to his back.

However, in another release, the Safety Council went much too far. It presupposed that "the surge of energy common to the primary stage of spring fever afflicts all women with an uncontrollable urge to clean house."

Nonsense! Women, heaven help us, clean house for a variety of reasons. But this maniacal process is never sparked by "the surge of energy common to the primary stage of spring fever." *Au contraire.*

As far as I have ever been able to figure out, a woman cleans house not because she is in spring's surging, vernal grip, but because she is boxed in by a feeling of dreary hopelessness that winter will never end, with its concomitant convictions that nothing matters, the world is going to hell in a hand basket, her new spring hat isn't really becoming, the children are savages, her husband isn't as attentive as he used to be, her bridge game is off and the whole house needs new curtains.

In this Slough of Despond, complicated by that rundown, end-of-winter, I-wish-I-were-dead physical lassitude, a woman attacks spring cleaning with true camp-meeting frenzy, because there is simply nothing else left to do!

Since she can't go South for a month or afford a series of facials, she rolls up her sleeves and starts slugging her house, egged on by atavistic, tribal custom and a determination to show the neighbors she still has it in her.

Such cleaning is an inherited characteristic of the American housewife. My grandmother, my mother, my aunts and all the female neighbors tore their homes apart every spring. (So do I.) As I remember, the menfolk, children and dogs ran for the storm cellar or the attic at the first signs. (They still do.)

At the end of a week all of us—big and little—were exhausted. But the house was spotless. And by some miracle we all woke up the next day to find that spring was here.

The night after the big blow we were certain to have for dinner one of Mama's chefs d'oeuvre, a burnt-sugar cake with opera cream filling, and we were safe for another year.

But I know the signs. One day in March I shall feel that my new hat is a hideous mistake, that I cannot endure another twenty-four hours of the weather and that I am too run-down to lift a pinkie. Then I shall pitch into spring cleaning and the linen closet out of sheer despair and general malaise.

"The surge of energy common to the primary stages of spring fever?" Never heard of it!

❀ ❀ ❀

My attention was called not so long ago to a splendid article by Stewart Alsop in the *Saturday Evening Post,* in which he sounded a ringing call for men to cease being mice and become monsters.

Well, not exactly real monsters, either. Mr. Alsop's clarion cry was for men once more to become masterly when faced with the outrageous treatment that so often passes for public service today in hotels, restaurants, buses, trains, stores—any place, in fact, where the general public is at the mercy of representatives of that nebulous, aloof, hidden power known only (as in a Kafka novel) as the management.

Mr. Alsop called for a public uprising, in righteous wrath, against what is known, for lack of a better term, as "being pushed around" by headwaiters, captains and bellboys, by hotel clerks, bus drivers, floor walkers, salesmen, ad infinitum.

That is something that has needed saying for a long time, and a subject upon which I grow quasi-eloquent from time to time.

Mr. Alsop even outlined a procedure by which one blows his top and becomes such a towering monument of indignation that even hotel clerks are cowed. It involves voluntary choking until the "indignee" grows magenta in hue, popped in eye and terrifying in voice and word.

Now this is just dandy, and I applaud Mr. Alsop for striking this forcible blow for liberty in a commercial world in which the going motto is: "The customer is always wrong."

But alas, what he has described, fine as it is, is for men only. When a man, goaded beyond endurance by sloppy, insolent and indifferent service, finally beats his breast and protests, people applaud him admiringly because "he is standing up for his rights in true American fashion."

But if a woman for just cause does likewise, everyone is frightfully embarrassed because "she is making a scene." And the unforgivable sin in a woman is not infidelity or gossip or biting her nails, but making a scene.

Heaven forbid that a member of my sex so far forget herself as to make a scene even though the hotel clerk insults her, the insolent waiter pours soup down her décolletage and the bus driver is rude beyond compare!

Ladies must not lift their voices, grow purple of countenance, jump up and down or appear in the throes of a seizure. This is fine for the boys, and more power to them. But ladies must be ladies if it kills them, and sometimes it almost does. I've chewed my tongue so often that it's raveled.

But, thank God, my sex is not helpless in the face of intolerable provocation. We have a weapon that I beg my sisters to use more often than they do: tears.

I used to hate myself for doing it. But when I discovered in my salad days that only men could make scenes, I hunted around for a womanly substitute. It seemed terribly unfair that only men could chew the rug in public.

However, about that time, I discovered that in extremis tears will reduce the bully on the other side to a frightened pulp. Dirty trick? Nonsense! No more so than Mr. Alsop's simulated fit. I keep an extra handkerchief in my pocket just for occasions when so-called public servants become so impossible there is nothing to do but cry.

The woman who makes a scene gets no place; but the world belongs to us leaky faucets.

I am forever reading another of those terribly depressing articles on the household revolution that science threatens to work in my home in the next decade. Nothing but push buttons and pot luck! Over my dead body!

That's what I said—over my dead body.

The granddaughter of the woman who was a so-called "slave" to a wood-burning stove is now in durance vile to so many labor-saving gadgets that she is on the verge of an urge to take an ax to the whole shiny agglomeration.

One more labor-saving device added to those already cluttering up my home and I shall never have time to come up for air or see daylight.

What really takes the toll of housewives is not so much the cost of keeping these monsters in the pink, as the hours we spend on our knees begging repairmen in their various fields to mend the frail, ailing creatures.

Up to a certain point, labor-saving devices are dandy. But there is a point of no return for the housewife. That point has been reached with the multiplication of these devices into mere gadgets that duplicate the effort and results of other contrivances, gather dust, take up needed space in the catch-all closet and finally wind up on the White Elephant table at the next rummage sale.

Automation in the kitchen is one thing, but confusion is something else again. That's what a multiplicity of gimmicks, each with but a single mission to perform, spells. The old-fashioned, all-purpose stove is, in retrospect, unequalled by the sum of its silly parts scattered from basement to breakfast. Man's work may be from sun to sun, but woman's work is never done because her life is so loused up with the coaxing and care of labor-saving gadgets.

Just about the time I was mulling over these truisms, Dean Judson White of William Woods College for women at Fulton, Mo., flattered me out of my wits by asking me to put my mind to work on the type of curriculum that ought to be offered college women in the sixties.

The dean feels, and rightly, that college curriculums were originally tailored for men only, and that women are merely added starters. In short, Dean White believes the time has come to study a curriculum oriented to women and not just thrust on them by custom and careless chance.

Truth to tell, at the time the dean got in touch with me, I didn't have any red-hot ideas for reforming higher education for women. But I did and do cherish one hard and fast conviction: As long as the world is worth living in, women will be primarily homemakers.

That doesn't bar the girls from law, medicine, the sciences, arts, government or any other exercise of their talents. But the inescapable fact, and to me a most happy one, is that no matter what the members of my sex do outside the home, they are primarily homemakers for their respective husbands and children.

So, on the above premise, it is obvious that what women need, educationally, to face the future is not less masculine-oriented education but more. If the American home is to survive, some philanthropist or foundation must double the size of Cal Tech, M.I.T., Rensselaer Poly and similar institutions, and fill the added facilities with women.

Unless the American wife of the future, and it's nearer than you think, is a master plumber, electrician, carpenter, architect and decorator, the American home by 1970 will be a complete wreck.

The handwriting has been on the wall a long time. But I didn't really get its message until Local 3, International Brotherhood of Electrical Workers, announced that it would go out on strike unless granted a four-hour day! As this is written, the lads already receive $42.90 in wages and benefits for a seven-hour day (i.e., a six-hour day plus one hour overtime).

Under a new contract such a seven-hour day would cost the householder anywhere from $60 on up. Some estimates run as high as $75 per diem.

The only answer is to send us women to technical institutions where we can learn to keep the mechanized, push-button household in working order. Never mind Chaucer and Kant and all that. What the modern woman needs is mastery of the monkey wrench, watts and amperes, hammer, saw, level and screwdriver. And she ought to be able to do a little lathe and plaster work on the side.

Last summer, when one of our air conditioners was ailing, the head surgeon received $10 per hour and his helper, who handed him the scalpel and sponges, drew $4.50 per hour, for a total of $14.50 per sixty minutes. It costs a trifle more to treat and put a dishwasher back on its feet.

Unfortunately, I haven't the slightest talent at do-it-yourselfing. Here is the blindest spot in my education. In the past ten years there's been many a day when I wished I knew less about Proust and Toynbee and a lot more about simple wiring. I grew up in the golden age of the handy man, who is, alas, no more.

What profit it me, Dean White, to bake a cake or parse Freud when I don't know a conduit from a circuit breaker?

🥀 🥀 🥀

Experts (i.e., politicians, statisticians and scientists) are always getting up on their big feet and telling the rest of us what marvelous changes the twentieth century hath wrought in even the most simple and familiar objects.

They dwell at length on the electrification of the egg beater and the razor, and the internal combustion engine in the surrey with the fringe on top.

But they have overlooked the updating of the farmer's daughter, who is identical these days with Liz Taylor, Grace K. Rainier, Audrey Hepburn and maybe Jackie Kennedy.

I have thought these long, long thoughts for some time, and especially since I went to the barn dance given by the Stanton N.J. Grange in Mr. Frank Bodine's barn.

Never saw so many pretty girls in one place in my life, neither at college proms in my salad days nor at the combined Stork, El Morocco and Persian Room in more recent years.

They formed a hep crew, as light on their feet in the cha-cha as in the jitterbug or the Virginia reel. They might have been so many of Marie Antoinette's ladies-in-waiting playing at being Trianon milkmaids. Only these kids really could milk. There wasn't a one of 'em at the dance who didn't know where the switch was in father's barn that turned on the electric milker!

And as for plowing: They could drive the tractor as well as brother any day in the week.

I looked around at the crowd in the big barn, 400 strong from the farms in Hunterdon and nearby counties. Real working farmers and their families, and they looked exactly like Park Avenue hillbillies in costume at an Elsa Maxwell barnyard ball.

All the ladies in fresh, starched cottons, expensive hairdos, bright lipstick and vermilion on their nails, both finger and toe. And the men in Levi's and blinding shirts.

You can't tell the city people from the country people today without a score card, except that the country folks look a mite more prosperous, and what is jingling in their pockets is money and not paper clips.

Then I looked at the faces of the young people, boys and girls, and began to wonder why so many modern Cassandras predict the end of America, not through wars and pestilence, but the decay of her people.

Never saw people who looked less decayed or frayed than these young farm folks. Never saw young people who looked brighter, more self-reliant or in fuller possession of all their buttons. Several of the boys were in uniform, home on leave from the Army, the Air Force and the Navy.

Everyone in the local Grange, including some of the boys home on leave, had pitched in earlier to help get the hayloft ready for the dance. Mr. Bodine's barn was the biggest in the neighborhood: The great loft, whose ribs arched upward like those of a Gothic cathedral, was 103 feet long, 38 feet wide and almost 35 feet high.

"It'll hold 150 tons," Mr. Bodine said, and that's hay.

The Grange charged only sixty cents admission to the dance. In one corner a customer could buy all the homemade cake he could eat for ten cents a big slice. There was devil's food cake with rich thick chocolate icing, fresh coconut cake, cream cakes and angel foods light as feathers.

"It's no problem keeping the young folks down on the farm today," said Mr. Bib Stanley, the dairy farmer who was my next door neighbor. "The kids go into New York, see the price of beef steak and streak for home to start fattening up the calves to sell the suckers in the city.

"The city slickers used to come out here to sell us Brooklyn Bridge," he continued, "but the traffic is reversed now: We go in to sell them Black Angus."

This is just to say that the traveling salesman and his hundred-dollar bills will get no place with the farmer's daughter today. A hundred-dollar bill to that doll is just the small change daddy brings home after selling a load of beef cattle or a ton of butter.

Aping the Lion

O, I would fain be in fashion
    And numbered with those best dressed
But the way is long and irksome
    And there's never time out to rest.

For fashion is hard and fickle,
    Now demanding our bosoms be ample;
Then again, in opposite mood,
    Frowning on so much as a sample.

O, woman is fashion's plaything,
   With skirts never steady or stable.
Are they long? Short? Full? Skinny?
   Who knows? Not me! Not Mabel!

We spend our life in pursuit
   Of a goal that's sure out of range,
For how can we master a problem
   Whose law is immutable change?

My recurrent beef is directed at woman's crowning glory. I once felt that if we could live through the shingle phase we would have passed our darkest hour. Only a year or so ago it appeared that nothing could top the Beehive, which imparted a completely egg-head look to my sex.

But I had reckoned without the coiffures variously touted as the Lion, Cloud, Pom Pom and/or Artichoke cut. They make me regard the crew cut as the good old days.

Let me get a good grip on myself now, before I try to describe the Lion cut. (Believe me, the king of beasts has a libel suit.) This coiffure looks like a hair mattress with a leak at the top. Again, it strongly resembles a rag mop worn as a wig.

The hair bristles up from the crown and then rides off in all directions. There is no visible part, with the result that a lot of hair falls forward over the face. This was always a trying style, even on Jo-Jo, the Dog-Faced Boy, or the English sheep dog, which originated it.

I believe one ground rule of the Lion forbids use of a comb. Instead, the hair is tossed, as in mixed green salad, or passed through an electric fan. The result is as casual as an unmade bed and creates the general effect of a hairdo two sizes too big for the noggin.

No one has yet told me the inspiration for this new cut. But I have a hunch that a sadistic hairdresser, thumbing through an old book of cartoons, ran across one of the crazy violinists who has just run a dead heat with "The Minute Waltz." And the Lion cut was born.

O, I would fain be in fashion,
  But I don't want to look like a Lion;
O, I crave to look à la mode,
  But not like William J. Bryan!

❀   ❀   ❀

Oh, East is East and West is West, but—Kipling or no Kipling—
the women of India and the women of the U.S.A. are met as victims
of a nervous tic.

It is occasioned by an anxiety syndrome, just to toss in a phrase
proving that a little learning is a dangerous thing. This shared tic or
syndrome can be traced to our clothes, although they are half a world
and light years apart.

At a small, private luncheon in New York for Mrs. Indira Gandhi,
daughter of India's Prime Minister Jawaharlal Nehru, there were a
half-dozen Indian women, slim, exquisite and dressed in a ravishing
array of saris.

And there were a dozen of us American women, looking by any
standard pretty mundane and—frankly—drab even in our best town
suits or wool dresses. That is, by contrast with the exotic butterfly
appearance of the guests from India.

Now I have long had a dreamy admiration for the sari, so feminine,
so becoming and so *stable*. So unaffected—need one point out?—by
the dictates of Dior or Givenchy. In the sari there is clothes security,
I have often thought wistfully, as I have paid another $50 (about three
times annually) to have my hems lowered or hiked.

A sari is a sari is a sari. They are handed, always in high style,
from mother to daughter. They are good, so to speak, to the last
fashion drop. And when one buys a sari, there are no measurements,
no fittings, no migraine. And no zippers! Or hooks and eyes, either. A
simple (for Indian belles) twist of the wrist and the sari is anchored
for the day.

Or so it seemed when Mrs. Gandhi and her five compatriots entered our hostess' drawing room and sank gracefully into chairs and sofas. They sat in complete repose, hands at ease, while their delicately manicured bare feet, in thonged sandals, beneath their saris "like little mice, stole in and out, as if they feared the light."

And what were we American women doing in the meantime? You know darn well! We sat there, animatedly chatting and unconsciously, every last one of us, trying to tug her skirt over her respective knees. At that moment, the sari never seemed more attractive or comforting.

This illusion might still be with me if our hostess, at the conclusion of luncheon, had not asked Mrs. Gandhi to tell us something of her work as former head of India's Congress party.

Mrs. Gandhi rose, a slim, petite woman in an especially beautiful sari of pale beige silk, embroidered in shades of brown and worn with the traditional short-sleeved blouse. Hers was of palest green silk.

But ninety seconds after Mrs. Gandhi began to speak, my disillusionment with the sari set in. For Mrs. Gandhi was tugging, too! Only she was tugging horizontally, whereas we Americans tug vertically.

The daughter of Pandit Nehru kept tugging at her gorgeous sari, the better to tighten it around her slender waist. The end of the sari, worn over the left shoulder, appeared to have a will of its own.

With a small, firm hand, Mrs. Gandhi kept pulling it more taut at the shoulder and constantly tugging it more firmly at the waist. And all the time, she was doing it as unselfconsciously as we Americans tug at our hems.

Nor did she seem to get any further with her horizontal pulling and hauling than we Americans get with our vertical yanking. Obviously, we are all frustrated daughters of Eve, longing for a better fig leaf.

If Seventh Avenue, the heart of the nation's garment industry, has an ounce of wit and gratitude it will hastily dispatch a bra and a big bunch of roses to Contessa Christina Paolozzi.

The nude portrait of this young woman in a recent issue of *Harper's Bazaar* is the greatest subliminal argument for clothes since Lady Godiva went horseback riding in her braids.

Without doubt, the magazine and the contessa, age 22, a member of the International Jet Set, have each achieved some kind of "First" with publication of the picture. To begin with, the sponsorship of nudity by a magazine whose *raison d'être* is female clothing is strikingly novel—but no more striking than the readiness of a woman to be identified by name in the magazine after posing for publication in nothing more substantial than Chanel No. 5.

Since the beginning of time, women—and I do not include professional models—have shown a sly, self-confident willingness to pose in the altogether for painters and sculptors. But even the willful Duchess of Alba, after posing thus for Goya, felt it the better part of valor to conceal the fact from her hot-tempered duke.

But we live in a franker age. The transition from "The Barefoot Contessa" to "The Bare Contessa" is only a matter of discarding the bikini. The really surprising result is that the bikini, once abandoned, clinches the argument that clothes are indeed a blessing in disguise. The contessa by first appearing bare and then fully clothed in the following four pages of the magazine offers incontrovertible proof of this thesis.

A real tour de force might have been achieved if the magazine had been able to persuade Marilyn Monroe to pose and Steichen to take her nude picture. Then charm, beauty, mystery and lyricism might have leaped from the page to delight the beholder. Instead, there is a snapshot of a young woman awkwardly posed and no more favored by nature than the average daughter of Eve.

The contessa's left arm is flung back in a gesture indicating that she is trying to scratch that inaccessible and often itchy spot between the shoulder blades. More's the pity there was no door jamb in the offing; she could have achieved the classic solution of her problem by backing up to it and experiencing the delicious relief of rubbing her fifth vertebra against the jamb.

Cyril Ritchard, starring on Broadway in *Romulus,* as the last Roman emperor, thus scratched his back in his first minute on stage. The whole audience settled back and sighed in happy empathy with Ritchard.

If the snapshot of the contessa had been captioned "Picture of a Young Woman Trying to Scratch Her Back," it would have been far more descriptive and eloquent than *Harper's Bazaar's* own defensive caption: "A photographic study of the nude by Richard Avedon, in the classic spirit which, from Praxiteles to Matisse, abhorring the demure and falsely modest, turns rather to a candor and forthrightness of vision that alone do homage to the elegant, mysterious beauty of the human body."

Seventh Avenue ought to get busy digging up the identity of the unsung genius who first said "No nudes is good nudes" and erecting a statue to him. That turns out to be a good, basic rule for the vast majority of women, with such notable exceptions as the duchess and Marilyn Monroe.

Harper's Bazaar, with its excursions into overexposure, has unwittingly proved that not diamonds but clothes are a girl's best friend.

Doubtless to cash in on the current craze for horse opera, a glossy weekly magazine not long ago ran a serial story in pictures and captions on the winning of the West. One chapter pretended to treat of the women who followed their men and the sun into the promised land beyond Missouri and Kansas. But it scarcely scratched the surface. In my childhood I was privileged to know many of these remarkable women, friends of my grandmothers and of my great-grandmother Fulton, who made the long, parched, exhausting trek across the Great Prairie and the mountain barriers.

They seldom if ever spoke of the cruel hardship or the loneliness, of the fear of Indians and the hostile land, of their isolation in time of sickness and need, of the threat of hunger in the years of the locust, of the total lack of comfort.

I have regretted all my life that in my youth I did not know how unique these women were and set down the stories of their respective lives. The men may have brought settlers and commerce to the West, but it was the women who brought civilization.

The number of true Westerners who are descended from formidable beldames who once sicked the dogs on the Indians is scarcely exceeded in this country by the Mayflower descendants. Despite the fact that the Mayflower families had a head start of some two hundred years and despite those long, cold, New England nights, the Western Aristocrats descended from gun-totin' materfamilias are now numbered in the millions.

And for pure snobbery, the descendants of those sturdy pioneer women have the First Families of Virginia beat four ways from the jack.

The men built the saloons and the gambling houses, but the women were the force that carved schools and churches out of the wilderness. And in that order. My grandmother, Mary Jane Callaway, always said that women first organized schools for their children and, on the following day, churches in which to worship.

Neither one of my grandmothers, nor my Great-Grandmother Fulton, was much larger than a cake of soap. They were small, dainty women who, like all pioneer women, did the work of ten whether they had been reared to such work or no. In a day when there were few doctors and no nurses, they cared tenderly for one another, delivered babies, set limbs, applied poultices and homemade remedies. No stranger was ever turned away from their doors, even when they scarcely had enough for their own.

In the twenty-four-hour task of keeping house, cooking, sewing, washing, ironing, scrubbing and preserving every scrap of precious food for their families, each still cherished her own vision of beauty. When the soil had to be wrested from the desert of Idaho to grow food for man and beast, Grandmother Callaway still wrested a little bit more for the lilacs, tea roses and pinks without which she could not live.

These were women accustomed to every hardship. Marauding Indians they took in their stride. Grandmother Callaway knew what it was to be alone when Indians went on the warpath in Boise Valley. Grandma Sinsel, the mother of one of my uncles, once hid her children under the floor of her first rude prairie home in Nebraska and sat with a gun over her trembling knees while a war party prowled outside.

They were all remarkable women, these and the thousands like them. And I hope some day that someone will finally immortalize the pioneer woman in a worthy and wonderful book.

See America First
(THEY'RE ALL TRYING)

Whatever the other distinguishing traits with which we North Americans have been endowed by the Melting Pot, one sticks up on the landscape like a sore thumb. That is the wide streak of gypsy in us, one and all.

We take to the open road like Romanies. If the national thumb is sore, it can be traced to overwork in thumbing directions or asking a lift along the way.

There is so much to see in this lovely land with its all but limitless horizon and variety that a lifetime is scarcely enough to encompass all of it. But no critic can say that we Americans aren't trying! The traffic jams caused by American tourists enjoying their birthright may be exasperating, but they are also heartwarming.

As one of the gypsy horde that takes to the road on vacation, I am constantly entertained, challenged, amazed and amused at our peripatetic population. Whole industries have sprung up to cater to its needs.

These tourist-inspired enterprises vary from that distinctly American phenomenon, the motel with wall-to-wall carpeting, teevee in every room and a swimming pool just outside the door, to ever-multiplying roadside Coney Islands for the children.

Years ago, in the trough of the depression, the head of the house and I drove across the nation. The contrast between that trip and our current ones was that between night and day. The cars we met along the way in 1934 were largely old, decrepit and held together by baling wire.

Tied to the old rambling wrecks, particularly those headed west, were all the family possessions, including dogs, crates of chickens, mattresses and cooking utensils. It was an exodus of desperation and despair.

These many years later, the nation's extraordinary prosperity fills the highways with sleek new cars whose occupants are not in search of Golconda because, obviously, they have found it at home. Now, we Americans are just going (1) for the ride, (2) for the fun of it and (3) for the pleasure of looking at our own country.

Endless statistics are published annually on the vast sums spent by touring Americans in Europe, South America and the offshore islands. But it is my guess that those who tour at home, who fill the roads, the motels, the national parks, the souvenir and postcard stands, the roadside rests, the hamburger bars and the gas stations spend so much more it would make the sum spent by the passport tourist look like peanuts.

I have a few friends in the East who have never been west of Buffalo, and some friends in the West who have never crossed the Rockies. I cry a pox on both of them. They owe it to themselves, but they owe it particularly to their children, to see this gorgeous, incredible, wonderful land that God has given us.

Deep in the Heart of Dixie

On one of our trips we drove deep into the heart of Dixie, all right. For one hundred miles the homemade signs advertising endless roadside eating establishments (if such they really be!) banished all nonsense about hamburgers, hot dogs or barbecue.

"Catfish, Hush Puppies and Turnip Greens," the signs, as one, advertised. And just to emphasize that we were in Tennessee, the home of "mountain dew," a poster near Knoxville advised us to "Stop at Moore's; See Real Moonshine Still." (No free samples.)

On this gold-and-blue autumnal day, drowsy with peace, we crossed a bridge over a placid stream, and glimpsed a river "baptizing." The preacher and his converts, robed in white, were hip-deep in the quiet waters—only a holler from a road marker pointing north and reading "16 Miles to Oak Ridge."

Such a trip is the finest instruction in American geography and history. In a single day, our journey encompassed the gloriously beautiful Great Smoky Mountains and a visit to "The Hermitage," the home of Andrew Jackson, warrior, President and, not least of all, devoted husband.

We took the Blue Ridge Parkway out of Asheville over and through the Smokies to Gatlinburg, a community so wholly devoted to tourism that I was afraid to get out of the car lest I be taken alive and forced to buy a hush puppy, a bouquet of straw flowers or a hand-hooked rug.

The Blue Ridge Parkway through the Great Smokies is one of the most beautiful drives in the U.S.A. The whole area reminded us of a sawed-off Switzerland, heavily wooded except for high, emerald meadows laced with swift mountain streams.

Sixteen green peaks in the Smokies rise above 6,000 feet. Whichever way one looks, the mountains roll away in ridge beyond ridge to the horizon. A gap here, a cut there in the mountains reveals a noble, far-flung vista at every curve in the highway.

More than 461,000 acres of this national treasure in beauty is forever protected as a national park. It is a joy to drive through it and find none of it defaced by billboards. How glorious it must be in spring when the redbuds, dogwood, the laurels and the rhododendrons are in blossom!

"Warning, Do Not Feed the Bears: Play Safe" is a discreet admonition posted throughout the Smokies. For some reason, I had thought this warning reserved solely for Yellowstone Park. But there are b'ar in the Smokies, beggars all. I kept my eyes peeled for them but, apparently, yesterday's visitors had fed them to satiety and they were sleeping it off.

"The Hermitage," home of Old Hickory, is a bonus award on this trip. I had not realized we would pass it on the way to Nashville. What a delightful and handsome old plantation home it is! Just what a damnyankee thinks such a house should be—warm, gracious and full of delightful prebellum mementos.

I especially pointed out to my Republican husband a ring given Rachel Jackson by her adoring husband—a ring set with diamonds, emeralds, amethysts and rubies to spell "dear." No wonder he was a fine President!

The Eighth Wonder of the World

In autumn nature puts her torch to the New England landscape. Hills and valleys flame scarlet and gold, with only here and there a clump of evergreens as counterpoint. Surely if the ancients who compiled the seven wonders of the world had been fortunate enough to see New England at this season, they would have placed it No. 1 on their list. There is nothing in all the world quite like the pageant on which nature and New England conspire each October. Nor is there anything either staid or puritanical about this mardi gras.

One memorable autumn, we drove for miles along the Mohawk and the Berkshire trails in Massachusetts and the Ethan Allen Highway in Vermont. Everywhere, under a silky blue sky fleeced with white clouds, the Berkshire hills, the Green Mountains and the low Taconic range rolled away like waves of molten gold overlaid with every shade of red from coral to maroon.

Each vista was more dazzling than the last. When we thought that nothing could ever be more beautiful than the last wide, peaceful valley, with the lacy spire of its white New England church rising from a base of scarlet maples, we came upon another hillside, another valley where the color was even more breathtaking.

Ours was a wonderful, two-day journey, compounded of peace and beauty, without a single billboard to mar the incomparable landscape. It was obvious that the fame of New England's autumn was at last beginning to attract the American tourist. We saw cars bearing license plates from all over the nation, from as far west as Oregon and as far south as Florida.

I wonder how many persons remember Pownal Center, Vermont?

Some time ago it enjoyed a moment of brief, international fame when the United Nations chose this quiet little village as epitomizing the deep and abiding peace which it, the U.N., hoped to achieve for the world.

The ensuing years have seen only strife and worse in a fear-torn world. The peace that still cradles this village between the gorgeous autumn hills has failed to bless the world. The tiny Vermont community still looks the peaceful ideal as it did years ago to the United Nations. In the Hoosic Valley, surrounded by New England's autumn, Pownal Center still can offer the world incredible beauty and a vision of peace.

Beat Me Daddy—Eight to the Barn

American citizens in the good old summertime who yearn to be couth and cultured have only to head the family car into New England to find themselves in the midst of the biggest, most diverse and concentrated culture klatsch in the nation.

Knock on any barn door north of Greenwich, Connecticut, and it opens on a box office. Displaced herds wind slowly o'er the lea, their barns filled with actors, musicians, ballet dancers, writers, painters, composers and assorted artists.

In the lyric embrace of Massachusetts' beautiful Berkshire hills there is music for everyone from the longhair to the crew cut. It is all rather wonderful and something to which the American can point with pride.

The music, for example, ranges from the Boston Symphony, whose eight-week seasons draw single audiences of as many as 14,000 paying customers, to the Berkshire Music Barn, where huge audiences of jazz aficionados gather to worship at this temple of modern jive.

For those who dig chamber music, there is the Berkshire quartet playing at Music Mountain. For dance fans, there is Jacob's Pillow, created in 1931 as the shrine of modern dance under the aegis of Ted

Shawn. It did not require the talents of a Delphic Oracle to predict that Jacob's Pillow would be mobbed every summer when that indestructible high priestess of the dance, Ruth St. Denis, gave recitals.

As for summer theaters, the lovely woods are full of them. They—the woods—are also full of students. The visiting fireman who takes a stroll thereabouts must be prepared to flush a violinist playing to a clump of birches or an embryo Markova doing ballet nip-ups in a sunny glade.

The Berkshire Music Center, an offshoot of the Boston Symphony's Berkshire season, was founded in 1940 to fulfill the ambition of the orchestra's late, great conductor, Serge Koussevitzky. Since then, more than 5,000 musicians have studied at Tanglewood, often aided by the Tanglewood Revolving Scholarship Fund.

Aaron Copland, distinguished American composer, is chairman of the center's faculty and head of its composition department. (He often guest-conducts his own works and the ovation is tremendous.) The Lenox-Stockbridge sector provides a great teaching as well as looking and listening center of the arts.

If the barns are full of artists and the woods of students, then every spare room in the area is filled with a patron. Inns, hotels, motels, "tourists accommodateds," restaurants and bars are jammed with customers drawn there by the arts.

Rooms must be booked weeks in advance. The license plates on cars tell a fine story of pilgrims from as far away as California and Georgia, all eager to enjoy fine music, dance and theater.

In winter, Boston may lay claim to the title of the Athens of America. But in summer, the title passes to the Lenox-Stockbridge sector, where the seven lively arts are active to the point of St. Vitus, and where they find ardent support from the American public.

Nauts to the Kiddies

Astronauts and cosmonauts may not want any advice from the likes of me. But I have a profound bit of counsel for them that may, in the long run, save them their sanity. Never, never go on a trip to the moon or anyplace else in space with a rocket full of kids. That was my mistake.

No matter how much the astronauts or cosmonauts know about their jobs, the kids will know more and will have no hesitation in saying so.

Now a trip to outer space, at least when I recently visited Atlantic City, New Jersey, is made in a long, shiny rocket that looks like stainless steel and seats thirty darling passengers. It didn't embarrass me to be the only adult in a crowd that was composed otherwise of sevens-to-elevens—it just made me mad. Grownups ought to show a little spunk, too.

No sooner were the doors of the rocket secured, than a warning sign appeared: "Fasten Seat Belts; Put Out Cigarettes." And no sooner did the sign appear than a small comedian in the back of the plane yelled, "Charlie, drop that chocolate cigar!"

"They do it different at Cape Canaveral," yelled the fat little boy opposite me as we blasted off.

"Where's the cherry-picker?" screamed a small fiend up front.

"My space suit ain't working," yelled the fat boy, determined not to be topped.

And all the time, through the simulated window in the front of the rocket, we were blasting through the heavens, past stars, comets, constellations. And I was straining to hear the smooth commentary that came over the intercom, explaining the sights like an American Express guided tour.

But I couldn't hear a word above the fat boy yelling, "Hold me Gertie, I'm weightless"; the child in the rear crying, "I'm yawing; watch me! I'm yawing!" and a moppet in back who seemed to be giving the rebel yell and announcing, "I'm the booster rocket; I'm the booster rocket!"

"Keep still!" I hissed at the fat boy. After all, I had come on this trip as an educational venture. I wanted to hear the sound track. But I was the only one who did.

"I'm in orbit!" the fat boy bawled.

"Naw, you aren't," shouted the little girl. "You're in New Joisey!"

In the window up front, another rocket passed us. Then a satellite. Next, a space ship.

"It's the Russians," cried my fat friend.

"Rat-a-tat-tat, rat-a-tat-tat," sounded machine guns as every kid drew a bead on the space ship.

At that moment, there swam into horrid view a dreadful monster from outer space. He looked like a cross between Gargantua and King Kong. And he drew back a huge iron club with which to break up our space ship.

"Yah! Yah! Yah!" sneered the fat boy, at the top of his lungs, "he looks like my father's mother." The space ship broke up, all right. The small fry would have rolled in the aisles, except for their safety belts.

There is little else to say except that when we landed, the fat boy wanted to know where the helicopters were and a sassy girl-child yelled "Fake" because she wasn't being picked up out of the water a la Gus Grissom.

When I climbed out of the rocket, I felt like the cub reporter at the fire who phoned his editor, "All is confusion, can learn nothing."

If confusion is to be avoided in the cosmos, leave the kids at home, is my advice.

On the College Circuit

Occasionally in my editorial enthusiasm for men—just any men—I am accused of overlooking the ladies.

The slight is unintentional. Under present circumstances it is quite impossible to achieve the former without an assist by the latter. Further, at least part of this story is strictly for girls. At Pennsylvania State University, where I once lectured, there are still 2.3 men students for each and every girl enrolled in the school.

This blissful proportion is far, far better than that in the state of Alaska, which has always had the reputation of being The Happy

Hunting Ground for my sex. The old theory operated on the frozen premise that if one cornered a man in the Klondike, he stayed cornered, thanks to distance, difficult escape routes and that, aside from the Malamute saloon, evenings tended to be lonely.

I am happy to report that this is approximately true of Pennsylvania State University, which is not as far as the Klondike but equally as remote.

The mountain fastness in which Pennsylvania located her State University is the geographic center of the commonwealth. Yet it is served by no known railroad. A visitor must debark at stations ranging from thirty to fifty-five miles distant, depending upon where it is decided to flag the fast freight.

There is fleet service over the mountains to State University by ox cart in summer and by dog sled in more rugged weather. When fog or hail in the Alleghenies makes it impossible to communicate with the outside world by smoke signal, there is emergency drum and/or carrier pigeon service to make contact Out There.

But all in all, a girl who runs a man to earth there has the Indian sign on him. It is almost impossible for him to get reinforcements from home in time to be of any real benefit. By then, he's roped and hog-tied.

Yet it is obvious that Penn State University has some kind of better mouse trap, besides the obvious one. At all odds, some 22,000 students beat their way across the mountain barriers to enroll there in '61-62. Parents find the locale especially comforting. Once an offspring is stashed away at Penn State U, parents need never worry about his whereabouts, as do paterfamilias in the Ivy League.

Its inaccessibility makes the State University an ideal place for either an institution of learning or a penal colony. After twenty-four hours at the school, I realized that if a kid or a con is set down there, it's a sure thing that either the Dean of Women or the warden can put a finger on one or the other in a jiffy. Escape is impossible.

On inquiry, I discovered that state officials had been as perceptive. Not only is the University located here, but the Rockview (so truly named) Penitentiary is just seven miles distant.

It's always difficult to tell whether students at Princeton, Harvard, Yale, Vassar and Wellesley are matriculating in Math. I or the flesh-pots of Broadway, which are so handy. But at Penn State U, an ed or coed is in for the duration.

The center of campus life, even as in my day, is the college dog wagons. Several students were kind enough to buy me hamburgers in the local Mermaid Taverns. Two great improvements in higher education since I got mine a generation ago are visible in such inns.

The hamburger remains constant, or at least the meat quotient does. But the other two chief adjuncts to a B.A. or a B.S. today are new. They consist of the juke box and the pinball machine which have replaced the gramophone and punchboard of my day. Higher mechanization, in keeping with the scientific age, has now taken over.

It is bound to produce a sharper, hardier breed. But the new educational sauce serves both goose and gander. The latter is going to be gone, real gone, if the former draws a bead on him in that remote fastness.

Mush By Day, Mush By Night

In my lifetime, the University of Wisconsin has always been touted as one of the most beautiful schools in the U.S.A., blessed with a campus of surpassing physical charm.

It was my misfortune to be unable to see the campus during a brief visit. A thick white blanket of foreign matter covered the landscape. I am confident that if they ever got this stuff scraped off the surface and coaxed the temperature up to zero the campus might indeed be very well worth looking at.

Anyone contemplating the dispatch of his offspring to the University of Wisconsin should be warned that in addition to the ordinary goods and gear required by the average college student, the Wisconsin student should be equipped with a bushel and a peck of pemmican and a good pair of sled dogs.

If the pemmican runs out during a really bitter winter, the student can always eat hot dogs until the pack trains get through in the spring.

Neither skis nor snow shoes are obligatory, but they help. And I noted that numerous young women attended classes in ski pants and boots. It is very *soigné* to wear pants casually tucked into boot or galosh tops. I struggled for two hours to make mine meet before I realized that I would either have to sew a cuff on the galoshes or a ruffle on my st-p -ns.

Some college professors stir up hydrogen bombs and others deal with the humanities. It is this latter group which has always interested me.

Two in this category have delivered themselves of particularly distinguished sentiments in the past few decades. Way back there, a Princeton professor advised the graduating class that the surest way to succeed was to marry the boss's daughter, than which no sounder advice was ever given a group of eager collegiate beavers.

The second and more recent sentiment was uttered by a lecturer in sociology at the University of Wisconsin, who said, out loud, that what college students need is a little privacy in which to do a bit of petting and to make passes at each other.

Students had never been hindered by the lack of privacy in the more than century of University existence. However, they were intrigued by the professor until it developed that he was all for setting aside a petting preserve on the leafy shores of Madison's lakes, and installing benches and lights, for heaven's sake.

(I assume the place thaws out eventually and leaves actually appear, although when I was there it seemed highly unlikely.)

The student body reacted sharply at the mention of lights. Students had been doing well on the shores of Lake Mendota without either benches or lights for several decades. The consensus was that if benches entailed lights, then what was good enough for grandpa and grandma was good enough for the current crop.

The long and short of it is that the preserve has never been set aside, and no one has yet complained of the dark. Robert Taylor, public relations director of the University, says it was decided "that there was no use mechanizing the thing."

However, Wisconsin is proud of the fact that the huge and handsome Elizabeth Waters dormitory for women, built just before World War II, is equipped for the amenities. Cozy little sitting rooms off the main drawing room allow a courting couple a measure of privacy.

The name of "Passion Pits" was so thoroughly tacked on these sparking parlors that when I asked a dignified University official about them, he reached into his files and pulled out a big folder marked—"Passion Pits."

It is doubtful if any alumni are more attached to their Alma Mater than Wisconsin grads. From time to time they return to Madison to be married on Picnic Point, a favorite campus trysting ground.

The romantic aura surrounding the point has not even been shaken by the former coed, married at the Point, who returned for a divorce on the ground that marriage is no picnic.

The Leer That Made Milwaukee Famous

Uncle Horace, the old rounder, always said Milwaukee's three most famous products were beer, German food and Gilda Gray.

Uncle, who was devoted to the good life, said as a cultural troika they beat Carnegie Hall, Grant's Tomb and the Metropolitan Museum all hollow.

"Show me a picture," Uncle Horace used to say delicately, out of deference to the children, "that can vibrate like Gilda!"

So I went to Milwaukee to savor all three. But I left a frustrated woman. Beer I had right up to my scuppers. But I never could get a mouthful of German food or within hailing distance of Miss Gray, although this Milwaukee girl was vibrating nightly in a downtown saloon.

Milwaukeeans, at least those with whom I came in contact, are so all-fired refined in this generation that the mere mention of German food makes them shudder.

They obviously prefer second-rate French food to the good first-rate German food that must abound in the place if one has a chance to get at it.

"Sauerkraut," they gasped, then trembled like reeds in the wind or broken zither strings. "Reely, Mrs. Robb, you cahn't be serious."

"Well, I am," I kept saying defiantly, "and what's the matter with sauerkraut, except maybe it smells a little? In New York, I get all the second-rate French food I can eat. In Milwaukee, I want hasen-pfeffer, sauerbraten and pigs' knuckles with sauerkraut in a tub."

"Pigs' knuckles," they cried in horror. "Oh, not reely."

I don't get it. Pigs' knuckles were invented in Milwaukee, and now the descendants of the good German burghers who made the town are so elegant that unless they are munching on third-rate frogs' legs Provençal or guinea hen under glass, they aren't happy.

"Okay, okay," I said, knowing when I am licked. "Forget the pigs' knuckles and the kraut and I will eat this pressed duck. But let us eat in time to go see Gilda Gray."

"And whom may she be?" they asked, and I quote correctly. They are so refined they don't even use "who" in polite conversation.

Manners are manners, but just how long do you have to be polite? I counted ten and then reminded the folks that most of them were shaking that thing as early as Gilda, a home town girl who made good on Broadway and then came home again to retrieve her broken fortunes.

But I couldn't win, not in Milwaukee; the mob I was with had no pride or patriotism. The argument that a girl of Gilda's age, who could still shake that thing, ought to have encouragement from her fellow citizens cut no ice. I was about to leave town, and still hadn't latched onto a pigs' knuckle or cased Gilda.

"She is performing in a saloon," said one of the grand dames, haughtily wrapping herself around her eighth Manhattan, a drink I regard as the kiss of death.

"Look who's talking," I said, loud and clear, and I caught the next plane home.

I should have known that this was not the true-blue Milwaukee crowd. True-blue Milwaukeeans only drink beer. To them, whisky is a dirty, six-letter word. But my acquaintances who rejected both ham hocks and Gilda also felt beer was quite, quite common. And martinis and Manhattans such refined, ladylike refreshments. Even when they were under the table, they still felt that way.

Well, sir, the next time I am in Milwaukee I am going down to police court, and there I can surely find a good, honest, native flatfoot with vulgar tastes in food and entertainment to match my own.

Laughing Water

During most of this century the white man's burden in Minneapolis has been a valiant attempt to live up to Henry Wadsworth Longfellow's ode to the noble red man, "The Song of Hiawatha."

In that interim, Minneapolis, together with the state and federal governments, has spent hundreds of thousands of dollars trying to coax a trickle of water over the city's most famous landmark, Minnehaha Falls.

The New England poet, who never ventured this far into the wild and woolly west, nonetheless described the falls with such feeling in "Hiawatha" that it has been a tourist "must" ever since the poem was published in 1855.

Every right-thinking American who ever mastered a third grade reader wants to see

> Where the Falls of Minnehaha
> Flash and gleam among the oak trees,
> Laugh and leap into the valley.

During the major share of the past four decades, tourists have been able to find the falls, all right, but they haven't been able to locate the water even with a divining rod.

The sad truth is that as the city expanded, the famous falls shrank, doomed by civilization's onward march. By 1914, the squalid facts could no longer be concealed: city sewers had drained the poetic falls, named for the red-skin Juliet, of their water supply.

It was no longer a laughing matter for either the falls or Minneapolis. There is nothing more embarrassing to a municipality than a naked waterfall with a national reputation.

Thus began the city's struggle to live up to Longfellow and keep the falls milling if not laughing out loud as in Henry's day. The first of the city's artificial respiration plans for the falls was undertaken: the construction of a reservoir to feed it.

From that time on, the city, state and federal governments tried, in a manner of speaking, one dam thing after another, to keep Minnehaha chortling.

By 1921, the city devised a faucet plan. The big waterfall was turned on and off for tourist benefit during the summer season. One of the tourists in the twenties for whom the city turned on the water was Cal Coolidge, a New England boy who wanted to see the falls.

> And beyond them stood the forest,
> Stood the grove of singing pine trees,
> Green in summer, white in winter, ever singing,
>   ever sighing.

Ever sighing, too, were the city fathers. They were continually adding sluice gates, dams, electric pumps and what-not to coax water over the dry ledge of Minnehaha. Sometimes the city didn't even have enough money to operate all the gadgets.

And so it went until a decade ago, when, for the first time in ages, Minnehaha Falls finally filled with what nature and the poet intended: water. The white man's burden was lifted that summer by the bounty of nature, heavy snows and rains throughout the year.

In these days of the great Red Skin Revival via teevee, the city's cup and the falls runneth over in prodigal abundance in April, May, June and sometimes July when:

> The Thaw, the great thaw water,
> Loosened from its Winter corset
> Floods the High Falls
> As it oughter.
>   (Courtesy I. Robb)

Only in those months is there any certainty that water in plenitude will hurl itself over the fifty-foot drop and race away in the narrow, tree-lined gorge as in the days when Minnehaha and Hiawatha—or their counterparts—did their sparking there.

In the spring, the torrent drops into a foaming pool. Spray and mist rise like a jeweled fog and catch the rainbow in a shining arch across the waters.

It is as lovely as Longfellow implied.

But, you are asking, how could Longfellow describe the falls so beautifully if he never saw them? Simple, my dear Watson: a young Chicago photographer, Alexander Hesler, took the first daguerreotypes of the falls in 1852. A mutual friend gave copies to Longfellow, who was so inspired he wrote an ode immortalizing a waterfall and impoverishing a city.

Ready for the Next Round

To fly almost directly from Moscow, Russia, to Moscow, Idaho, is not unlike being shot forward in a time capsule. It is a unique experience to be catapulted by plane from a nation under rigid control to the great open spaces of the free and easy West where there is still a premium on rugged individualism.

Our Moscow is the home of the University of Idaho. Indeed, both Moscows are the sites of universities, but with a difference. The University of Moscow, Russia, is one of the show places of the nation, partially housed in an enormous wedding-cake skyscraper of which the Russians are inordinately proud.

Russia's Moscow University has everything: buildings, laboratories, parklike campus, 24,000 students and a good faculty. It has everything, that is, except academic freedom and the right of students to seek and know impartial truth.

Idaho's university has only 7,000 students and not a skyscraper to its name. But it has academic freedom pressed down and running over. Its students have the right to stick their inquisitive noses into any facet of learning that may strike their respective fancies.

Here is the chief difference with a capital "D."

My presence on this campus, which is spectacular in its mountain setting, was both joyous and a trifle melancholy. I went there to deliver the commencement address at the university I attended for two years in the sweet long ago. Such an invitation is always flattering until one realizes that such solicitations only come to those who are, to say the least, mature. For a woman, such an invitation is an emotional mixture of the bitter with the better.

What does one say to a graduating class in these times? Ever since I can remember, the gist of commencement orations has emphasized the fact that the world is in a precarious state, thanks to the folly of the preceding generation.

The graduating class of the University of Idaho heard no such sad old song from me. If these youngsters are smart enough to be graduated from college, they know the world is in a precarious state, living in a frightening balance of terror.

Nor did I fly west to apologize for their fathers and their grandfathers. It is my conviction that each generation, picking up the loaded dice, does the very best it knows how in a world that is increasingly complicated. The most that can be asked of any graduating class is to face its problems and do the best it can, even as other generations before it.

The present generation of graduates is sometimes as unfairly tagged the beat generation as mine was named the lost generation. Lost? Shucks, I was confused a few times. But lost? Never.

This generation is no more beat than mine was lost. The few beatniques around rouse in me a fervent urge to kick them in the seatniques. I have no use for this group, full of self-pity at having to grapple with a world it never made. No one has ever yet made the world he inherited. Half the fun and challenge of life is trying to make something better out of that helter-skelter inheritance.

The beatniques can't change the world by withdrawing from it in untidy silence. One changes the world by standing up to it and not feeling sorry for himself. Of all the emotions, self-pity is the most corrosive and shameful. No generation was ever beat, really beat, that has been ready to climb up off the canvas and try for a haymaker in the next round.

Brush Work

The Sunday painter is a national phenomenon that has swept the country like a prairie fire in the last two decades. Young and old, rich man, poor man, beggar man, thief: Everybody daubs.

Until I went to Cedar Rapids, I thought the craze had developed like baby dear: "Out of the nowhere into the here." Now I believe I have traced the origin of this craze, which rivals that for the twist and hot rods.

The late Grant Wood, one of the most famous of American artists, was conducting a painting class for Cedar Rapids businessmen as early as 1929.

Not out of the effete ateliers of the East, but out of the pragmatic Midwest prairies came this urge to express himself in paint on the part of John Q. Citizen.

The story of the starving American artist in the midst of plenty, unappreciated by the nation's grass roots Babbitts, is one of this nation's stock literary figures.

But it didn't and it doesn't happen that way in Cedar Rapids, which, by literary rights, ought to be inhabited by Philistines (i.e., bumpkins who don't know their pigs from their Picassos).

Maybe the literary longhairs ought to take another look at the Midwest. The people of Cedar Rapids always loved Grant Wood and gave him, a home town boy, their loyal support from the time he was a young artist. Long before he had gained national or international fame, the home folks in this town of 90,000 souls liked his work and bought his canvases.

Long before the world thought he was good and great, his neighbors did. There were a dozen men and women there who saw that he got to Europe to study and who even invented commissions that would take him abroad.

Several hundred of Grant Wood's canvases, including his famous portrait of his mother ("Woman with Plants"), are owned and hung in this little city.

Some seventy canvases hang—of all places—in the most unusual art gallery in the world: the Turner Mortuary or funeral home, or undertaking parlor. I had to go all the way to Cedar Rapids to find a funeral parlor in which I think I could lie still long enough to be decently buried. And this because Grant Wood canvases replaced, in this mortuary, the standard potted palm.

The late David Turner, funeral director and native of Cedar Rapids, must have been an extraordinary man, and I am only sorry that I never met him. But his son, John B., a delightful young man, showed me through the Turner art gallery or, if you will, mortuary.

It was Dave Turner who finally persuaded Grant Wood, poor as a church mouse, to quit teaching school and devote all his time to painting. It was Dave Turner who gave him a studio apartment in what had been the hay loft of a Gay Nineties carriage house and is now a garage for the funeral cars. It was Turner who bought forty-four Grant Wood canvases before such paintings as "American Gothic," "Daughters of the Revolution," "Midnight Ride of Paul Revere" and "Stone City, Iowa," were painted in the hay loft and made Wood internationally famous as an American regional painter.

Mr. Turner had faith in Grant Wood, but so did a lot of other supposedly money-grubbing, unaesthetic Midwestern highbinders. They loved him, too, and they speak of him now not so much as a great artist but as a dear friend whom they miss profoundly.

But the people of Cedar Rapids didn't stop with Grant Wood.

People out there buy pictures as unself-consciously as Onassis buys Great Masters. Marvin Cone, friend of Grant Wood and famous in his own right, is a local boy whom the home folks have always esteemed. Not only that, they buy his stuff. The same was true of John Noe, a most successful businessman who began as a Sunday painter.

To the eye, Cedar Rapids looks prosaic, but I wouldn't be surprised if it isn't one of the real art centers of America.

We Ain't Mad But—

The Vigilantes have ridden again in defense of the fair name of Saint Paul. Thus one more chapter is written in the desperate feud and long rivalry between St. Paul and Minneapolis, an affair whose savagery makes the Hatfield-McCoy clans resemble kissin' cousins.

The rivalry between these two Midwest metropoli outdoes in ferocity even that between Dallas and Fort Worth in Texas, where everything is bigger and better. Down thar, with thirty miles between the two, Texans have to sight each other through telescopic lenses. But in Minnesota, with only the lovely upper Mississippi River flowing between the two cities, irate partisans can draw a bead on each other with a squirrel gun.

Citizens of the St. Paul half of the Twin Cities were fed up with the hard fact that a hamlet immediately to the east, which shall remain nameless as long as St. Paul can manage (but which is known locally as Minneapolis), seemed to monopolize all the publicity and take all the bows.

Consequently, a few years ago a group of St. Paul residents formed an organization called the Wambuts, with the laudable aim of intimidating any individual, group or organization that through ignorance, carelessness or malice slighted St. Paul in favor of Minneapolis.

The Wambuts broke down into (cap W) we ain't mad, (cap) but (uncap) . . . Off to a fast start, they soon intimidated such formidable organizations as the House of Morgan, the New York *Herald Tribune,* the investment firm of Merrill Lynch, Pierce, Fenner and (then) Beane, and a galaxy of railroads, airlines and resort and travel agencies.

For years before the Wambuts came into being, St. Paul citizens had done a slow burn about a lot of injustices. For example, although they paid half the upkeep of the Twin Cities' International Airport, tickets always read simply, "Minneapolis." Stewardesses made the heinous error of announcing, "We are now about to land at the Minneapolis airport."

The Wambuts went to work on that. As a result, air tickets now read Minneapolis and St. Paul, and any stewardess or pilot who makes any announcement about the "Minneapolis airport" is apt to have a Wambut in her/his hair, screaming like crazy.

When the sacrosanct House of Morgan addressed a letter to "The First National Bank of St. Paul, St. Paul, Minneapolis," the Wambuts, after repairs to individual blood pressures, went to work. Nailed the Morgan hide to the door, in a manner of speaking.

In fact, the House of Morgan was so intimidated it didn't even try to apologize in a routine letter. It assigned its Poet Laureate, one Al Foote, to write a properly apologetic ode in retribution.

Reader's Digest, Kiwanis magazine and the Duncan Hines group were all given what-for by the Wambuts, too. And each promised to reform, lead a better life and give St. Paul a square shake from then on.

An innocent bystander visiting the Twin Cities could wish the rivalry between the two not quite so intense. It is ridiculous to be put to the trouble of placing what amounts to a long distance call if you want to phone from one city to the other, when only a river separates them.

Even the sun and the rain do not fall alike upon the twain. It's according to which community you're in whether the sun is warmer and more blessed, the rain wetter and more dreary. And a St. Paul girl will remain an old maid rather than lower the flag and marry a lad from Minneapolis, or vice versa. Oh, they're twin cities all right—but don't insult either by pretending they're identical!

Girls, Go Southwest

This is the day I ask Horace Greeley to move over. I have a message for the ladies. Go Southwest, girls. Texas, that is. The Lone Star State has the most of everything, including men. Yippee! There are more single men than women in Texas. These are glad tidings indeed. Nothing in recent years has grieved me more than the ugly fact that in the fifties for the first time in our history women outnumbered men in these United States.

But not in Texas! The pickin's are good. Not all Texas men are oil and cattle barons. But they all aim to be. Texas is full of women, whose diamonds now clank when they walk, who helped their respective husbands get a start in the oil fields by taking in boarders, roomers and washing.

I don't want to inch into the field of Miss Ann Landers and Dear Abby, but a gal with spunk who is dying on the matrimonial vine could do worse than thumb her way to Texas.

In my travels through the Lone Star State is was interesting to discover that the Big Rich in Houston are just as much figures of legend and fun to the rest of the state as Texans in general are to the rest of the nation.

The remainder of Texas was chuckling not long ago at the predicament of Houston, growing like a weed in all directions, and with virtually no zoning ordinances for the protection of property owners.

An attempt to create zoning ordinances was defeated when one of the Biggest Rich denounced such ordinances as communistic interference with the right of private property!

Texas is full of wonderful stories, some true, about its rich. It tells them with the same relish as do we poor relations in the forty-nine satellite states.

There is the tale of the Yankee visiting Houston, who went for an early morning walk and met a little boy delivering newspapers before school. The child was making his free throw at each door stoop from the back of an imported sports car.

When the Yankee looked his surprise, the liveried chauffeur explained haughtily that "Master Tom's parents wish him to experience the benefits of work and thrift."

This story may have its roots in the fact that Texas' rich and handsome former governor, Allan Shivers, did take over his son's paper route in Austin when the little boy had a cold and delivered the papers from a gold-plated heap.

Then there is the story of the Dallas man so near-sighted he had worn glasses since childhood. Recently he got into his air-conditioned car with a friend and started down the highway. After a few miles he took off his glasses.

"Cripes, Joe! Put on your glasses or you'll kill us," his friend yelled. "Relax!" bawled Joe. "When I brought in them last two gushers, I took this car down and had the windshield ground to my prescription."

I might as well admit at the beginning that I went to Houston, the home of the Big Rich, only on sufferance, and was pledged to keep a civil tongue in my head. I had a very difficult time getting a visa for Houston, merely because I live in the same town, New York, as Miss Edna Ferber, author of *Giant*. There was some talk of guilt by association.

Houston has some of the richest citizens in the United States or the whole world, including Texas, for that matter. It is also the only city with poor millionaires who are sad sack characters with more than one but less than ten millions in the bank.

Middling millionaires are men with $50,000,000 or better, and the Big Rich, for which this city is noted, must have a minimum of $100,000,000 to make the grade.

It is difficult for Houston to understand that wealth in such profusion is apt to stun visiting firemen. It even stuns other Texans, such as the gentleman from Fort Worth who attended a party there at which his host pointed out to him a profusion of Big Rich.

Finally his host pointed out a man and said: "Sam over there is worth about two million."

"On relief, I presume?" the Fort Worth citizen asked.

"No," said his host, "Sam's wife is a good manager."

It's this kind of story I wish to avoid, because it makes the Proper Houstonian feel he is misunderstood and that outlanders may even be having a little fun at his expense.

The trouble is that foreigners like myself are left a little breathless by incidents such as a conversation to which I was privy. I was quartered in a huge swimming pool with hotel attached. As I stood waiting for an elevator to waft me to the lobby a man and his teen-age daughter, both in bathing attire, waited with me.

"Daddy, my prescription sunglasses don't match my bathing suit," the young lady said petulantly.

"For Pete's sake, don't bother me about it. Get another pair!" her Paw ordered impatiently.

It is manifestly unfair to tell such stories about Houston, merely because people elsewhere have to make do with any old pair of expensive sunglasses.

In all seriousness, the endless flow of oil has enabled Houston's Big Rich to be the most generous persons in the world; they give millions to worthy causes with less thought than the average citizen shells out $5 to the United Fund. One result of this generosity is the Houston medical center, one of the finest in the nation.

The trouble is that impoverished visitors like myself are more apt to be impressed with the Big Rich hostess I met at a dinner party who said it was no trouble to keep her house filled with flowers.

She just goes out in the garden, points out to her gardener what blooms she wants cut, then has her secretary call Mr. X., who comes to the house and arranges them expertly at $50 an hour.

Onion Orgy

Spring comes to Oklahoma, the only state in the nation named for a musical comedy, heralded not by April showers and May flowers, but by the annual wild-onion feast of Oklahoma's many Indians. In this generation the noble red man lives in an air-conditioned tepee, drives a convertible and, if he is an Osage, treasures his grandmother's mink blanket as a family heirloom.

But the wild-onion feast of spring is as meaningful to him as the Thanksgiving turkey to his white brethren. Before civilization blessed the red man with the can opener and the home freezer, he spent the long winter months existing on hominy and smoked meats and longing for a taste of green sass.

As soon as the onions were large enough to pull, whole Indian families, young and old, went to gather the succulent little onions. They were cleaned, boiled until tender and then drained. Finally, they were mixed with scrambled eggs in an early American version of the French omelette aux fines herbes.

I was lucky enough to arrive in Tulsa one year in time for the annual wild-onion dinner given by the Indian women of the Witt Memorial Methodist Indian Mission, a mission whose membership represented twenty-one Indian tribes.

The little mission borrowed the Boston Avenue Methodist Church, the biggest Methodist church in town, for its wild-onion dinner. More than 400 men, women and children, ranging from full-blooded Indians to others with no more than a proud thirty-second degree kinship, sat down to the feast patterned after the dinners of long ago.

It was a delicious, homey banquet with only two modern innovations: fruit salad and coffee. Otherwise the dinner was traditional: the *pièce de résistance,* scrambled eggs and onions; baked ham, squaw bread, hominy and grape dumplings. If Lo and his wife and children wanted a real touch of the old days, they scorned coffee and took either sofkey or sassafras tea.

The church's modern kitchens bustled with a dozen busy Indian women a few hours before the dinner as they put the finishing touches to the feast. Here were women so accustomed to modern kitchen gadgetry that they would have been helpless trying to get a meal over a camp fire.

Squaw bread, one of the skillful cooks explained, is really baking powder biscuits rolled into flat, round cakes, and fried in deep fat. The bread came out puffy, and a luscious deep golden brown.

"Our grandmothers used their knees as a bread board for rolling out the dough," one of the women laughed. The other women smiled and nodded.

Grape dumplings were new to me, too. Another Indian woman in a starched cotton frock, enveloping apron and chic patent leather pumps, explained that they were made like ordinary dumplings except that grape juice is used in mixing them instead of milk or water.

"Of course, our parents and grandparents used wild grapes," one of the women explained, as she showed me the rich purple dough. "I think they used to be called 'possum grapes.' "

The dumplings are also boiled in grape juice. They can be served hot or cold, and top off an Indian meal. I thought them delicious. I took the sassafras tea instead of coffee. It carried me back to my childhood when the sassafras teapot boiled on the back of the stove for six long weeks each spring and we children drank it regularly and liked it.

I tasted the sofkey, but I fear I would have to learn to like it. It tasted like the water in which hominy had been boiled for a long time. Grains of corn floated around in the liquid.

"As a matter of fact," said one of the women discreetly, "some like sofkey when it has aged a bit and is a trifle—well—more sour in taste."

Let me see now, what is Cherokee for corn squeezin's?

San Francisco I Love You

I'm in love, I'm in love, I'm in love with a wonderful city, San Francisco, and I have been for as long as I can remember (I first set perambulator in San Francisco at six months, and it was a case of love at first sight).

Ever since I have been carrying on a violent affair with this jewel of the commonwealth, this peerless pearl of the Pacific. All good Americans go to Paris when they die, but I would like to make advance arrangements for four months out of the twelve right there.

What has The City of Light got that San Francisco lacks, except a head start and, possibly, the Eiffel Tower, the Tour d'Argent and Brigitte Bardot. In addition, everyone in San Francisco speaks English and it is possible to get a cup of American coffee and eggs sunny side up without any argument. And the taxi drivers don't seem animated by homicidal intent.

Mind you, now, I have every intention of going to Paris, post mortem, but only on a part-time basis; three months in Paris, three in Venice, three in Marrakech (at the foot of the Atlas Mountains in Morocco) and three in San Francisco.

San Francisco is the most fascinating and beautiful city in the Western Hemisphere, and I am in no mood to entertain any outraged squeals of protest from such outlying districts as New Orleans, Quebec, Victoria, Rio de Janeiro, Buenos Aires, Santiago or Charleston, either S.C. or W.Va.

Indeed, on its steep hills rolling down to the Golden Gate, San Francisco is one of the few really unique and lovely cities of the world. Most cities are man-made. Only a precious few, such as Rio de Janeiro and Marrakech and San Francisco, owe their beauty to God.

Venice, so enchanting it wrings the heart, is man-made. But San Francisco, so lovely it lives in the heart, owes its breathtaking beauty to nature and nature's God. Man has built well in San Francisco, but it is the awesome combination of mountains and rolling hills and jewel-like bay that makes it America's "eternal city."

As one crosses the bay from Oakland, San Francisco in the sun is a gleaming white city rising tier by tier on her many hills, like Algiers rising out of the Mediterranean.

It is a city in which every prospect pleases and even man doesn't seem quite as vile as usual. It is a cosmopolis presiding over one of the greatest natural harbors in the world, rivaled only by Rio and Sydney and Seattle.

Man has only to lift up his eyes to see the green hills across the bay from the city and to look down to see the waters in between, spanned by two of the most spectacular bridges in the world.

Three quarters of a million persons live in San Francisco homes perched on hills that only a goat or a cable car can climb. Here is one of the world's few large cities in which inhabitants look out upon gardens, flowers, green hills and blue waters—providing there isn't a fog. And only unfriendly people mention that. Here there are hedges of calla lilies, growing like weeds, walls covered with climbing roses the size of dinner plates, California poppies and lupines in every crevice and violets at a bargain at flower stalls that have brightened the same street corners as long as I can remember.

Like the phoenix, San Francisco sprang from the ruins of its earthquake (oops—fire). Much of what man had built was gone, but what God had wrought was untouched and is San Francisco's claim to immortality.

I never go to San Francisco but that I make a pilgrimage up Telegraph Hill after dark to pleasure my soul with one of the most spectacular night panoramas in the world.

The land and the water sharply separate in the jet of night: the myriad lights on shore stand out against the black expanse of the water. Alcatraz and Treasure Island are anchored there like sturdy battleships. Spanning the Bay are two vast, shimmering necklaces of lights, outlining the famous bridges that are spider webs by day.

To the west of Telegraph Hill are the brilliantly lighted expanses of Nob Hill and the city's sparkling skyline. Across the dark water, embedded like jewels in a velvet box, are the gleaming cities of Richmond, Oakland and Berkeley.

It is fairyland, and the lucky, lucky people who call San Francisco home can see this incomparable sight any old time just by driving up Telegraph Hill.

Come to think of it, scratch Paris and make it six months in San Francisco.

Jewels of the Northwest

If the audience will please come to attention, we shall rise and sing "America, the Beautiful" before launching into the business of the day.

I remember arriving in Seattle, metropolitan jewel of the Northwest, after a flight from San Francisco. The journey was so fantastically beautiful that it calls for all stops out on superlatives. I felt not unlike the Baedeker scout who first spotted the Taj Mahal.

Americans save their pennies for years to go to Europe to marvel at sights that can't hold a candle to the poetic grandeur of the Cascades, that vast range of blue, often snow-capped mountains that lift endlessly into the sky as far as the eye can see.

Passengers on the flight to Seattle pay merely for comfortable service between two of the most beautiful cities in the United States. What they get in addition is an incomparable panorama of one of the world's most impressive mountain ranges.

For $40 worth of ticket—and what can you get today for $40 except perhaps a four-rib roast—passengers on a smooth, clear flight see the gleaming, snowy peaks of six of the most majestic mountains in America: Shasta, Jefferson, Hood, Adams, St. Helens and Rainier, lifting their heads from masses of cumulus cloud.

By flattening one's nose against the window, it was possible at one time, after taking off from Portland, Oregon, to glimpse five of those snowy fingers reaching into the sky. From that vantage point, 12,000 feet up in a clear and sunny sky, we could glimpse all but Shasta, which had long since melted into the air.

We took off from San Francisco, where the wondrous green hills lift themselves so abruptly from the sparkling waters of the Golden Gate.

We flew northward over the green, fertile valley of the Sacramento River until suddenly we were over wooded mountains and the great white bulk of Shasta loomed chaste and remote to the east.

The world was now so beautiful and unfamiliar that I pawed frantically through all that useless printed matter with which air carriers provide passengers. But I could not find the one thing I wanted most: a map. However, the obliging stewardess went forward and came back with the pilot's map and the reassuring word that he knew the way and didn't really need it.

So in awe and wonder I was able to identify Crater Lake, that blue sapphire then set in glistening white at some 8,500 feet above sea level. And that great system of inland lakes, curling like blue fingers among the greening mountains, turned out to be Shasta Dam, one of the nation's great engineering and irrigation projects.

Then as the massed Cascades receded into the east like an endless blue ocean, there followed in stunning white succession Mount Jefferson, 10,495 feet high; Mount Hood, hovering over Portland at 11,245 feet; Mount Adams, 12,307 feet; Mount St. Helens, 9,671 feet, and finally the twin peaks of Mount Rainier, 14,408 feet.

Mount Rainier, 246 feet higher than Shasta, is the peerless monarch of the Cascades, towering like a pristine guardian above Seattle. Because of its twin peaks, it looked like a Titan's saddle, covered with an ermine throw.

Like Shasta, it rose resplendent in the sun from a froth of white clouds at its base. When we landed in Seattle, we had lost the giant, for the cumulus hid it from the city. But we who had been above the clouds had seen not only Rainier but the other five white peaks in all their beauty, bathed in sun.

Never before in all my life have I had so much beauty for $40 (including tax). And if anyone is thinking of taking the wife and children to Europe to see the sights this summer, think twice before going thataway. Won't hurt, for once, to come thisaway and see what America, the Beautiful, has to offer free of charge.

Say It Ain't So!

I forget now whether it was Los Angeles or a giraffe of whom the incredulous farmer said, "There ain't no such animal!"

For one who dwells among untrodden ways in the quiet backwash of New York, Los Angeles is a confusing, high-octane community of stars, bars and drive-ins. Celebrities come in bunches there, like grapes or asparagus, and my mouth was perpetually at half-mast at the sight of Jayne Mansfield, in person—not in a motion picture—and in a sweater, and Peter Lawford in a simple blue serge suit.

This is the city in which the waitresses in the drive-in eateries, all more elegant than Maxim's or Le Coteau Basque, make more per week in tips and found than starlets.

The lady car hops often find $300 in their weekly take-home pay, I am told. And one such hamburger belle, who took some effective shots at her husband a few years ago, was found to be living in a $25,000 home which she was buying out of earnings.

If I were ten years younger, I would be tempted to switch professions. And to the drive-ins rather than the studios.

One never knows how the other half lives, but I had a faint glimpse at a Hollywood luncheon that demonstrates how tough things are in everyone's backyard. An old friend, Perry Lieber, invited me to lunch on the RKO lot with Shelley Winters, Farley Granger, Janis Carter, Jack Beutel, Harriet Parsons, then the only woman producer in Hollywood, Ruth Herbert and Virginia Kellogg.

A very large bouquet of flowers, an impressive set piece of roses, stock, carnations, camellias and what-not, decked the table. The luncheon, after all, was for me, and I had visions of RKO sending the flowers back to my hotel with me.

But I reckoned without Miss Winters who said to me, "You don't really want these flowers, do you?"

"Not more than my right eye," I said promptly.

"Well, goody," said Miss W., a tasty dish in well-fitting sweater and slacks, "then I shall just take them home with me. I am having a party tonight, and I can use them on my dining-room table."

A waiting lackey came to snatch the flowers. I remarked a little bitterly that she could at least leave them on the table until the guest of honor was out of the room. But Miss Winters said a girl had to get flowers where and when she could.

So the bouquet was snatched and put in her car. Then Miss Winters, spotting me as the domestic rather than the glamour type, asked:

"Is a fifteen-pound ham enough for thirty-five people?"

The party, she explained, had grown from five or six guests to thirty-five, but the ham had remained stationary.

Miss Winters said she did not think she had enough cups, either. But I saw her fixing her large, limpid eyes on the commissary manager. I have a hunch she went home with cups snuggled in among my flowers.

Naturally, this commissary luncheon was on RKO. You could tell it by the way the hired hands ate. The Misses Carter and Winters, who looked so dainty, tore into the free food like farm hands, consuming in midday a sirloin steak each, accompanied by tomato juice, salads, coffee and grapefruit.

The Messrs. Granger and Beutel also ordered up free steaks, with suitable accompaniment of other costly viands. I guess no matter how much you earn today, a free steak is a free steak.

Mr. Granger seemed a nice, shy young man and Miss Winters confirmed it by saying that the first time he went to a party and met Ava Gardner, the femme fatale, he fell into the punch bowl.

"He probably would have drowned right then and there," she said cheerfully, "if friends hadn't pulled him out."

California Is a Nice Place to Visit

Whenever I bid a fond farewell to California, I feel like expressing my sentiments by quoting the immortal words of the Okie who, heading his jalopy toward home, painted on the side of his beat-up car:

"I'm going back to Oklahoma and the hell with your six-foot geraniums!"

I'm certain that Okie must have been as awed and admiring of the six-foot geraniums in the beginning as I was. But a man can stand just so much of anything, including sunshine and six-foot geraniums.

I think I know what prompted the Okie's abrupt valedictory to the geraniums: He was homesick. Home is home. And Oklahoma and New York City may not be such a much in the eyes of Californians: nothing but oil and Osages in the former and stone and sharpers in the latter. A poor thing, but mine own, in the case of both the Okie and myself.

Every Californian is his own Chamber of Commerce! Native Sons assure me that the No. 1 prime target for an enemy nuclear attack is God's Country (California! You should ask!).

Everything in California is so much bigger, better and more important that an enemy with anything but rocks in his head will never waste bombs on New York City when he can get at the West Coast. Anyway, that's what the boosters say. So I always return to my home in the East feeling that we have nothing to worry about from H-bums as long as the geraniums hold out.

All in all, California is a marvelous place and I am glad it took the rest of us into the Union. Where else can a thirsty customer lay the dust with a "Banana Cow," an alleged cocktail made with equal parts of ripe banana and aged rum blended in an electric mixer? Don't ask me what it tastes like! You think I got rocks in my head?

And where would the nation be today, may I ask, without the California ranch house? Still stuck in that old New England salt box, probably.

What has happened to the California ranch house in the last ten years should happen to Debbie Reynolds. What with glamour and picture windows, the new and improved California ranch house doesn't even bear a coincidental resemblance to the Californy ranch house I was born in, on a real, working Californy ranch.

Grandpa's house was a respectable, middle-aged two-story white farmhouse with the requisite number of porches. Since that day the California ranch house has lost one story and spread in so many directions and over so much territory that the new models are now sold with built-in electric scooters.

When I was in Los Angeles, I was shown the newest model ranch house, owned in its entirety by Edgar Bergen, if I remember rightly. The point is that the house was so rambling that people in the kitchen wing couldn't see the library except on a clear day, or seldom.

San Fernando Valley was a surprise, too. I honestly thought it was farm country, where mo'om picture people really raise cattle. But San Fernando Valley is just another big suburban real estate development with miles and miles of row houses, all alike. There isn't room enough to swing a cat, much less a cow, in the valley.

At night the valley is a solid mess of neons. If there are any cowboys, they are employed solely in throwing a neon-lighted bull.

All in all, I like California and Californians just fine, even the ones from Iowa. But you know how it is: It's a nice place to visit but I wouldn't live there if you gave me all the six-foot geraniums in the place.

The Care and Feeding of
a Dodger Fan

The care and feeding of a Dodger fan, immediately after the worst has happened . . .

"Now remember: When he comes home this evening, just pretend nothing has happened," I instructed the household jewel. "Just make like normalcy."

"Mr. Robb is going to be mighty disappointed the Dodgers didn't even win the league pennant today, Madam," said the jewel. "He was set on it."

"Into each life some rain must fall," I murmured, "only the trouble is, he isn't ever prepared for the cloudburst. Hide the evening newspapers before he gets here and just act as if life can not only be beautiful but can go on."

"Yes, Madam, I think I get the pitch," said the jewel.

"No, no! Not that!" I cried. "Don't even mention anything that might remind him! And, in the meantime, lock up all the knives and any sharp instruments, including razor blades and broken glass."

"You mean he's going to feel that bad?" asked the jewel, nervously.

"You should have seen him in 1952 when they kicked away the World Series!" I said. "Manic depressive, if I ever saw one. Then when they flubbed it again in '53, he went around talking to himself for days. And when they bollixed it again in '56, he began developing a persecution complex.

"But," I added as cheerfully as the circumstances permitted, "he's only a threat to himself, not others."

"I never worked for Dodger fans before," the jewel said, her voice edged in anxiety.

"They're really not bad," I assured her. "I've lived with this one since September 16, 1929. It's just that all Dodger fans are intensely emotional and apt to react violently when the boom is lowered.

"And while you're about it," I continued, "fill the ice bucket and put it on the table next to his chair while I get the Scotch and soda. And when he comes through the door, you rush up and tell him we're having a $13.90 steak for dinner."

"You want to kill the boss?" asked the jewel. "And, anyway, that steak only cost half that much."

"Yes, I know, but I'm trying psychology. I read the other day to try counter-irritants to take a person's mind off his miseries. I tried loving kindness in '52, and sympathy in '53 and aspirin and cold compresses in '56, and none had any effect.

"So now I am going to try this counter-irritant suggestion. He'll be so mad about the $13.90 steak, it'll take his mind off the baseball miseries for a while."

The jewel shook her head doubtfully.

"If I may say so, Madam, you're tampering with fate," she opined.

"Well, we can't just let him sit there and suffer," I cried. "And when the $13.90 steak begins to wear off, I'll tell him I'm afraid you've cooked it well done instead of medium rare, and that's good for another fifteen minutes.

"And then I'll tell him that I went shopping today and just couldn't resist the sweetest little twilight blue mink coat, and such a bargain at only $5,450, plus tax."

"Madam, you're going to kill that man!" gasped the jewel, in genuine alarm.

"You don't understand," I said patiently. "Mr. Robb is apt to come home in a state of shock, and I am merely doing what this psychologist suggested. I am providing a counter-irritant to keep his mind off his real misery."

We both heard the key in the lock.

"And," I cried triumphantly, "if the steak and the mink don't work, I've got an ace in the hole. I'll tell him I think Jimmy Hoffa should be the next President."

☙ ☙ ☙

These are days of sartorial triumph for the head of Clan Robb. By reviving the derby hat, fashion once again has caught up with him —and don't think he isn't looking as smug as a bug in a jug.

Man and boy, the master of the manse has been a hard-hat man to my certain knowledge for thirty-two years. So I have been amazed by the headlines proclaiming "Derby Hat Is Back." Such is Add's addiction that I didn't even know it had been away!

"I have been faithful in my fashion to the derby," he said when I asked him how come he had clung to it in the years of its decline. "It looks good with dark street clothes for occasions that just miss being formal, and besides," said my Scotsman, "a derby never wears out. Or, hardly ever. I've been getting my money's worth out of my investment."

"Well, I'm impressed," I said. "Right here in the paper it says 'Most often the derby can be glimpsed around the most elegant midtown regions of Fifth, Madison and Park Avenues. A man has to be well dressed to look good in a derby.' "

"Naturally," agreed my husband, as the canary feathers began to sprout around his mouth.

"This article also says that while the black derby is the biggest seller today, there are navy blue, brown, taupe, gray and salt-and-pepper derbies," I went on. "Would you wear . . ."

"Only over my dead body!" he snorted. "The brown derby should be preserved as a memorial to Alfred Emanuel Smith, and all others save black restricted by law to the chorus line. Only Milton Berle would be caught alive in a salt-and-pepper derby."

"Do you favor the tightly rolled umbrella and guardsman's mustache as proper accompaniment for a derby?" I asked my Beau Brummel.

"Only in England," he replied, and added, "Don't get funny with me and my derby!"

I guess it's hard for women to take men's hats seriously. They all look alike, no matter what kind or type. The boys can't even tell 'em apart themselves. Once, at a small dinner party, an early-departing guest wore home my husband's dark blue Homburg. It took forty-eight hours for the two to discover the inadvertent swap. Imagine that happening to two women!

Certainly, out in the great open spaces of Idaho, when I was young, gentlemen's hats were all identical. My father and every other Western gentleman of his generation wore a Stetson—and wore it summer and winter.

Until the day of his death, Papa entertained dark suspicions about the antecedents and motives of any man who wore a straw hat. To him there was something unmanly, if not downright underhanded, about a straw hat and its wearer.

When my bridegroom came West to marry me, I implored him not to wear a straw hat, lest Papa forbid the banns. (And not to smoke cigarettes, either. Papa was a cigar man, with a low opinion of cigarettes and their fly-by-night smokers. Now, more than thirty years later, I'm still surprised that sometime during his ordeal, Add didn't set the barn afire!)

As for the derby—well, if Add had got off the train in Caldwell, Idaho, in a derby, I'd still be a spinster. Papa would have seen to that!

❀ ❀ ❀

It is with a considerably jaundiced eye that I keep scanning all those reports picturing the little woman not only as the chief purchasing agent of the family, but also of her husband's clothing.

There is general agreement in the reports that the American wife owns everything that isn't nailed down, that she does eighty to eighty-seven per cent of all the buying for her family, and that the spineless nincompoop to whom she is married is lucky if he gets to select a shirt once per annum.

Of course, the inference is that the housewife does all these chores because she is greedy, grasping, domineering and, frankly, unbearable. It is obvious, also, that the gents who write these reports have never sat down long enough to figure out that they are painting the members of their own sex as a lot of jellyfish who darnwell deserve the hand-painted neckties they receive under this system.

Naturally, I can speak only for Chez Robb, but if I tried to buy a suit for the head of the clan, my arm would be in a cast. In all the years in which our hearts have beat as one, the nearest I have ever come to selecting any raiment for him is a length of English or Irish tweed or Bermuda doeskin for sports jackets or slacks.

Once I went wild and bought him a French vest that he still treasures, and twice, Canadian sweaters (imported from England, natch). He is sufficiently indulgent to wear the neckties I buy him as lagniappe from time to time. But that ends the recital.

Sartorially he is his own man, and welcome. Within a month after our marriage, I made a stunning discovery that has, at least as far as we are concerned, contributed vastly to a happy marriage. That discovery is simple and to wit: Never, NEVER, well hardly ever, go shopping together! Whether for clothes, furniture or groceries!

At least, in the purchasing department of Chez Robb one head—and it doesn't matter whose—is a lot better than two. And a lot better than verbal fisticuffs in public over a green vs. a blue carpet, or lamb chops vs. beef stew or a brown dress with ruffles (ugh!) over the navy blue with the leather belt.

We discovered early enough to profit by it that we are both persons of strong personal likes and dislikes and opinions. Better he should buy his clothes and me mine than make a shambles of a store and a federal case out of a new hat. He would die rather than wear a Hawaiian floral shirt; I would kill myself before I'd appear in slacks.

As for major household purchases, such as a new highboy or sofa, we talk it over in the privacy of the home, where the walls are padded. Then one or the other of us scouts the market and narrows the choice before the party of the second part goes along to help in the final selection. Neither one of us bullies the other—much. About fifty-fifty, I'd say.

Our plan has made for peace that passeth understanding. I think he dresses handsomely; he thinks I dress becomingly, and we both love our home. So I guess the program has worked.

If there are women who have to do the whole job by themselves, even choosing their respective husbands' raiment, I feel sorry for 'em. Who wants to be wedded to a worm?

〰 〰 〰

What follows is, in a way, the story of my life for the last thirty-two years. It is a real washboard weeper, a tale of heartbreaking struggle, hand-to-hand combat and constant defeat in my unceasing efforts to persuade, cajole, plead, threaten and bribe the countless laundries of New York City not to starch my husband's shirts.

I am encouraged to write this personal memoir only because a crusading New York firm that specializes in gents' furnishings—Wallachs by name—fearlessly brought to light this grave domestic issue in a series of advertisements in local newspapers.

Wallachs innocently began its great crusade in an ad that read: "Why is it that laundries are so passionately addicted to starch? Why is it so hard to get back a shirt without at least a veneer of starch in the collars and cuffs? Is it true that laundries have one worker whose job it is to find and destroy all pinned-in notes that say, pleadingly, 'no starch, please'?"

Aside from the fact that the American Institute of Laundering and every individual laundry in the five boroughs called on Wallachs with passionate denials, the firm has been doing just dandy, because the customers started crying "bravo!" "hurrah!" and "you took the words out of my mouth!"

As for me, I am sobbing with gratitude to Wallachs for pinpointing the only real problem, aside from baseball (which is only seasonal) that has clouded my married life. The head of Clan Robb hates starch in his collars. Ordinarily the mildest of men with a divine disposition, the mere sight of a starched shirt turns him into a snarling paranoid.

At such times he is prone to beat his breast, to the accompaniment of crackling starch, and cry aloud for justice. I hope Wallachs gets it for him; heaven knows, I have been unable to.

For years, every weekly laundry list has started with the injunction: "Please, please, do not—repeat do not—starch Mr. Robb's shirts," and has ended with the plea, "please, no starch in shirts."

Fifty per cent of the time, the shirts return with the look and feel of white-washed sheet steel. That is the cue for the rest of the household to hide out until the storm blows over. At such times, I wonder how many innocent wives have been beaten and children maimed by a paterfamilias gone berserk. The school of hard knocks and hard collars go hand in hand.

Everyone except the laundry industry knows the boiled shirt is kaput, save for weddings and wakes. It—the laundry biz—is living in a dream world of boiled shirts and matching customers that ended years and years ago. It is an interesting sociological note that the only man I actually have seen looking extremely respectable in a hard collar by daylight in recent years was in the dock in England, standing trial for a series of wholesale murders.

Starch in shirts—and the solution does not lie in changing laundries (that way lies madness)—can be a domestic issue as grave as the farm problem, inflation and inadequate schools. More power to Wallachs for bringing the issue to light. It deserves full marks for having drawn to public attention a facet of the average American wife's life and hard times.

"Did you know I am worth a minimum of $92,307.68 on the hoof, right this minute?" I asked the head of Clan Robb.

"Would you repeat that again, slowly," he said, as he dropped the evening paper.

"Did you know that I am worth at least $92,307.68 in my stocking feet, not counting my engagement ring and my wrist watch?"

"Of course, of course!" he said, rattling the paper. "I am simply surprised that you place so little value on yourself. Tell me the name of the dastard who is low-rating you and I shall have at him!"

"It's a big insurance company, the Northeastern Life. And it says that if I am one of the 22,413,000 working women in the United States today and am earning $3,000 annually I am worth $92,307.68.

"The company says it takes that much capital at three and one-fourth per cent interest to earn $3,000 a year."

"It figures," said Mr. Robb. Then added cagily, "Does this insurance company say anything about a man being able to choose between one of those 22,413,000 working women and $92,307.68 in cash?"

"What a horrid, commercial question! Are you thinking of trading me in for part cash and a new model?"

"Actually, no," said the head of the clan. "I was just asking for one of my friends."

"Don't get his hopes too high!" I cautioned. "It says right here in the brochure that if a man is forty-three years old, earns $10,000 a year, has a wife who doesn't work, and two children of three and four and a half years of age respectively, who are also unemployed, then the wife is worth $64,418.80."

"He'd do better financially with the working model. More trade-in allowance," Mr. R. remarked.

"This wife is worth $64,418.80 because the insurance company figures that if the husband had to hire a housekeeper at $200 a month for fifteen years, or until the youngest child is 18, he'd be out $36,000.00," I said.

"Yes," Mr. R. agreed. "Where can a guy dredge up a housekeeper today for $200 a month? If Northeastern can find a housekeeper who'll touch a family with two kids for less than $250 a month it's in business as an employment agency. They have low-rated that wife. She is worth at least $45,000 in housekeeping fees."

"This wife saves her husband $28,418.80 as income tax deduction, too, by the time he's 65," I added, "so it adds up to $64,418.80, if you take the insurance figures or $73,418.80 if you apply Robb's revised figures."

"Does the company say anything about how much a loving husband, who is a good provider, is worth?" asked the head of the clan.

"Goodness, no. Everyone knows such a paragon is worth his weight in gold," I assured him. "But do you really think I am worth $92,307.68?"

"Certainly!" declared Mr. R.

"Then," I asked, "do you think I could borrow $25 on account?"

Mr. R. handed over the money.

"I walked into that trap," he said.

"Honey, I appreciate the fact you've been trying to save money. But don't you think you've been overdoing it?" asked Mr. Robb.

"This is a gag," I said. "But don't mind me. Have your little jest."

"No, I'm serious. I realize that other women spend hundreds of dollars, sometimes thousands, to get their faces peeled for beauty's sake . . ."

"Shelled," I said, "shelled, not peeled."

"Shelled or peeled, they pay out a lot of money to get the hide taken off," said the head of Clan Robb. "But you just stick your head in a gas oven, light the fire and whoosh—your skin is off because it's gone."

I touched my peeling nose, my frayed lips, my tattered forehead, with a bandaged hand.

"If this is your idea of cheering me up, I don't think much of it,"

I said. "I look a mess and you know it. I haven't got any eyebrows or any eyelashes, and I need a new transformation."

"Oh, I don't know. On you, no eyebrows look good. And when your front hair starts growing out again, you'll have a fringe, just like Queen Mother Elizabeth, only," he added loyally, "cuter. I never thought she was the cute type."

I just sulked.

"And maybe this will cure you of making garlic bread," he said cheerfully. "I never did like the stuff, really."

"I don't think the oven blew up in my face just because it didn't like garlic bread," I snapped. "I think the oven was faulty or the gas was leaking or something.

"And if the oven was going to blow up, I wish it had blown up before I had stood on my big flat feet all day cooking dinner for twenty-five people. If it had blown up in the morning, I at least wouldn't have worn myself out over a hot stove all day!"

"Why, honey, you love to cook for a crowd," said my spouse reproachfully. "That's what you always say. I never saw a crowd have a better time."

"I never heard a crowd have a better time," I groused. "There I was upstairs on my bed of pain, and everyone downstairs laughing and yakking and carrying on like crazy. And you right down there yakking with them!"

Mr. R. looked pained.

"Well, you told me to go downstairs and see that everyone had a good time," he protested. "I was just doing what you told me to do. You said to give 'em something to drink and to get the food on the table, and I sent you up a martini."

"It was a three-martini burn," I said coldly.

"Why didn't you yell?"

"I did. But you were all yak-yakking so much, no one heard me. You'd have thought everyone was celebrating his own wedding anniversary, not mine. Some of 'em could at least have come up and asked how I was!"

"But the doctor said you should be quiet," said Add.

"Quiet, with that mob? Ha! Fat chance!"

"You're being very cross and unreasonable," said my spouse.

"This flattery will get you no place."

"And besides, it was my wedding anniversary, too," he continued. "And how do you think it made me feel to tell guests you'd stuck your head in the oven and tried to blow yourself up after all these years with me? That's the kind of thing that makes a man leave home!"

"Well, it's an anniversary we're not apt to forget," I said soothingly.

He just groaned.

I have been moody recently, wondering how I would be able to hold up my end of the conversation this autumn when our mob reassembled and the chitchat switched to "what I did during the summer."

The Robbs are apparently the only people who stayed home. Everyone else fled to Europe, Africa or fell off a yak in the Himalayas. So it seemed pretty obvious that we would have to sit clamlike, unable to retaliate, when friends started on their summer travelogues.

But some recent happenings have lifted me right out of the doldrums. I believe we shall be able to chatter with the best of them now. I feel reasonably certain the Robbs are the only persons in their set who tiled a bathroom this past summer. And some other woman may have blown herself out the window with a leaky gas oven, but I'll bet I'm the only one who sat on a wasp.

We were swept into the bathroom deal when a friend of ours named W. Lawrence Freeman, a plastics expert, came to visit and said, "You, too, can tile a bathroom."

If anyone ever took a poll of the most fatal words in the English language, the phrase "You, too, can . . ." would win in a walk. More innocent persons are hooked into more impossible deals by those three words than by "I love you." There should be a law.

The Robbs are not gifted individuals who can make an eighteenth-century English breakfront out of two old orange crates, a pot of glue and a keg of ten-penny nails, as explained in the ladies' magazines. "Nothing imparts an air of greater distinction to a room than an eighteenth-century English breakfront," the magazines always say. "Now you, too, can have one. Simply follow the diagram and instructions on page 209. All you need is two old orange crates, a pot of glue, a keg of nails and a little spare time."

So ten months and 6,000 man-hours of hard work later, what do the Robbs, who have followed the diagram and directions, have? They have something that looks identical with two old orange crates, a pot of glue and a keg of nails.

Anyway, at the end of two years of unremitting moil and toil, Mr. R. succeeded in tiling the shower. Then he made a mighty vow: he swore to finish tiling the bathroom before frost was on the pumpkin if it killed him.

Naturally, with the passage of two years, the gook that holds the tiles to the walls had gotten a little tougher, stringier and harder to handle.

But there is absolutely no truth to a snide local rumor that on the day we ate luncheon in the bathroom, Mr. R. inadvertently cemented himself to the floor when he unfortunately got more gook on it than on the walls. What if he did have to cut his way out of a pair of sneakers? It was an old pair.

While Add made ready to abandon sneakers, I carried sandwiches and coffee up to the bathroom, and we had a very fine picnic. If you are considering a picnic, give a thought to the bathroom: no sand, no fleas, no red ants, no mosquitoes, no poison ivy, no hostile dogs or cows. And running water in every faucet.

But is the bathroom finished? To be honest, no. We ran out of tile. Seems unlikely now that we can match the same pattern. Oh, well, nothing like a piebald bathroom for a picnic!

As for the wasp: Yes, it is true that I sat on a wasp and that it died doing what comes naturally. However, thanks to great advances in Medical Science, I ate off the mantel for only twenty-four hours. As I look back on the event, it undoubtedly was an interesting experience and will be a conversational boon.

But I'm not talking for less than a dinner!

"Is that another new hat?" the head of the house asked suspiciously.

"Frankly, yes," I said. "I am trapped like a rat and willing to give myself up. It is a new hat. But I bought it for a noble purpose."

"Is that so? And what noble purpose pushed you right into Sally Victor's and twisted your arm?"

"I will thank you not to be funny," I said. "I bought this hat purely as a patriotic duty, to fight communism."

"That," said my spouse, "is the most fascinating story since Baron Munchausen's demise. Now I have heard everything."

"Well, I did buy it to fight communism," I insisted. "The whole story was in the papers. This labor leader—I forget his name—came home from Europe and said he would not be at all surprised if all Europe fell prey to communism because women over there aren't wearing hats."

"Take it easy," said the head of Clan Robb. "Take your time; there must be a point in this story some place."

"Well, it's just as I said. This labor leader came home and said hatmakers all over Europe are out of work because women are either not wearing hats at all or are just tying up their heads in scarfs."

"Where does communism enter the case?" Mr. R. inquired.

"Why, naturally, if these poor hatmakers are out of work indefinitely because of the foolish whims of women, communist agents will go to work on them and pretty soon all the hatmakers will be communists and maybe that will be the beginning of the end."

"This is indeed a serious situation," my spouse said. "One fraught with danger to all concerned, including the American husband."

"I'm glad you brought that up, because this labor leader said if American women didn't wear hats and keep the American millinery industry busy night and day, the communists might take over here, too."

"So you rushed out and did your bit?"

"Of course. I knew you wouldn't want people going around saying your wife is a subversive because she doesn't wear a hat," I said.

"Perish forbid!"

"And you wouldn't want the neighbors thinking maybe I'm a spy or anyway a communist courier because I tie my head up in a handkerchief."

"No, no, a thousand times no!" said the master emphatically. "That would probably ruin my credit just as easily as the hat.

"But have you thought what you women are probably doing to the scarf and handkerchief business by rejecting them and reviving hats?" he asked. "Have you thought that the scarf and handkerchief business may soon be at a standstill, thousands of men unemployed, their wives hungry, their children ragged and all prey to communism?"

"Well, no," I said uncertainly. "You see, this labor leader was only interested in hats."

"That's the trouble with the modern world," the head of the house said. "Selfishness, selfishness, selfishness! Dog eat dog! Hat eat scarf, and communism take the hindmost."

"Do you think I ought to buy some new scarves and hankies, too?"

"Certainly!" he said. "Go out and buy more hats, more scarves, more handkerchiefs, while I, impoverished, ragged and hungry, go seek sanctuary with the comrades."

"Oh, poo!"

"That's right, make fun of me," he cried. "What does it matter if I am driven to the party if you save two or three industries by spending us blind? What is one broken individual against thousands?"

"Honestly," I said, "you make me so mad!"

"It's mutual," he said, as he withdrew behind the evening paper. "Anyway, it's a pretty hat. And I'm at least grateful your labor leader wasn't connected with the diamond cutters' guild or the mink makers' union. I can only afford so much sympathy."

Probably more than most city dwellers, New Yorkers have to stifle their pack-rat instincts. The Collyer brothers syndrome is a flourishing exception to this rule. But their number is negligible.

Only a handful of city slickers who still own town houses, with the luxury of attic and basement, can indulge the ancient human instinct to squirrel away stuff that "is simply too good to throw away" or "may come in handy someday." And that really isn't and never does.

What the human pack rat lacks is the strength of character to part with possessions he no longer needs or uses. It is easier to tuck it away than to chuck it out.

True to a solemn vow we made last spring, the Head of Clan Robb and I have been engaged this summer in Operation Ruthless. This consists of tackling, one by one, our Fibber McGee closets and ruthlessly discarding such treasures as an old No. 2 iron, a lamp base made of a coconut sent us from Florida by a misguided friend twenty-five years ago, and one too many receptacles in which food is supposedly kept warm by candle power.

Under this program, there left Chez Robb forever, in the custody of the Salvation Army, one of my few Walter Mitty dreams of grandeur that materialized in the too, too solid flesh—or rather in the too, too solid leather. For what marched out of the apartment to begin life anew in a Salvation Army shop was a resplendent set of matched alligator luggage.

Although I had owned the four glittering pieces for twenty-two years, the sheen of newness was still in the rich, dark leather and the pale, silvery gray silk linings were pristine. The set ranged from a cosmetic to a pullman case built on the general dimensions of a steamer trunk.

En masse, they would have done credit to a Vanderbilt, a Rockefeller or a Morgan. And that, as I soon discovered, was their fatal drawback. Only a Vanderbilt, a Rockefeller or a Morgan could afford the upkeep on so much magnificence.

In the days before World War II, when a twenty-five-cent tip per bag would send a porter hysterical with joy, I soon discovered that anything less than a dollar tip per alligator bag sent the redcap fraternity hysterical with rage.

Indeed, I got the feeling that anything less than a dollar-per-bag was selling capitalism short. Even when I traveled on a swindle sheet with my alligators, the sight of so much money going down the drain used to goad me into ordering the small rather than the large sirloin as an economy measure to redress the balance.

Nor was this the only expense. The alligators were not only magnificent but as heavy as lead. A wrestler could have trained on them. (And I began to get weary of redcaps who snatched at the pullman case and then asked me accusingly, "Lady, you got bricks in here?")

The real expense was in excess baggage on the airlines, even in a day when the weight limits were more generous than at present. The four pieces weighed sixty-six pounds with nothing but air in 'em. When packed, the excess baggage charge resembled the original cost of the plane, and was so maddening to the office auditor that he finally said the alligators must go—but not by plane!

So for twenty years the alligators blushed unseen on the top shelf of a closet. Some years ago I saw a movie in which a second-hand dress suit transformed the lives of several persons, including Edward G. Robinson. I can't help but wonder what impact my lovely alligators will have on their new owner, short of breaking his back and bending his bank book.

The head of our house, an amateur photographer, has been on a light diet, interspersed with rest periods, ever since Santa handed him a new German camera so elaborate that only a graduate of M.I.T. or Cal Tech could cope with it.

I have never seen anything outside an airplane cockpit equipped with more knobs, dials, meters, gauges, timers or levers than this camera. It boasts a built-in light meter and hot and cold film. It came in a peddler's pack with filters, sunshades, sable brushes to dust the lenses and a lock equipped with a burglar alarm.

This camera bears about as much relation to a Box Brownie as a peashooter to the H-Bomb. I have been vaguely aware that camera manufacturers have added a few improvements to the basic Box since my childhood. But I never dreamed that they had perfected something so intricate that it would require thirty minutes just to set the dials, read the meters, adjust the filters and equate the focus before pressing the trigger.

When my husband saw that the peddler's pack included a 90-mm lens for distance pictures he cried aloud that if only he had had such a lens the day Queen Elizabeth II was crowned his pictures of the Coronation procession would have been sharp and sensational.

But it is my private opinion that by the time he had twisted the knobs, turned the dials, read the meters and consulted his slide rule, Her Majesty would have been back in Buckingham, taking bows from the balcony.

Make mine a Box Brownie, say I. There was a reliable, simple instrument, the only camera I ever owned. The only problem it posed, when I was a kid, was getting up the money for film. Once you had put the film in the black box, all you had to do was look through the little hole to make sure you were cutting off feet instead of heads, and then snap the trigger.

A man with a camera could really be trigger happy in those days, whereas today's owner of one of these intricate new machines develops an inferiority complex the minute he realizes that the built-in electronic brain is smarter than he is.

It is a malaise of our society that now the machine is competing with man. I was the master of my Box Brownie, give or take a few lost heads. But it strikes me that Mr. R. is going to take a lot of back talk from his new camera before he achieves any clear-cut decision. Something tells me it's going to be a long, hard fight. But my man is in there punching and I hope he wins.

👹 👹 👹

The head of Clan Robb cast an appraising eye over all the department store boxes, the tissue paper and the new goods and gear covering the bed.

"I guess you really did clean out the store this time," he said. "Anything left by the time you staggered out?"

"A few odds and ends," I said lightly, "but you know the funniest thing happened . . ."

"Funny to whom?" he asked as he surveyed the loot.

"Well, you know that terrible rainstorm we had the other day, with all the wind? And how it just fell in sheets, and the gutters on Fifth Avenue were full in ten minutes? And it just poured and . . ."

"You don't have to give a commercial for the weather. I remember. But what's so funny about it?"

"Well, it's a very funny thing but during that very storm, I was caught in this department store with my charge account open. It was absolutely, positively impossible to get a taxi and I would have drowned if I had tried to walk. So I was just kind of trapped."

"The victim of circumstances, eh?" asked Mr. Robb with that Chesterfieldian kind of politeness that can be so infuriating in a husband.

"Certainly. And I just couldn't stand around half the day getting tireder and tireder when all the chairs were taken except those in the dressing rooms. And I couldn't go into a dressing room and monopolize the chair without trying on some clothes," I explained.

"How can you manage to rest your weary bones in a chair and still try on clothes?" asked my spouse. "It sounds like a trick with commercial possibilities if they ever really revive vaudeville."

"Wouldn't you like to see what I bought?" I countered.

"Sure, the suspense is killing me. I might as well know the worst now as the first of the month. I suppose I ought to be grateful the storm was over before you bought a hand-embroidered fly swatter."

"I've got a surprise for you," I said, pawing through the tissue paper and coming up with a fly swatter hand-embroidered in robin's-egg blue wool yarn around the edge, with an American beauty rose embroidered in the center, and the handle wrapped in more blue yarn.

"A real, genuine hand-embroidered fly swatter and only $7.50!" I cried.

Mr. Robb buried his head in his hands. "I can't believe it. I can't believe it," he kept muttering. "Seven-fifty! Did the salesgirl wear a mask? And why did you buy it?"

"Mainly because ever since we've been married, every time I go shopping you say 'Where's the hand-embroidered fly swatter?'

"And the other reason I bought it is because it's almost as horrible as that Venus de Milo with the clock in her stomach that Uncle Horace tried to give us for a wedding present."

"At least the clock would tell time. But this isn't worth a darn. You kill a fly with this and you'd have to send it to the cleaner," said my spouse. Then he looked at me suspiciously. "Did you really buy this abomination or did you make it for a gag?"

"Honestly, I bought it," I said. "The salesgirl told me it came with a shipment of American arts, crafts and novelties."

"All right, you've had your fun," said the head of Clan Robb. "But a man can only stand so much before he puts his foot down and mine is down. In the morning, take that thing back to the store. Back it goes! Understand?"

"Yes, sir," I said, with becoming meekness.

"And the next time there's a cloudburst," he ordered, "get caught in the five-and-dime."

Would that nuclear warfare were the only one momentarily threatening the American way!

But a short while ago I felt duty-bound to expose a movement in the garment industry and haute couture charted either to bring back long underwear or revive opera gloves for every-day—and fur-lined at that.

My gripe was aimed at the campaign to foist on American womanhood a coat without sleeves, a situation as logical as specs without glass or autos without gas.

Or have the times passed me by? Was I out of step with the fashion parade because I still thought of a coat as a garment worn for warmth and not for place or show? Was I the only woman who didn't cotton to a coat with built-in ventilation? Or hadn't Seventh Avenue ever heard it's cold outside? Goose pimples are chic, maybe?

In my attempts to buy a coat I was consistently shown garments that even ten years ago would have earned the designer a free ticket to the disturbed ward and a year's consultations with a head shrinker, criminal division. Not only did the new coat of distinction have no sleeves or else real short ones, but it was as drafty as a condemned tenement. Any breeze would whip through it like a gale, for the simple reason that designers were too lazy to sew up the seams.

The result was an outer garment consisting mainly of a collar, to which floating panels were attached fore and aft. In a brisk zephyr, milady would resemble a series of pennants at half-mast, or a Maypole with wet wash. Maybe even a helicopter in full sail. I saw coats slit all the way up the back as well as the front, and likewise all the way up the sides. Look, ma, no seams!

It certainly dates me to admit that I was brought up in an era when a coat was regarded as a garment designed primarily for warmth. There was a working premise that anytime it was cold enough to wear a coat, sleeves right down to the wrist bone were a necessity.

The corollary was that anytime it was too warm to wear such sleeves, it was too warm to wear the garment to which the sleeves were attached. "Button Up Your Overcoat" was not so much a song as a premise. "A stitch in time saves pneumonia" was the ever-present rule about seams. But antibiotics have changed all that.

In the repertoire of Joe E. Lewis there is a famous song, "Sam, You Made the Pants Too Long." I kept wishing as I shopped that he would update it with a verse dedicated to shivering womanhood, "Sam, You Made the Sleeves Too Short."

Oh, I've got my love to keep me warm, all right, but what about a coat to match?"

Variation on a Theme
or
Woman's Prerogative

Same Scene
Time: Six months later

"I certainly saw the silliest thing in seven states today," my lord and master said recently, as he curled up with a good briar and a book after dinner.

"I was crossing Fifth Avenue at Forty-ninth, and here was this woman getting out of a taxi in a fur coat with short sleeves. Can you beat it?"

"My goodness, no!" I said. "I have never even seen a taxi with muskrat trim. And one in a full length mink . . ."

"Okay, smartie pants," said my spouse. "So the fur coat with the short sleeves was on the woman. What I am getting at is this: imagine some fool woman chopping off the sleeves of a good fur coat at the elbows. What won't women do next!"

"So what's the matter all of a sudden with short sleeves?" I asked.

"Look, honey, you don't get it," my spouse said patiently. "This was no summer seersucker this woman was wearing. The temperature was down to zero. Near freezing. Presumably this gal was wearing a fur coat to keep herself warm. But from the elbows south, she was hanging out of this fur benny, exposed to the ravages of winter. It didn't make sense."

"Was she wearing gloves?" I asked.

"How do I know if she was wearing gloves?" yelped my spouse. "All I am trying to tell you is that I saw a silly woman uptown whose I.Q. was showing in a fur coat with short sleeves."

"What kind of fur?" I asked.

"What difference does it make, what kind of fur?" demanded my spouse. "It looked like mink and for all I know some sucker paid through the nose for mink. But for my money, any kind of a fur coat, mink, rabbit or skunk, looks silly with short sleeves."

"They're very fashionable this year," I said. "Givenchy and Balmain and everybody has designed fur coats with short sleeves."

"Okay, so Givenchy and Balmain have designed fur coats with short sleeves. It isn't the first time those French designers have made monkeys of American women. But I thought American women had enough brains to balk at the ultimate in absurdity. Fur coats with short sleeves!" he snorted.

"Well, my goodness," I said, "keep your shirt on. All the girls have had their fur coats remodeled with elbow-length sleeves, Annie and Sara and Lizbeth and . . ."

"That bunch of dizzy dames!" he said with a gentleman's approximation of a Bronx cheer. "I wouldn't expect any more of them. In a pinch, none of them could tell their ankles from their elbows, hot or cold."

"Hmmm," I hmmmed.

"Those cookies pay $4,500 for a mink coat and then chop off $750 worth of their equity the first time some Frenchman says it's fashionable to have chapped elbows! What clucks!"

"But you don't have to have chapped elbows," I said. "What the furrier chops off, he either makes into elbow length fur gloves or into a lovely, big, warm muff for $500 with an option of one fitting and a pure silk satin lining."

"All right, so for $500 the girls can get a pair of gloves or a muff, but short sleeves on a fur coat are still silly," my spouse said, as he lit the briar and opened the book. "And let me tell you when I saw that woman on Fifth Avenue today with the sleeves cut off her fur coat, I thanked my lucky stars I was married to a sensible, level-headed woman with enough gray matter to wear sleeves as God intended.

"By the way," he added, "where is your fur coat?"

"Why, it just came home from storage today," I said brightly, "and you lie perfectly still while I model it. Because I've got a surprise for you, honey! A great, big surprise!"

The Fodder of the Country

When the July temperature idled in the nineties out in Caldwell, Idaho, in the long ago, Mama knew what to do. She gave me a nickel, attached me to the little red wagon and sent me up to the ice plant for a hunk of ice, to make a freezer of ice cream. In fact, in those days, a nickel's worth of ice would freeze the two-quart freezer full twice.

Land's sake—we only bought a dime's worth of ice for family picnics when we used the six-quart freezer and made the washtub full of iced tea to boot.

Those were the days when ice came in hunks, not in one hundred-cube lots done up in sanitary cartons and price-pegged at $1.50 per carton. Mama always put yesterday's newspaper in the little red wagon, and the man at the ice plant always carefully wrapped the ice in it, not for sanitary reasons but because the paper acted as insulation.

When I got home with the ice, Mama and I tackled the problem of making little ones out of the big one. We slipped the ice in a gunny sack kept for such purposes. Then out on the black lawn, we went to work on the sack with a big hammer. That's how ice cubes were made in olden times, Junior.

Mama made the best ice cream in the world, although she had a stiff time defending her title from Grandma, Aunt Nell and Aunt Kit. Mama had a secret weapon, a Jersey cow named Effie. Mama also had an old church cookbook with a recipe for angel food cake that began "First find an angel."

Mama said all ice cream recipes should begin "First find a Jersey cow." Even before I went for the ice, Mama had already made the custard, the base of her ice cream, with Jersey milk, fresh eggs and sugar, and put it out on the back porch, where the honeysuckle bloomed all summer, to cool.

Then she added thick, clotted Jersey cream, and I gave thanks to Effie. Mama's vanilla ice cream on a hot July day was ambrosial, her strawberry ice cream was a dish for the gods, but the one I remember as the most paradisiacal of all was her black raspberry cream.

It was my job to pick the blackcaps as well as go for the ice, and I ate as many of the sugar-sweet berries as ever I put into the pail. The patch out by the woodshed was big and what a little girl put into her mouth, and into the pail was a secret between herself and her stomach.

Mama washed the berries, mashed them and strained the seeds out of the pulp before she added it to the custard and the cream. Then she was ready to pour the Lucullan mixture into the freezing can and to lower it into the freezer.

Now we were ready to pack the freezer with ice and rock salt, adjust the handle and begin to crank. It never took more than five to ten minutes to finish the two-quart freezer.

Who cared when it began to grow harder and harder to turn the crank? That signaled the great climactic moment—the removal of the dasher. What treat does the modern, streamlined child know to equal the exquisite thrill, the rare delight of licking the dasher?

Life, on a hot July afternoon, can hold no further joy, no greater fulfillment.

While I was disposing of the dasher, Mama was packing the freezer with rock salt and additional ice and wondering if two quarts would last the afternoon or if she should start a new batch of custard for the evening ahead.

I don't know why I have thought of all this, except I just emptied some store-bought ice cream into the freezing tray of the refrigerator, and darned if there's any fun licking a cardboard carton!

There are unenlightened Americans whose idea of a gastronomic heaven is New Orleans and Antoine's, New York and The Colony, or Paris and Tour d'Argent.

Poo! Such fallacies are based on simple ignorance and the fact these fellow citizens have never eaten in the Boise Valley. Scratch a housewife there and you uncover a latter day Escoffier.

What has the Tour d'Argent got that the average Valley housewife hasn't? That's easy: a duck press. But I guarantee if you give the local ladies a duck press and even the sketchiest instructions, they will turn out in no time pressed duck that will make the Paris institution blanch with envy.

Probably make it with wild duck, too, since Idaho is one of the last great game preserves in the Union. If a visitor sighs for pheasant, duck, elk steaks, pot roast of venison, bear filets, salmon, trout or a chop of mountain goat, some friend is almost certain to rummage through his deep freeze and come up with the delicacy.

I met an old school friend, now a doctor, on the street the last time I was in Boise. He said, to my amazement, that he thought I looked a mite peaked and pulled out his prescription pad. He wrote with a flourish, handed me the prescription and departed.

It proved on order for four pheasants from his locker.

And once when I was in Nampa with my Aunt Kit, the next door neighbor came in with five trout, none under fifteen inches in length. He was mad, too, because he had had to drive thirty-five miles to a good fishin' hole.

"Damn streams are fished out," he said disconsolately. "Used to be able to drop a hook any place around and get trout. Now a man has to drive an hour or two before he can get a nibble."

Salmon fishing is still fairly good, he continued, mainly because the dudes who are beginning to flock to this earthly paradise and vacation dreamland aren't used to using their feet. The best salmon fishing is in Idaho's vast wonderland, its primitive area, where even the horseback trails finally end and a man must hoof it over rugged terrain to reach the better fishing holes.

"God help us if the dudes ever learn to walk!" the neighbor said piously as he stowed the trout in Aunt Kit's refrigerator.

As I say, scratch a woman in Idaho and you find a chef. In addition, all the old friends with whom I went to school apparently labor under the impression that Easterners, particularly New Yorkers, live from hand to mouth in a district devoid of really edible vittles. This is an attitude I cultivate and encourage since the moment I return, friends and relatives start cooking to "fatten me up."

Mrs. Hunter, the next door neighbor, came over within an hour of my arrival with a chocolate cake that was pure ambrosia. Subsequent offerings included a marble cake with chocolate frosting from Lucie Thometz, cookies frosted with fudge from Peg Shaw and banana bread made with black walnuts from both Hattie O'Connor and Fran Knipe.

Madge Erstad dropped by with the zephyr-like Parker House rolls in which she specializes. It was only a matter of time until Nellie Hartley showed up with one of the culinary masterpieces of all time: a chocolate angel food cake.

In the meantime, Aunt Nell and Aunt Kit were not idle. There was ambrosial fried chicken three times a day, for instance. And since I was smart enough to be home in the cherry pie season, both aunts turned out an array of such delicacies, fit for the gods.

We eat high on the hog in Idaho, and the hog is cooked to perfection, to boot. Not only an apple in his mouth but a marcel in his tail. Any unmarried gentleman with matrimony in mind should head thataway. All the girls can cook like angels.

There is a rumor among gourmands that the man who digs his grave with his teeth dies happy.

Hm-m-m-m—, well, yes and no. I suppose it would depend somewhat on an adequate supply of bicarb and a digestive tract modeled after that of the Capra hircus or garden variety goat.

Our progress on one trip into the Midwest was slowed up by something we ate. To be specific, it was something we ate in Shartlesville, a somnolent village in the heart of the Pennsylvania Dutch country.

For some years before I had been reading and hearing constant paeans in praise of Pennsylvania Dutch cooking. It was touted to me as a strictly high-class cuisine, superior in quality and endless in quantity.

Now I am ready with a firsthand report.

Around noontime as we rolled through a harmless looking village named Shartlesville, I spied a sign announcing that the village restaurant was strictly from Pennsylvania Dutch in the menu department.

We moored alongside and went in. Instantly, one could see that this shrine was dedicated to the Strong, Silent Eater, with napkin tucked under triple chin (and matching stomach under the table). Men, women and even little children attacked mounds of food in a holy hush broken only occasionally by the smacking of lips or an honest burp.

My spouse and I tiptoed to the family style table where an occasional eater looked up pityingly at our cadaverous, one-chin chassis. My spouse poked me in the ribs and whispered "Isn't anybody here but us gluttons."

A dour waitress slapped a menu in front of me, and right away, from the rich gravy spots on its surface, I knew we were in for a treat. We told the glum Hebe to bring us the regular luncheon, with roast beef for the gentleman and turkey for the lady.

In a trice, she slapped before us enormous bowls of chicken noodle soup, not only steaming with a great deal of locked in goodness but— wonder of wonders—with innumerable large hunks of chicken swimming in the rich broth and snuggled among the pale yellow homemade noodles.

"I didn't know they still put chicken in chicken soup," my spouse said in awe at the lavish use of fowl in the liquid.

"I'm full up already," I whispered as I finished the soup. "It was a meal in itself."

The man across from me speared his fifth ear of corn as the

waitress snatched away the soup plates and substituted in the space in front of us two kinds of hot rolls, butter—both sweet and salt—homemade cottage cheese, fresh peach marmalade, apple, grape and currant jelly, a dish of celery, pickled beets, a dish of sweet and one other of sour pickles, and containers of French, Russian and mayonnaise dressing.

Next came Add's roast beef, gently lapping over the plate, and accompanied by roasting ears, sliced tomatoes, string beans in cream, rice, a delicious cold mixed vegetable salad, summer squash, sweet potatoes glazed in maple sugar, carrots and marvelous white potatoes mashed with onions boiled to a pulp. And a boat of gravy. And a pint of coffee.

My turkey arrived with the same accoutrements, plus oyster dressing, cranberry sauce and mashed turnips.

Twenty minutes later, my spouse leaned over and sneered: "You giving up?"

"No," I snapped, "but my belt has."

For dessert there was nothing but five kinds of pies, three kinds of ice cream (homemade), devil's food, angel food and mocha cake, strawberry and peach tarts and apple strudel.

"You know why that waitress looks dour?" Add asked as he paid the $1.50 each for the luncheons. "She's got indigestion," he said, prophetically.

And so have I—at the thought of that day. Sort of hors d'oeuvre de combat, you might say.

Every time I go South to visit I am tempted to return, on a permanent basis, as a carpetbagger in hope that some of the prosperity will rub off on this pore No'th'ner. Everyone there lives so high that, I declare, they're going to have to start building taller hogs! The vittles there are just wonderful!

"Would y'all have a red snapper befo' dinnah?" asked our Jackson,

Tennessee, host, in the living room before we went in to dine. I thought it was rather odd to serve this elegant fruit of the sea before dinner rather than as part of the meal. But I reasoned "different climes, different customs."

So I said, "Yes," since I am always on the hunt for new and interesting ways to serve food. And whadda you know? When the red snapper came it wasn't a fish at all; it was a Bloody Mary by another name.

"Red snapper sounds so much more refahned," explained my hostess, and so it does!

There was no more give left in my girdle after a prolonged diet of grits and gravy, spoon bread, buttermilk biscuits, Tennessee ham, chicken in a folded "handkerchief" of pie crust, butterfly shrimp, crab cakes and Black Bottom pie, with a million calories per square inch.

I had my first encounter with a three-crust lemon pie there. And to think that I had lived in ignorance of this marvelous delicacy all my life, convinced that one crust to a lemon pie was the legal limit.

Not down there it isn't! The third crust goes in the middle. Where else? And is this pie eaten with luncheon or dinner? No, indeed. It is consumed with the midmorning coffee break. Sort of perks up the appetite for luncheon—after a breakfast of fruit, grits, gravy, scrambled eggs, country sausage, biscuits and jelly.

And if one feels a little faint in midafternoon, after a luncheon of shrimp gumbo, fried chicken, biscuit, moulded salad and a Tennessee Special (a dessert one drinks) he can have a little snack of three-crust lemon pie at the afternoon coffee break. The Special is two scoops of vanilla ice cream and a jigger of brandy tossed in an electric mixer for a few seconds. Serve in champagne glasses and let yourself go.

Southern hospitality is just as factual as it is legendary. As a result, I have been having some long thoughts about one facet of Southern life. Apparently all who live in a Southern clime, whether Latins or Americans, don't need sleep.

Obviously, sleep was invented for Northerners who, perforce, must hibernate for long periods of the year because of climatic conditions. Two or three hours of sleep every twenty-four hours seems ample for gregarious Southerners. When Edison said that only women, children and idiots needed eight hours of sleep a day, he should have added "and Northerners."

☙ ☙ ☙

Some critics of the middle South are known to refer to it patronizingly as the "Bible belt." But those of us with affection in our hearts are apt to think of it as the hot bread belt.

There is no law against cold bread, particularly if homemade. But a housewife in that region can get the reputation of being shiftless if she puts cold bread on the table more than a half-dozen times a week, and any man who can prove that his wife serves him cold bread for breakfast is entitled to an uncontested divorce and the sympathy of bystanders.

This is a region rich in many things, but particularly in a variety of hot rolls and biscuits ranging from beaten to buttermilk. With butter running in golden rivulets between the top and bottom halves of sour cream biscuits and with homemade black raspberry jam oozing in royal purple from same, it does not take a washboard weeper on the radio to prove that "life can be beautiful."

Mrs. Lyda Frazier, a famous cook of the region whom I've mentioned before, has always believed that a few hot rolls are indispensable to tamp down one of her baked ham dinners. On the 1,200-acre farm she has been running with her son, Cavella, the farm kitchen has always been as modern as tomorrow.

Like many a superb old-time cook, Mrs. Frazier clung to her old-fashioned wood-burning stove despite the resplendent shiny electric model in her kitchen.

"I like it for baking," Mrs. Frazier said of the old wood burner.

Mrs. Frazier has for many years had the reputation of "setting a good table," and when guests get squared away for one of her dinners of incomparable Missouri hickory smoked ham, they need time both to eat and digest.

"I always have baked sweets and mashed whites," said this small, brisk, neat woman. "It gives folks a little choice. Then I have three or four green vegetables. You know, whatever's in season or is handy in the freezer. That way, there's something for all tastes.

"Some people like fruit salad. Some like lettuce or green salad. It's just as easy to mix two as one. Gives people a little choice.

"Then I always think a few pickles and a little relish are nice for something extra, and that's what you put 'em up for, anyway. And a little homemade jelly or jam is always nice with hot rolls.

"When it comes to dessert, I just give folks simple fare, either cake and ice cream or pie and ice cream. I favor pie and ice cream, and I say you can't beat a good cherry or apple pie served a bit warm so's the ice cream melts and runs into the cracks.

"You know, the New England states and Missouri are the only sections of this country where you get pie for breakfast.

"I get a real pleasure out of a little slice of apple pie with my breakfast coffee."

No one in this region bakes a finer apple pie than Mrs. Frazier. She says it's easier than falling off a log.

"Peel and slice your apples," she said. "Any good cooking apple will do. Cover with sugar and a sensible amount of nutmeg and let the apples set until juice forms. That's the secret of this pie. Peel the apples far enough ahead so's the sugar can draw the juice out of the fruit. Makes a better pie and in addition it doesn't take so much sugar.

"Now when the apples are ready, you line a pie pan with a real rich crust, and you spoon the apples into the crust, being careful not to spoon up the juice. That way, it doesn't boil over and make a mess of the oven.

"Next, I put a lattice work top on the pie and bake it. In the meantime, I put the excess juice on the stove and boil it down until it's like syrup. Now when the pie's baked, I put it on the bread board and pour into the pie, through the holes in the lattice-work crust, all that syrup I've been boiling down on the back of the stove.

"If I do say so myself," said Mrs. Frazier modestly, "it makes a real good pie and has for years."

🌀 🌀 🌀

Apple pie is one of man's few attainments that is perfect in and of itself. It has no rival as an American dessert.

This Kohinoor of the American kitchen stands pure and undefiled as the peak, the Everest, of the nation's cuisine. Any attempt to pair it with champagne is merely carrying coals to Newcastle, or eyebrows to John L. Lewis.

The apple pie as we know it today began its march toward perfection with the Pilgrim mothers. Within a decade after the Pilgrims landed at Plymouth the apple pie was assuming the role of comfort and compensation in the wilderness.

(When my Great-Grandmother Fulton made the Westward trek by covered wagon her long red braids were saved from a hungry, marauding Indian and his knife by her quick-thinking sister who thrust a warm apple pie into his greedy hands.)

Today any housewife can buy all the ingredients, packaged and in quick form, in any grocery store. But there are still those who make it from the ground up and who even prefer—for a tender, flaky, golden crust—old-fashioned lard rather than the new-fangled shortenings.

As for apples there are Duchess and Greenings for "green" apple pie. Then there are Jonathans and Wealthies for the perfect pie, since the ideal apple for this American masterpiece should be tart and juicy.

But Winesaps and Rome Beauties will make a splendid pie, too, if the cook will but add a dash of lemon to supply the tartness these two lack.

And who, like myself, can remember the wonderful flavor of apple pie made from dried apples, dried because that was one means by which our ancestors could preserve fruit through the year.

A well-meaning but completely misguided German vintner announced not long ago that American wine grapes are capable of producing any kind of wine, including new vintages yet to be perfected. So far, so good. If Mein Herr had only quit there he would have been way ahead of the game. But Folly and the sound of his own voice beguiled him into the prediction that he could even perfect a champagne to drink with apple pie.

Champagne with apple pie? It would but profane a national monument as perfect as the Parthenon, the Coliseum and the Alhambra.

In sterner days he could have been summarily hanged for such blasphemy. The mere suggestion that apple pie, the earliest and purest American art form in the national heritage, needs champagne or could be improved by this beverage, is a heresy that will shake all right-thinking, 100 per cent Americans from medulla oblongata to metatarsals.

The only beverage any dedicated American would tolerate in the presence of apple pie is coffee, hot as fire, black as night, clear as a mountain stream and strong as sin.

❀ ❀ ❀

Maybe a gourmet eats better elsewhere than in San Francisco. I don't, and I don't want to argue on a full stomach. All I know is that if I gain another pound, I shall be soldering gussets into my clothes.

Pick any hill in the city limits—Nob, Telegraph or Twin Peaks— roll in any direction and you are certain to fetch up at the threshold of a restaurant of superior quality, be it French, Armenian, Mexican, Greek, Italian or steak house à la U.S.A.

The Armenians, for instance, are never going to be a downtrodden minority as long as George Mardikian wrestles the pots and pans at Omar Khayyam's. And having tested George's menu over the years, I doubt that they ever were.

As for fish houses—Law me! On Fisherman's Wharf, a man can tie into such West Coast delicacies as minute shrimp (a hundred or so to the cocktail), oysters no larger than a nickel (and you know what's happened to the nickel recently), abalone steak and sweet, big West Coast crabs, which are the size of the average Maine lobster.

When I walk out on the wharf and see the same big old black cauldrons where crabs are cooking as usual, I always feel better about the world situation. There are the same sidewalk counters, piled high with the cooked beauties, pale coral on top and pale yellow underneath.

The housewife can always carry home a crab—big enough to make a meal for two persons—for seventy-five cents up. It's like giving away diamonds at seventy-five cents a carat.

Just beyond the counters and the cauldrons, the fish houses and the hungry tourists, the fishing fleet at night lies snug against the piers. From that fishing fleet eighty-five or ninety years ago grew the one inimitable native dish which is the pride of San Francisco.

It is cioppino, San Francisco's answer to the bouillabaisse of Marseilles. The outgrowth of the fish stew that Sicilian sailors, who came to California decades ago, first cooked over little charcoal stoves on their fishing vessels in the gold rush days, cioppino is now a "local" dish.

Not even Mrs. Murphy's chowder, reinforced by overalls, is a more delicious, rugged, life-giving substance than cioppino. It should never be eaten without an all-encompassing bib, for cioppino fans— and that includes all San Franciscans—insist that for true enjoyment a little cioppino must get in the ears, as with corn on the cob.

Tarantino's, one of the flossier restaurants on Fisherman's Wharf, serves a sumptuous cioppino. With bibs.

Here is a recipe for this stunning dish with which the housewife rather than the chef can cope.

One-half cup olive oil, one tablespoon minced onion, two to four cloves garlic finely chopped, one tablespoon minced parsley, one number 2½ can solid pack tomatoes, two eight-ounce cans tomato sauce, one-half cup sherry, one and one-half cups water, one-half teaspoon sweet basil, one-half teaspoon marjoram, one teaspoon monosodium glutamate, salt and pepper to taste.

One and one-half to two pounds uncooked rock cod, halibut, sea

bass, sole or other white fish cut in bite-size pieces, one pound uncooked large shrimp in the shell, two pounds clams well scrubbed,
two cooked crabs, cleaned, cut in pieces and with claws cracked.

Heat oil in Dutch oven. Add onion, garlic and parsley; sauté slowly
until golden brown. Add tomatoes, tomato sauce, sherry, water,
sweet basil, marjoram, monosodium glutamate, salt and pepper. Bring
to boil, then cover and simmer gently one and one-half hours.

Add cut-up white fish to simmering sauce, cover and cook gently
ten minutes. Add shrimp (do not stir), cover and cook twenty minutes.
Add clams and crab (do not stir), cover and continue cooking ten
minutes.

Serve in heated soup plates, sit back and sigh. In San Francisco,
man does not live by bread alone!

In this best of all possible worlds, in spring—if ever—come perfect
days for the man whose demigod is his belly. There is a time to fast
and a time to feast, and a time to mask numerals on the bathroom
scales, if not actually to destroy the monster. The voice of the turtle
is heard in the land, calling man to the table to enjoy the bounties
of spring.

Summer's warm abundance and autumn's ripe plenty may seem
more bountiful, but it is spring that blesses us with the delicacies of
asparagus and strawberries. Can anyone ask for more?

Who could demand a more fitting celebration of the rites of spring
than plump, tender asparagus in hot butter sauce, followed by scarlet
strawberries sweetened by the sun?

Asparagus is a queen among vegetables and a beauty queen at that,
with its pale green stalk flushed with violet clear to its delicate tip.
Who, if he casts a seeing eye upon asparagus, can be surprised to learn
that it is a member of the lily family and a double cousin of the lily
of the valley?

It is a delicacy that civilized man has enjoyed for millenniums.

Cato the Elder, in his book *On Farming,* gave the Roman world rules for its cultivation that have not changed much in 2,000 years. If Lucullus left none of his recipes for its preparation, neither did he have a pressure cooker, which I favor in preparing this superb vegetable.

Sixty to ninety seconds, according to the size of the stalk, at fifteen pounds pressure is my favorite recipe for this jewel.

It should be cooked until it is tender; only that and nothing more. It is a major culinary crime to reduce this gem to pulp, to boil it until it is soggy, dispirited and tasteless. It must retain its shape and its *esprit.*

It must be taken steaming hot from the pan, put on a hot plate, treated to hot butter or hollandaise sauce and served immediately. The family should already be seated at the table, reverently and expectantly awaiting this treat, and should fall to the minute it is served. Asparagus should not be asked to wait on time, tide or a tardy diner.

Who, with his roots in the country, does not remember asparagus, cut in two-inch lengths, and served up swimming in a hot cream sauce? You can't hardly get that kind no more. It was delicious when done by a master—say my Aunt Nell.

There are those who like their asparagus cold. Vinaigrette, for example. Ah, well, it takes all kinds to make a world.

As for strawberries, they deserve a sonnet in themselves. And whoever invented strawberry shortcake (I am a true believer in short, short, unsweetened biscuit dough) should long since have been elevated to the Hall of Fame.

And now there is no time to hymn spring's other treats, young scallions, radishes, Bibb lettuce, the first tender peas, the succulent carrots no bigger than a thumb . . .

Eat, my friend, and be merry. You can always diet tomorrow.

Do you ever wonder why no American poet has ever written an ode to corn on the cob? What more noble, more typically American subject could a native poet wish? Something like:

> O, Corn! Good for man or beast,
> Fit for humble meal or feast,
> Fine to drink, or fine to eat,
> Better now than pie or meat.

I am no T.S. Eliot, but if this gives him an idea, I shall be happy to have him run with the ball, or the cob.

To sit at table the last days of August with a platter of hot corn and a pound of country butter, front and center, is to savor life at its sweetest and pity Lucullus, who was born 2,000 years too soon.

O, happy day when the Pilgrim fathers stumbled on the Indians eating this strange vegetable of the New World. What peak in Darien is comparable to that memorable moment when the daring white man first sank molar into the creamy pearls festooned upon the cob?

Imagine the historic scene that followed, with the Pilgrim fathers begging a few sample ears—perhaps from Pocahontas' pa—to take home as a treat to the wife and children.

Picture some Pilgrim father coming home, dumping a half dozen ears in his wife's lap and saying:

"Get yourself a load of this, Martha, and then say that trip on the Mayflower wasn't worth it!"

If America had given the world no other gift, no further boon, than corn on the cob, the world would still be in her debt. The heat of August is made durable by the thought that it is ripening a delicacy better than caviar or *pâté de fois gras* and within the purse of even the poorest.

During the corn season in the U.S.A., every man eats like a king, or, as a king would like to eat, if only he could get his royal hands on some of the American specialty. Let the upper classes have their wicked demitasses, let the Vanderfellers wallow in guinea hen under glass. I will envy no man as long as the roasting ears lie in smoking, golden heaps on the luncheon and dinner table.

There is an old wheeze that describes the unluckiest man in the world as the one who works for his board and room and then loses his appetite and develops insomnia.

I know a far unluckier man, now out back weeding the corn patch. It is Old Bill, who helps with the garden. If you have tears, prepare to shed them now! His upper plate is busted.

When I passed the corn, like molten sunshine, to Bill at lunch, he shook his head sadly.

"Dropped my upper plate last week," he mumbled. "Broke clean in two. I took it to the Doc who made it and says 'Hop to, Bub, it's corn season and time's awastin'. Vulcanize this thing and let me go eat.'

"But he called me last night and says 'Bill, I sure am sorry to break the bad news, but this is a riveting job, and I got to send it clean to Newark to git it repaired. Man, I sure hope you like soup.'"

"Let me cut it off the cob for you, Bill," I said.

"Nope, nope," said Bill. "If'n I can't chomp, I won't munch. A man's got his pride."

The world is dark, indeed, and wide. The Russians are mean as dirt. The Chinese are a caution. Taxes are eating up the land. Politicians are ruining the country. The younger generation is a handful. But the corn is ripe, the crop is big and most of us have a good upper plate.

❀ ❀ ❀

Life today is comparable to the kid with the apple who said, "There ain't gonna be no leavin's." The boys in the white coats in the nation's laboratories are seeing to it that there is no waste matter in the world that can't be transformed into one of two popular substances—plastics or cocktail snacks. Sometimes, they're indistinguishable.

After the scientists put waste matter—just any waste matter will do—through the smelter, they roll it out and let it cool. Now the official taster enters the picture. He comes along at this point and samples the residue. If it is palatable—it doesn't have to taste real good—and can be salted, then it is shredded, packaged and sold as cocktail fodder under some such taste-tickling title as "Slurp-up with Burp-up."

The stuff has to be positively revolting to a goat before it is discarded as a cocktail possibility and further refined into a hundred different kinds of plastic. A man who wants to live dangerously today has to do no more than eat his way through a hors d'oeuvre tray. The guest who boasts that he eats anything can prove it anytime the sun is over the yardarm and cocktails are ready.

Many an unhappy refugee from Alcoholics Anonymous took to drink only after rattlesnake filets were put on the market some twenty years ago as an hors d'oeuvre dainty. This was the point at which I began taking my crackers straight. Since that unhappy day, hostesses have tried to lure me with everything from *ravigote* of seaweed to *pâté de* praying mantis.

That brew stirred up by the witches in the fourth act of *Macbeth,* a hash to poison dreams, isn't a patch on what the laboratories turn out as cocktail snacks. Remember?

> Fillet of a fenny snake,
> In the caldron boil and bake;
> Eye of newt, and toe of frog,
> Wool of bat, and tongue of dog,
> Adder's fork, and blind-worm's sting,
> Lizard's leg, and howlet's wing,—

In retrospect, that sounds wholesome and tasty compared with some of the canapés I have encountered.

Shakespeare was ahead of his time.

Grandma knew how to parcel out vittles fit for man or beast. We got the pot roast and the parrot got the sunflower seeds, the pig the pumpkin seeds and the chickens rated the cracklin's.

Today, the hostess with the mostes' on the ball pays $1.98 per pound for dehydrated, shredded and processed sunflower and pumpkin seeds. No canapé tray is complete without this American caviar.

Farmyards have been bare of chicken feed since scientists discovered that it can be reactivated and sold, for seventy-nine cents for a six-ounce jar, to any potential Perle Mesta.

By and large, beware of Greeks bearing gifts and hostesses toting canapés. That way, a citizen has at least an even chance of dying in bed.

There are times when I am convinced that we who live in New York are almost as provincial as our critics insist. For some time my sister, who migrated to Memphis a few years ago, has on her visits here talked about "finger food."

That's a catchy phrase—finger food. Try it on for size. Both my sister and I like to cook. While we may not haunt Escoffier, let me say without false modesty that we don't rattle the pots and pans in the amateur section. So when she talks of food I listen, with pencil poised.

When Cathryn (and if you think that's a torturous way of spelling Katherine, consult her! There are years when she wishes that Papa hadn't named her for her great-grandmother!) spoke of finger foods, my mind turned to the tried-and-true, before-forks fodder such as fried chicken, frogs' legs, corn on the cob (ah! sweet mystery of life!), artichokes, asparagus, sandwiches, ice-cream cones, pickles, olives, salted nuts, cake, bread and butter, cookies and all the other legitimate "use your fingers!" bait.

Otherwise, if we used our fingers in the dining room, we got a smart rap across the knuckles when our parents were trying to turn their young savages into civilized human beings. Mama was a strong-minded woman who had vaguely heard that fingers were made before forks but placed no credence in such a wild rumor.

If there were persons who had ever used their fingers with which to eat, Mama certainly wouldn't have recognized them in either time or place. She would have felt that their parents were delinquent. When

Charles Laughton made such a tremendous hit in that old film, *Henry VIII*, we kept Mama away from the movies.

The first time Henry or Charles tossed a bone over his shoulder at table, Mama would have been on her way to the box office to ask for her money back.

I can hear her argument, too, to the guardian of the box office— to the effect that if this was the cultural lag of the medium, the movies had best shut up shop and not debase audiences. (Frankly, we protected Mama from the harsher things of life. It would have been unthinkable to take her to anything vaguely resembling a play by Tennessee Williams.)

Well, I started out with finger food, and here I am conjuring up Tennessee Williams. But there is logic behind this, however, because I think that's just how grim finger food is. I finally realized that finger food is just another and sneaky name for that curse of civilization, canapés, and their identical twin, hors d'oeuvres.

Just calling the gook finger food doesn't make icebox seepings any more attractive to me. When a woman scrapes out the peanut butter jar, adds the last of the piccalilli and mayonnaise and then moistens it all with the juice of the maraschino cherry jar, it makes no difference to me whether it's called "finger food" or Ptomaine Tidbits.

The ingenuity that women use devising ways and means to use left-overs in "finger food" would, if concentrated on a worthy cause, get a man to the moon in the next twelve months. If the nation is to survive not nuclear war but finger food, women's energy is going to have to be channeled into some constructive effort.

It has been years since I have gone to a cocktail party, but I catch the finger food routine during the cocktail hour before dinner. There we see honest vittles such as cheese and crackers, little hamburgers, sausages, miniature chicken sandwiches, etc., etc. It is when the hostess runs barefoot through the icebox, combining and inventing as she goes, that trouble starts. Finger food? At that point, it's all thumbs.

Well, sir, I know I'm licked before I start. But here goes Señora Sancho Panza, full tilt.

This time I am riding against lettuce in sandwiches, hot or cold. Such monstrous misuse of this noble salad green ruins both it and the sandwich, and why one was ever introduced into the other, to the destruction of both, beats me.

When the Earl of Sandwich invented his namesake in the eighteenth century, he slapped two pieces of bread around a hunk of meat, the better to eat at the gaming table. Did he put lettuce in it? Ha! Not that purist. He took his straight, and that's the way I want mine. Only try and get it.

St. George had it easy with the dragon compared with a customer trying to get (1) the waiter and (2) the chef to PLEASE OMIT lettuce from the cream cheese and chopped peanuts on pumpernickel, the tuna-fish salad and mustard pickle on marble cake, or the bacon and egg with cream dressing on whole wheat toast.

Apparently, in sandwich schools all over the country, student chefs are taught that lettuce is the indispensable or secret ingredient of sandwiches, more basic even than bread and mayonnaise. Once behind a counter, they cling to this totem with the dogged and unswerving devotion of a zealot.

Not even oil and water mix as reluctantly as lettuce and a sandwich made with toasted bread. Basically, they are antithetical and savagely destroy each other. A chunk of lettuce slapped between two pieces of toast wilts like Sweet Alice, Ben Bolt, at fear of a frown.

But the lettuce, before it gives up the ghost and wilts into a tough and flabby substance, has its revenge. The lettuce, cold and clammy with refrigerator mortis, spreads its icy damp through the toast. In a gustatory *Götterdämmerung,* the two antagonists, locked in deadly embrace, expire together in limp defeat. So does the diner.

It is my hunch that lettuce, now universal in sandwiches, first crept into this alien field via the tea shoppe, which must also stand before the judgment seat and answer for the cream cheese and canned pineapple salad. It's a 100-to-1 that some tea shoppe proprietress, seeking to gussy up a self-respecting, perfectly decent sandwich, first added the lettuce and was carried away by her unwholesome handiwork. Since then, the practice has spread like chickweed. No sandwich or customer is really safe. The diner who orders a sandwich without lettuce or a steak without French fries has a fat chance of achieving either. Addiction to both is regarded as a fundamental and basic American trait. The customer who demands no lettuce and/or French fries is fobbed off either as crazy or subversive. Don't think any dog wagon or tea shoppe has even the slightest intention of catering to such outlandish whims. He'll get lettuce and like it. Ditto, French fries.

I like lettuce and I hate to see it abused. But my earlier campaign against spurious French dressing has wrought no great nationwide reforms. A sort of rust-colored lava, it still reduces anything in its path to rubbish not even fit for the compost heap.

So I am hardened to getting lettuce in sandwiches until I die. But no one can say I haven't tried.

Grin and Bear It

Windsor Wedding

Most wedding dresses wind up in the attic or at rummage sales. But the most famous wedding dress of our troubled times rests in the Metropolitan Museum of Art.

The "Wallis Blue" wedding gown of the Duchess of Windsor was presented by Her Grace to the Museum, at its request. Presumably it will, over the years, give the Rubenses, Raphaels, Goyas, Whistlers and Da Vincis a run for their money.

The Duchess' dress is housed in the Museum's Costume Institute, together with other historic gowns. It may even come to pass that the pale blue wedding dress of the former Baltimore belle, Wallis Warfield, will rest ruffle by flounce with the exquisite court dresses of Queen Alexandra. Her Majesty was the beautiful Danish bride of King Edward VII, grandsire of the Duke of Windsor, briefly Edward VIII, of whom it has been said "like grandfather, like grandson."

In point of protocol, Her Majesty's gowns may outrank Her Grace's. But in point of public interest, rack one up for the Duchess. Probably no dress in modern times has been copied so widely, in such a vast price range, as that designed by Mainbocher for Wallis Warfield Simpson's wedding to the former King of England.

In my capacity as a reporter, I covered those famous nuptials on June 3, 1937, the biggest event since the original chariot race in *Ben Hur.*

I have always regarded it as a great tribute to the alertness and mass production methods of the American dress industry that three weeks after the wedding, any enterprising American girl with $3.99 in her pocket could buy a fair duplicate of the Duchess' wedding dress.

It graced the windows and was for sale at that price in a half-dozen shops along Fourteenth Street, the poor man's Rue de la Paix or Fifth Avenue.

Granted, a dollar was worth more and went farther in those days. Still, at twice the price, it was little enough for a dress that probably cost $850, FOB Mainbocher, where a kitchen apron retails at $325. The dress's instant duplication on these shores is not only an indication of American know-how but a bow to the larceny in the hearts of all of us.

After he had completed the Duchess' wedding gown, Mainbocher tore up the pattern. He never duplicated it himself. The thousands of designers, manufacturers and village dressmakers who did were forced to work from newspaper and magazine photographs and descriptions. All of which goes to prove what a useful and valuable part the printed word and picture play in our lives.

The Metropolitan Museum of Art hankered for the Duchess' wedding gown for some time before it finally got up enough courage to make the pitch by cable. By return cable the Duchess said she would bring the gown with her the next time she returned from France to the United States. When she arrived at the Museum, not only did the Duchess present the dress but also the little sandals and the off-the-face halo hat of "Wallis Blue" that completed her wedding ensemble.

At the time the dress was new, there were many and dire predictions that the marriage would not last a month, six months, a year. But the Duke and Duchess are now celebrating their Silver Wedding anniversary.

Once, after the marriage had long been a going concern, I asked them if they would do it all over again—if he would give up a crown for love, if she would brave the slings and arrows of outraged critics as she did in 1936–37.

"Yes! Yes!" they cried in unison.

"I'm afraid a great deal of wishful thinking went into predictions that our marriage wouldn't last," the Duchess added.

"Now we're just a very happy, very middle-aged couple," the Duke said.

Often since that interview, I have chuckled over an amusing sidelight that never saw print. While I was writing the interview, I had an anxious telephone call from His Royal Highness.

Would I, he begged, as a great favor to himself and the Duchess, not mention the fact that she often cooked their Sunday night supper —and sometimes their Sunday luncheon—on an electric two-burner plate they had smuggled into their suite in the Waldorf-Astoria? (On such occasions, the Duke had told me, it was his job to put up the card table and set it properly.)

Only a day or two before, the Duke confessed that the Duchess, a famous cook, had been unable to resist cooking on both burners to speed things up. As a result, every fuse in their apartment blew. They had been hard put to explain the matter to the hotel authorities, since cooking by guests in the hotel is strictly forbidden.

"Since then," said the Duke conspiratorially, "we put the card table right by the stove and service is direct from burner to consumer."

Please, the former King-Emperor petitioned, would I strike out all reference to the outlaw stove!

"If the hotel found out, it might dispossess us," he said with genuine concern. "And it does give us such pleasure to have a meal at home."

It killed me to kill an amusing story. But perhaps it was worth the sacrifice. At least the Windsors appear to have lived happily ever after. When last I glimpsed them, they were holding hands. The gesture did not appear to be in the mood of the wary couple who held hands for twenty-five years because each was afraid to let go.

The Modern Message

Madison Avenuemanship reached a new peak, in one woman's opinion, with a series of advertisements that boldly recast American mores and manners in the modern mold.

Do you wish to clobber a first husband? Insult an old suitor? Lie to a second-string beau? These daily situations, ignored by the present books on etiquette, were incisively outlined for those who "Live Modern" in a series of advertisements for Crane's stationery. For the timid or the socially insecure, Crane's offered an invaluable public service in a field too long ignored.

Let us take, for example, the problem of properly pulverizing a first husband. The picture accompanying this ad looked out upon the terrace of what could only be an impressive seaside mansion. And the legend read: "Gloat on Crane's—'I'm turning the beach house over to you. Stuart and I will be married at his villa in Capri, Celeste.' "

Beneath this was a brilliant explanatory sentence, "When it comes to impressing first husbands, a stinging little note on Crane's paper does more for your ego than alimony."

As anyone can see, this little comedy of holy terrors is right out of Noel Coward. And, believe me, Celeste isn't going to have the last word, if I know Noel. I'll guarantee that by return mail Celeste will receive a note, written on even better bond with a higher linen-rag content, from that first husband.

Ignoring the fact that Celeste's use of "will" rather than "shall" in her message is a revealing Freudian gaffe, No. 1 writes, "Give the beach house back to the Indians or your parents. Millicent and I are sailing for the Orient on our honeymoon aboard her yacht. We go via the Mediterranean if the Suez is wide enough to take the *Vagrant*."

The next ad in this series that struck me with its modern approach was called "Fib on Crane's." The accompanying illustration showed a young artist, suffering etched into his handsome face, striding through a meadow, accompanied only by his easel, canvas and paints.

"Knowing how sensitive you are, Briggs," for such was his name and this was the note that sent him into the meadow, "I simply couldn't put you through the ordeal of my rather plebeian wedding— my conventional relatives, the stuffy country club. Much as I once . . ."

The situation was further explained as the ad continued "When it comes to being most diplomatic or hiding your true feelings, a letter on Crane's impressive paper carries off white lies with great finesse."

It is too early to tell Briggs that he is jolly well rid of this witch-in-wedding-rig. All he can understand now is that she was ashamed of him and didn't want an artist cluttering up her wedding to the son of the town's most prominent banker-industrialist. (And why she should be ashamed of Briggs when he was obviously dressed by Brooks Brothers escapes me.)

If the first drama was pure Coward, this second is prime John O'Hara territory. Briggs looked too much of a gentleman to take sheepskin and send a message reading "And may all your children be certified public accountants!"

But it is pretty obvious that Briggs was saved from a fate worse than Beth. It is only a matter of time until the bride and bridegroom, bored to death, start romping in alien Wamsutta, and the O'Hara fat is in the fire.

This Crane campaign is certain to revive the old admonition "Do right and fear no man; don't write and fear no woman." And it also should do more for Western Union than a government subsidy.

Go South, Young Man

The more Palm Beach changes, the more it is the same in at least one respect: It is still the No. 1 happy hunting ground in the U.S.A. for ambitious gigolos (i.e., ambitious not to work).

It is still the cold-weather haven for more lonely widows and misunderstood wives, all richer than Croesus, than are congregated in any other spot in the nation. The dangerous age in this community is the point at which any restless wife or widow begins to believe the collegiate type when he says, "But you have never really *lived!*"

Any number of lads to whom toil is repugnant have gone to Palm Beach in the past three decades as dance instructors for a fairly famous New York dance emporium and have wound up marrying money with a capital "M."

I was treated to a firsthand run-down on the Lonely Hearts situation there and am in a position to report that the Palm Beach soap opera, like every other soap opera on the air, just keeps repeating itself.

I latched onto the preview at a typical Palm Beach cocktail dansant. A four-piece orchestra played soft music for dancing in the patio, bathed in artificial moonlight. Three bartenders saw to it that the boys and girls in the back room and around the swimming pool had something to sustain them at the witching hour. And a buffet table, a half block long, was loaded, too.

A collegiate type in a good tweed jacket and flannel slacks asked me to dance. He danced much too well to be a hard-working American businessman or an average American husband on vacation. He wanted to know at once where I lived, if I were misunderstood, if I were happy and would I have dinner with him at a small, cozy rendezvous down the pike.

"Look, son," I said in my blunt way, "that tall, dark man in the corner is my husband. Alas, he understands me. I am happy as a lark. Besides, we're sharecroppers, and in addition I'm a reporter."

"Gad, have I got a story for you!" he said, without missing a step. "I've been trying to market it, but I might as well give it to you. You ever hear of Bunny X?" he asked, naming the middle-aged heiress to one of the biggest industrial fortunes in the country.

"She got married four weeks ago, to a boy I introduced her to," he continued, steering me over to a marble bench. "I not only stood up with them at the wedding, but I loaned the guy the suit he wore and three shirts to go on his honeymoon.

"Four weeks ago he didn't have taxi fare to the beach and today he's got two domestic convertibles and a foreign sports car she's given him, and $50,000 in cash as a wedding present. Four weeks and he's got all that!

"But I'm telling you, she's loaded with money. Her old man left her a bankful of tax-exempt securities or bonds or something when he died, and she just sits there with the money rolling in and hands it over to this Joe I introduced her to."

"That was your mistake," I pointed out to him. "You should have played it smart and not introduced competition into your Eden."

"What do you mean?" he muttered, but he began to turn scarlet in the artificial moonlight.

"Don't give me that!" I said. "I'm an old Palm Beach hand. You're sore because you lost the grand prize. You down here as a dance instructor?"

"He was," my collegiate type said sulkily.

"Don't waste any more time on me," I ordered. "See that middle-aged debutante over there in the purple tulle, the diamond necklace and the white mink stole? (Author's note: Ermine is for peasants in Palm Beach.) That's your dish. Get to work, and better luck next time."

The head of our house, when I told him the incident, said I ought to be ashamed, sicking a gigolo on a poor, innocent woman. But I say no woman is either poor or innocent who wears purple tulle, a diamond necklace and white mink to a cocktail dansant.

The Southern Belles Are Ringing

It is safe to say that the only public utilities company ever to suffer both brassiere and bookie trouble simultaneously, a parlay unique in the history of free enterprise, is the Southern Bell Telephone and Telegraph Co.

How this respectable, middle-aged corporation ever got mixed up with blondes and bangtails in the first place—but let us begin at the beginning:

Southern Bell was stunned a number of years ago when it was discovered that the company was being stolen bra-blind by some of its lady employees. The girls had hit upon a simple cash and carry, share-the-wealth plan. They were taking home rolls of silver deposited in the old First National Bank, which, in recent years, has moved north from the stocking top to the bra area.

Southern Bell, still punchy, had scarcely begun to recover from the nationwide mirth about falsies, padded figures, double-entry systems and the cup that runneth over when the Dade County grand jury returned an indictment naming the public utility as "an accessory to the operation of gambling houses."

This particular grand jury laid about it with a big stick in an effort to run the hoods, racketeers and gamblers out of Miami and Miami Beach. In addition to indicting fifty-four persons, including former Sheriff James A. Sullivan, it put the slug on Southern Bell.

It is not very often that a reporter gets to feel sorry for a public utilities magnate. So I went around to the Southern Bell offices to try on the feeling for size with J. M. Phillips, district manager of the company. Mr. Phillips turned out to be a man with heavy gray hair and a public utilities suit and necktie. Until he was transferred to Miami from Nashville, Mr. Phillips was a happy family man who didn't know an uplift from a No. 2 cup or a horse parlor from a hole-in-the-wall.

"My goodness alive, the telephone company has not been aiding and abetting gamblers," he said as he sat behind his neat desk. "We are no more aiding and abetting gamblers than we are actively helping the criminal who uses the telephone to plan or execute a crime."

"You wouldn't have handy the name of a good hayburner in the second at Pimlico?" I coaxed.

"My goodness, no!" Mr. Phillips said. "And it is certainly not true as charged that bookmakers got phones and service during the war when they weren't available to other subscribers."

I winked. "Southern Bell got any hot tips on the next Kentucky Derby?" I asked. Mr. Phillips threw up his hands.

"Now about the brassieres . . ." I began.

"I can even laugh about it myself—now," he said. "It's been a field day for the comedians all over."

Three of the girls involved were convicted in the case of the clanking brassieres and others were to face trial. Miami loves and insists on telling of the confused, fatherly Deputy Sheriff, talking police parlance to one of the girl defendants, who urged her to make a clean breast of the business and get the whole thing off her chest.

I asked Mr. Phillips if the female employees of Southern Bell were now forbidden to wear bras.

"My goodness alive, no!" he said, and then public utilities officials or no, Mr. Phillips couldn't resist his own yak, "but we sincerely hope there won't be any slack in 'em."

Look Ma, I'm Dancing

I keep reading that the American Legion boys aren't what they used to be. The veterans of World War I have succumbed to hardening of the arteries and falling hair, so the papers say. And the veterans of World War II and Korea are all young men with a purpose, dignified as judges, who never toss furniture out of hotel windows and always forewarn citizens by yelling "Bombs Away" before dropping paper bags filled with water from the eighteenth floor.

Maybe so. Still and all, when the veterans assemble in convention, I now take protective cover and retire to my apartment for the duration. Maybe the boys have simmered down, but I want guarantees. They were too much for me some twenty years ago and I am in no mood to take a chance again.

The Legion, holding its annual convention in Boston, overwhelmed me with the most humiliating defeat of my reportorial career. I have been able before and since to cope with war, fire, flood, murder and the general run of five-alarm violence, disaster and human cussedness.

But that time the Legion forced me to toss in the towel and yell "Uncle." No matter what time and tide have done to the lads in the interim, they were full of fun and frolic in those far-off days.

I was young enough to dodge the falling furniture and enter into the spirit of things when Legionnaires commandeered the citizenry for snake dances.

As I look back on it now, I see that what defeated me was a combination of Legionnaires and technology. That was the convention at which the veterans came armed with an electric gadget known only as "the buzzer." This was a sort of stick, powered by a battery, that the boys applied, without discrimination, to the anatomy of men, women and even little children.

The Legionnaires preferred the rear façade as a target, and, naturally, ladies had priority. It is only fair to say that the buzzer livened up both the victim, Boston and the convention. Once contact had been made, the victim rose straight in the air, like a helicopter without props, emitting blood-curdling cries both on the ascent and descent and then indulged in a lively *danse macabre*.

The streets of the Athens of America soon resembled a Comanche massacre in sight and sound. To say that I was terrified is begging the question. I cowered in my hotel room with the blinds drawn, listening to the shrieks of the victims and the lively rat-ta-ta-tat of their heels on the pavements. At the end of the second day, I knew I was licked. The ceaseless cries of women taking off with the speed of jet propulsion had completely unnerved me, the hotel room had begun to pall and I knew every detail of a bad reproduction of "The Blue Boy," hanging over the washstand.

So I called the boss in New York and tossed in my chips.

"You may fire when ready," I sobbed into the phone, "but I would rather be in the army of the unemployed than dancing in the streets!"

After he pieced together my broken story, the editor was surprisingly sympathetic. He said I might come home and he would dispatch a big, strong, brave male reporter to Boston to ride herd on the Legion convention.

"Is there anything he ought to know?" asked the boss.

"Yes," I said tearfully, "he ought to know enough to wear a book in each pants' pocket."

Maybe the Legion has lost its sting and there isn't a buzzer in a box-car load these days. But discretion is the better part of valor. I stay home for the duration of such conventions.

Once More into the Breach, Dear Sophs!

In view of the fact that Shakespeare is generally regarded as the premier dramatist of the Western world, it is odd how seldom he can find a Broadway producer. Or maybe the dearth is in dedicated Shakespearean actors.

This, apparently, is the first generation in which Shakespearean actors have been an under-the-counter item. Sir John Gieguld and Sir Laurence Olivier from time to time devote their talent to Will, but not in the whole-hearted and more-or-less continuous tradition of Sir Henry Irving and Edwin Booth, if we are to believe Grandma.

Or even in the latter-day tradition of E. H. Sothern and Robert Mantell who trooped the road with Shakespeare for decades. I arrived in New York too late to see John Barrymore in what the critics generally regard as the best *Hamlet* of our times. However, I do remember seeing Robert Mantell as Macbeth, a performance that scared the wits out of me only because the actor was by that time so venerable I would have taken odds that he would be finished before the play. At that, it was a photo finish.

But I am blessed with two scholarly friends who can remember Mantell in his prime when, as spear carriers in the actor's production of *Henry V,* they reversed Mantell, Shakespeare and history.

The year is 1905; the scene, Columbia University. The first of the dramatis personae to enter is Mantell's casting director. He went to the University to recruit from its Shakespearean classes the French and English armies that clash in the Battle of Agincourt, in which Henry V, in the person of Mantell, was once more to lead the English archers to resounding victory.

Callous to class distinctions, the director unfortunately recruited the French army first, and from the sophomore class in Shakespeare. He then compounded the tactical blunder by enlisting the English army from freshman devotees of the Bard.

Both John Wheeler, a newspaper syndicate chief after that, and the late Henry Snevily, subsequently his general manager, were members of the sophomore class. As Snev remarked, after the first rehearsal it became apparent that indignant and proud sophomores were about to rewrite history and the Bard. They were in no mood to be pushed around by freshmen in the interests of art or accuracy.

The sophs sent a committee to remonstrate with the casting director. However, he was a hardened sort, indifferent to the cloistered nuances of university life. He pointed out that they were getting fifty cents a night and the chance to see a great thespian work, so what?

It was plain that the sophs in the livery of the French would have to redress their own grievances. Before the third night's performance, they threw down the gauge to the frosh and each class packed the galleries with its own adherents.

From the moment the famous combat scene began, it was a battle royal. The swords turned out to be tin and bent too easily to inflict any real damage. The opposing armies took to fisticuffs. Warriors, locked in battle, fell into the orchestra pit, and innocent musicians went down like nine-pins.

In the meantime, the freshmen and sophomores in the gallery were joyously beating each other up. Blood streamed from a hundred noses. Mantell had hysteria and ordered the curtain rung down, but an enchanted audience pelted the curtain and demanded that it go up and the fight go on.

"We French sophs rewrote Shakespeare and history that night," Snev recalled, "and for the first and only time on record, the French beat the hell out of the English at Agincourt.

"You wouldn't know it to look at me," he added modestly, "but I am one hell of an actor, and I haven't ever enjoyed Shakespeare so much before or since."

War Reunions are Hell

"In the countries where American Military Government teams were charged with administration, there has been no appreciable showing or growth in communism," said General Lucius D. Clay, standing behind a red, white and blue bouquet at the speakers' table. "That is your legacy and your monument," added the General and sat down.

The alumni of American Military Government, plus their ladies, stood up and applauded warmly. They had come from every part of the nation for this reunion in New York. The applause died away, chairs scraped on the floor of the hotel ballroom and everyone sat down again.

"So I got out my uniform and had it pressed and I was going to wear it to the reunion tonight," said the attractive man on my right, who, on close scrutiny, turned out to be my spouse. "And I could get into it all right, but I couldn't breathe, so I said what the hell . . ."

"Well, that's very interesting," said the man with the curly gray hair across the table, who had come from Detroit for the reunion. "But when I tried to get into my uniform, I says to Belle here"— nodding to the buxom blonde on his left—"I says to Belle 'If Uncle wants me again, I hope he gives me a trade-in allowance and $250 for new uniforms.' I could get into the uniform, all right, but it wouldn't zip."

"We were stationed in Tuscany for a while," the thin, dark young man from Sacramento was saying earnestly to Belle, "and all the women there, young and old, had wonderful posture from carrying things on their heads."

"Yeah?" said Belle. "And what did that get them?"

"Well," said the thin, dark man, a bit bewildered by Belle's vehemence, "it got them wonderful posture."

"Yeah?" countered Belle, "I can tell you what it gets those women:

It gets them the privilege of carrying things on their head till they drop dead. Give me round shoulders and a redcap, every time!"

"Yessuh, Ah read *A Bell for Adano*," said the colonel who had come all the way from Mississippi to see his old friends in AMG, "but Ah could nevah find any practical application fo' its lessons in mah districts. Wh' Ah was mostly stationed, the people didn't need a bell nearly as much as they needed plumbin' and sanitation, and I guess there isn't a best seller in plumbin' and sanitation."

"There was for Chic Sale," said Belle.

"Sure, you remember the public baths in Turin," the Detroiter argued with the former AMGer from St. Paul. "They were right around the corner from headquarters and down that little back street called Via del something-or-other."

"No," said the stubborn man from St. Paul. "I don't remember where they were. I wasn't in Turin long enough to take a bath. I was only there two weeks."

"Now you take this party," happily said the Mississippi colonel, "It is shu' 'nuf typical of American Military Government. Everything has been snafu from the beginnin'. The martinis were hot and the soup was cold. Ah declare! It takes me right back lak Ah never left Italy!"

The man from St. Paul shook with laughter.

"Remember when we designed that insignia for the AMG?" he asked. "By God, we didn't miss a thing. It was an overstuffed rocking chair on a dais."

"And so I said to the girl, 'But all I want done is my laundry. Laundry,' I says, and I spelled it out," came from the man on my right, "and then I showed her the bar of soap. And she started yelling and three or four men ran out of the house and they yelled, too.

" 'What do you take our sister for, a servant?' they screamed, and I just kept backing away and saying, 'But all I want done is my laundry.' "

"And if Uncle Sam needs you again, what are you going to do?" the man from St. Paul asked the thin, dark young man.

"Well, I still got my address book," said the veteran from Sacramento.

A Woman of Conventions

Since the political conventions of 1960, I have formed a group called Conventions Anonymous. Its membership is confined to newspapermen and newspaperwomen who always swear off after every quadrennial political season and yet seem unable to kick the habit. The agonies of covering a Republican or a Democratic conclave tend, like those of childbirth, to fade too fast.

Thus, we of Conventions Anonymous are pledged to help each other go straight in 1964. If one of us weakens, he has but to call one of the brethren who will hasten around, with a sash weight if necessary, to save the backslider. The trouble is that we tend to forget the blood, sweat, tears and toil, and even the oratory. We remember only the educational side bars, such as how the Bloody Mary was invented and the composition of The Salty Dog. Or rather, that's what I remember, that and His Imperial Highness, Prince Mike Romanoff, commuting my sentence in the salt mines.

This is a wonderful country, full of democracy. Anyone can go to a political convention. That explains the presence of Georgie Jessel, a professional Democrat, at this particular Republican stampede, that I recall, in Chicago. What Prince Mike was doing there is not quite clear, except that he didn't appear to be running either from or for anything.

It is to Georgie that I owe the educational side bar about The Salty Dog and the Bloody Mary. One day during the GOP convention, while girding myself for further jousting, I met Georgie in the Pump Room, which is to Chicago what the Colosseum is to Rome or moonlight to the Taj Mahal.

Georgie was fortifying himself against Republicans with a strange potion in a champagne glass. He let me taste it. After bystanders had used the fire extinguisher on me and successfully resorted to resuscitation, he explained that the liquid fire was known as a Salty Dog.

"It is a little something of my own invention," he said with the casual pride of Galileo fingering his telescope. "Just a soupçon of fresh grapefruit juice and a dash of salt in a glass of vodka, and you think any Democrat can win."

As for the Bloody Mary, Georgie claimed to have invented and christened it years ago in Palm Beach after a resplendent night of champagne, even in the fountains. On the morning after, doghair was indicated, but Georgie discovered that he had only a bottle of vodka and a can of tomato juice to work with. Fifty-fifty, it worked wonders he discovered, and the Bloody Mary was born, recondite tribute to the elder daughter of Henry VIII.

The Bloody Mary is a confidence builder, too, Georgie said. It once inspired him with the conviction he could not only nominate but elect Averell Harriman to the Presidency.

As for H.I.H. Prince Mike, I walked on air after I encountered him in the lobby of the Blackstone during the same political convention. The prince spoke to me! He was regal and aloof to be sure. But still, he spoke. In that moment, the lobby of the Blackstone vibrated with a reconciliation more touching than the 1961 meeting between former President Truman and former President Eisenhower at Independence. I had been in a social Siberia for years, banished by Prince Mike.

My fall from imperial favor occurred at the Kentucky Derby in 1940, when I innocently wrote that Prince Mike was on hand, waiting as usual at the clubhouse gates to get inside on someone else' thumb. Those were the days just before Prince Mike became a West Coast restaurateur and one of the most successful men in America.

However, it was not until January, 1941, that I learned of my banishment. At that time I was up to no particular good in Hollywood and felt I had found the right medium when I read that Prince Mike had been tossed into the pokey for violating his parole. I disremember what he was on parole from, except the police.

To me, this seemed an ideal time to journey to the jail and interview the Prince. With nothing but love in my heart and a cross-cut file in my muff, I arrived at the jail and sent in my card to His Imperial Highness.

Imagine my chagrin and embarrassment when Prince Mike refused to grant me an audience. He sent back curt word by the warden that I had grievously offended him by my coarse reference to him at the Derby when, all the time, he was the guest of Darryl Zanuck. Or was it Sam Goldwyn?

At all odds, he spoke to me in Chicago! I was restored to grace and favor and my cup ranneth over.

It was at another convention in Chicago, this one Democratic, that I was forever confirmed in my suspicion that equal rights bode no good for my sex. At such political upheavals, meals are a catch-as-catch-can problem for a newsman.

On this particular occasion, I was having dinner at the Blackstone at 1 A.M. with a half-dozen male confreres, including my old and dear friend, Paul Gallico, and one politician, the late Jesse Jones, so rich that even other Texas millionaires showed him deference. During the unfortunate and previous twenty-four hours, at least unfortunate for me, as you will see, a group of militant female politicians had besieged the Democratic platform committee to include an equal rights plank in the finished product.

Now I will fight on the barricades for my privileges. But I won't walk across the street for my rights. Women have so many of 'em now that they have taken to wearing pants, a perversion of nature and an abomination before the Lord.

I was in the midst of a quite impassioned speech to this effect, when I had the ill luck to cry "After all, what are equal rights for women?" My timing could not have been more unfortunate. At that moment the waiter presented the check and Paul did not miss the cue.

He took the check, handed it to me and said, "This is they." Or maybe "them." And all the men, including Jesse Jones, just sat there with fishhooks in their pockets, while I learned the harsh truth that with equal rights it is the woman who pays and pays and pays.

At still another convention, I learned one of life's most valuable lessons: Never trust any tip from the feed-bag or the horse-owner's mouth. Again I was at luncheon in the Pump Room, from which any knowledgeable reporter can cover a Chicago political convention in far more comfort and authority than 'way out there at the Amphitheater or Convention Hall, hard by the stock yards.

This time it was Alfred Gwynne Vanderbilt who stopped by the table. He modestly admitted that he had a horse, of which he had highest hopes, and that he was testing those hopes at a Chicago horse track that very day. Although I am not a betting woman, this information seemed comparable to me to a whispered confidence from the president of American Telephone and Telegraph that the company is about to split its stock and raise its dividend.

Instantly I peeled five dollars off my scanty roll and asked a luncheon companion, Mr. Bob Considine, to place every penny on Mr. Vanderbilt's horse's nose. Unfortunately, Chicago at the time was in the unaccustomed grip of reform, and Bob spent every minute until race time trying to find a horse parlor instead of a presidential candidate. In the nick of time, he found a man willing to take my wager.

In a wink of time, my fiver was gone. Mr. Vanderbilt's horse was not the hopeful type. But it was a useful lesson, reinforcing the dictum that a penny saved is a penny still to be spent and that difference of opinion not only makes horse racing but paupers.

Although I am the founding member of Conventions Anonymous I'll say this: At conventions I usually got as good as I gave.

Alphonse and Gaston à la New York

Nine out of every ten visitors to New York carry away the unhappy and not altogether true conviction that we who dwell in this vast metropolis are not always neighborly or friendly, polite or courteous toward one another.

An English newspaper columnist here on business for the *London Daily Express* wrote his paper implying that a New Yorker could drop dead on the sidewalk and even his next of kin would simply step over the body and go on about his business.

Any way you slice it, this is harsh criticism, implying lack of heart and humanity on the part of all of us. But so the indictments go, with no one ever rising to say a few words in behalf of the defendant.

But I have a tale this day to prove how hot is the milk of kindness racing through our veins and how superbly our politesse and humanitarianism rises to the exigencies of city life.

Let us take the case of Liza, age five, and her vitamins. Liza and her family live in a large, new apartment house. The residents of this cliff dwelling have long known that the water riser connecting the bathrooms, stacked tiled tier on tiled tier, acts as a perfect sounding board, and that any conversation in any bathroom is instantly broadcast throughout the building.

Now the tenant in the apartment above Liza and her parents is a charming gentleman of the old New York school, meaning that he minds his business and expects the neighbors to mind theirs.

However, a few days ago, Liza, for whom the doctor had prescribed vitamins, and her mother were in the bathroom, in the process of getting the first vitamin tablet down Liza. This was a tough job, as Liza is a modern, highly articulate child. She was determined not to take the pill and said so loudly and repeatedly the more her mother pleaded and threatened.

At the end of ten noisy minutes, Liza still hadn't taken the pill. Then suddenly a disembodied voice, vibrant with power and authority, filled the bathroom. In measured, awesome tones it said, "Liza, this is God. Take that pill!"

Liza looked at her mother, who nodded solemn affirmation. Liza took the pill without another word.

When Liza's mother wrote a letter of appreciation to the old gentleman she received, in turn, a note that simply said, "I am always happy to be of service in emergencies."

Virtue in Red Lights

Is it possible that one-way streets, lack of parking space and the traffic congestion common to all great American cities keep alive the puritan tradition in the United States?

Is the automobile the guardian rather than the wayward destroyer of native morals? Or, rather, the traffic jams it causes in American megalopolises?

By the way, let us pause for a moment to consider that word: megalopolis. We had best become accustomed to it, since it is now the fashionable—really, the intellectual—epithet for big city or metropolis. In recent months I have been unable to pick up any magazine or book dealing with the life, times and problems of large cities without at once coming across megalopolis.

This noun, with its good Greek root, is now a dirty word for New York, Chicago, Los Angeles, St. Louis or other big city in any book or article with pretentions to solving urban problems.

But now, back to the traffic impasse, the guardian of virtue. When I went to see *La Dolce Vita,* picturing the decadent life of Italy's café-society set, the picture's force as a first-rate modern morality play overshadowed its other facets for me.

Its portrayal of sin actually as ugly as sin obscured temporarily for me the fact that Roman members of café society restlessly raced from one scene of bored turpitude to another of half-wit debauchery. "Raced" is the key word here. Eventually I began to wonder how those dissipated Romans ever did it. Raced, that is.

Since the war I have never been in Rome when traffic wasn't at a standstill. The Vespas have the illusion of speed only because they make so much noise. So the more I thought about *La Dolce Vita* the more I wondered how Roman society, even jet-propelled, got around —not to decadence, but to so much of it—in any given twenty-four-hour period. Perhaps, with luck, they could make it to two orgies per day, but the rest of the time they were surely standing still in Roman traffic, doing nothing more censurable than nail biting and cursing.

That conviction became certainty the day I sat in New York traffic, twiddling my thumbs, as I tried to get to a tea party for a friend from England, a cocktail party for a friend from California, a dinner party, the theater and a supper party.

With superhuman effort I made the tea, the dinner and the theater. Traffic did me in, and sent me home at the end of the evening but a shadow of the blithe woman who had set out at 4 P.M. on a round of pleasure. I was in bed by midnight, the hour for any worthwhile orgy to get under way.

Ever since that day, I have been contemplating the role of traffic as Mrs. Grundy in this and other megalopolises. Give a thought to the dedicated rounder or Don Juan. He leaves one rendezvous, with a scant fifteen minutes to get to the next, and finds that he is parked on a one-way street, going in the wrong direction.

By the time he is headed in the right direction, he is already late. And when he arrives at the proper cross street, he discovers a sign reading "No left turn till 5 A.M." Thirty minutes later, as he draws up in front of his lady's apartment house, a sign reads "No parking on Thursdays" and this is Thursday.

Next he seeks a neighborhood parking lot or garage and meets only signs reading "No vacancies." He is now two hours late, exhausted and in no mood. So he goes home and spends what is left of the evening with a good book. Virtue and the combustion engine have triumphed.

Never Ask for Whom the Dinner Bell Tolls

As a small-town girl who came to New York to seek fame and fortune, the one unchanging aspect of the ever-changing metropolis that impresses me most is the constant quantity of corn in its behavior pattern.

In the movies, New Yorkers look frightfully sophisticated. And in the Park Avenue branch of its literature, they sound overwhelmingly recherché. But New York is composed of persons who hail from Ohio and points West. Galloping sophistication seems to assault very few, no matter what their trade, or how long they live here.

These long thoughts were reinforced one night when I went to a dinner party on Park Avenue, which at once establishes that the gathering had class. But the hostess was fighting combat fatigue because of the parochial character of her glittering guests, representing finance, politics and the seven lively arts.

A bona fide New Yorker, her mistake was to ignore the fact that in a city of more than 8,000,000 souls, the grapevine is so cozy and efficient that sixty guests in widely divergent fields are as fully aware of what each is doing as if the whole kit and kaboodle lived in Caldwell, Idaho. And you just can't explain it by extrasensory perception.

Her next mistake was to invite twenty-four persons to dinner and the rest of the sixty to join the first group at 10:30 for midnight supper. That was the signal for all hell to break loose.

When word percolated on the party line, the guests invited at 7:30 for dinner assured the guests invited at 10:30 for supper that they, the 10:30 contingent, had heard incorrectly. Nonsense! said the 10:30 mob; it was the 7:30 guests who needed hearing aids.

Then each group got to thinking that perhaps it was in the wrong. So sixty persons called the hostess to find out whether the party was at 7:30 or 10:30 P.M.

When the situation was finally straightened out and the phone quit ringing, the hostess began to wonder if, in fact, these people were her friends and what had ever made her think them so attractive in the first place.

Next, as it must to all hostesses, this woman discovered seventy-two hours before the dinner that she was in desperate need of that scarcest of all the world's scarce commodities, an extra man. In fact, she needed two extra men to balance the dinner table.

Her mistake was not to draw fresh blood. But in New York, an extra man is an extra man. There were two such on the 10:30 or supper list. These she called and invited to the 7:30 dinner.

So now, in this enormous town, where firmly fixed legend says no one ever knows his neighbors, word quickly spread that the hostess had changed her mind and invited all the guests to dinner. That's when the dam gave way.

Supper guests who had planned to come after the theater hastily canceled tickets and phoned to say they would arrive on the dot of 7:30 P.M., despite their previous misunderstanding.

Well, the long and the short of it is that the telephone company declared an extra dividend, that the number of confused supper guests who came to dinner nicely balanced the number of confused dinner guests who arrived for supper and that the hostess, after tearing up her guest lists, went to Jamaica to recuperate.

Flying by Covered Wagon

When my California and Idaho grandmothers used to gather the young folks around them in my childhood and tell wondrous stories of the winning of the West, it always made me sad to realize that I, when it came my turn to sit in the chimney corner, would have no tall tales to tell.

But the advent of the jet air age has saved me. The fact that Trans World Airlines and Pan American World Airways fly passenger planes between New York and Paris in six hours thirty-five minutes at a speed of 575 miles per hour has taken me off the hook.

Surely all the younger members of the family will gasp in amazement when they hear old Aunt Inez tell of blazing an aerial trail between the two nations in an elapsed flying time of twenty-nine hours forty-nine minutes, and at an average speed of 156.6 miles per hour.

"But why did you fly so slowly?" they will probably want to know.

So I shall be forced to point out that when this flight was made in June, 1939, it forged history as the first plane ever to carry a cargo of passengers across the Atlantic, and the speed was regarded as sensational.

That 1939 flight inaugurated the age of transocean air travel. Pan American pioneered the way with its justly famous flying boats, the Clipper ship. Slow and clumsy they may seem now, but almost twenty-three years ago these vast seaplanes were as much an aviation marvel as the passenger jet was when it went into service.

In 1939, the world was awed by the fact that it took the "Atlantic Clipper," backed by a stiff tail wind, only fifteen hours twenty-eight minutes to reach its first refueling stop, Horta, in the Azores, after its take-off from Long Island Sound near Port Washington.

Twenty-three years ago it was a marvel that the big flying boat could buzz into Lisbon from Horta in only seven hours eleven minutes! The fact that a passenger plane had spanned the Atlantic in 22 hours 30 minutes flying time was worth eight-column banner heads on the front page of newspapers the world around!

Passengers and plane spent the night in Lisbon and next day flew on to Marseilles in seven hours ten minutes flying time. The elapsed time, since take-off from Long Island Sound, was forty-two hours twenty-eight minutes, and the press of both the United States and France rejoiced that now the two nations were only two days distant from each other.

Just to prove that one could go from Broadway to the Champs-Élysées in forty-eight hours, the French government sent a plane to Marseilles to carry us passengers to Paris in a three-hour flight.

Miracles are so numerous and so commonplace in this machine age that it seems preposterous that planes could once have been so slow and the air journey so long! But I shall be able to make a very good story of those pioneer days when the supersonic age may have arrived and I am one of the survivors of the flying covered wagon that lumbered through the skies to blaze the trail.

The Reds May Have Edge in Science,
But They Lag in Cheer Leading!

For those Americans like myself who are vitally interested in improving the quality and depth of American secondary-school education, there is splendid news and a ray of hope from the Southland.

The University of Alabama conducted a two-day "Clinic for High School Cheerleaders," a coeducational meeting attended by 1,600 intellectually ambitious, hard-working high school students from all corners of the state.

When the University first initiated this clinic, only 250 students showed up. However, such is the intellectual ferment generated in the interim by the nation's admitted educational crisis that more than six times as many eager-beaver students attended a recent conference. The worthy purpose of the clinic was "to show the youngsters the art of crowd control, with a positive approach to cheering."

Without doubt cheerleading is a science and it is in the realm of science that the honest critics of American secondary education have pointed the finger of despair. So it is gratifying to learn that science departments, at least in Alabama, are being fortified by cheerleading.

As instructors in this new science, the University's own cheerleaders, together with those from other parts of the country, were drafted. Such a program certainly faces up to the plea of the nation for beefing up science curriculum and instruction.

How are "outstanding high school cheerleaders" spotted in the first place? Well, I have a hunch that a new burden was placed on the shoulders of Alabama U. scouts who case high school football material for players worthy of athletic scholarships or direct aid from some generous old grad.

Scouts probably were told to keep their eyes open for the best scientific material available for training in "The Power of Positive Cheering." And who pays for the two-day cram course "in the art of crowd control"? I wonder—the parents? The high school? Or some home town civic organization that also gives a helping hand in the delicate financing of the local football team?

One thing is certain, and it should be a great consolation to the U.S.A. Russia may annually be turning out two or three times as many scientists and technicians in the race against time as we are. But she isn't producing any cheerleaders "with a positive approach" to the job! We're leading the world in this field.

We also lead and lap the field in drum-majoretting or the scholastically sanctified strip tease which has made burlesque as obsolete as vaudeville. Who is going to pay to see burlecue when the autumnal price of a football ticket entitles the holder to witness not only the power of positive cheering but the delights of educational flesh-peddling?

We need better education in this country and fewer frills, such as foreign languages and mathematics. Let's have less of such "sand-box" activities as instruction in the mother tongue and in such stuff as history. Come on, all together now:

"Siss-boom-ah-h-h! Erudition! Erudition! Ha, Ha, Ha!"

On Burning Books

Before World War II, we Americans were properly and proudly scornful of the Nazi book burnings and of Japanese thought control. We beat our chests vigorously and spoke of civil liberties and of the inalienable American right to read and think as we pleased.

Those were the good old days. As for the right to think as we please, it takes a stout and determined citizen today to espouse an unpopular viewpoint—just any unpopular viewpoint, political, social or economic.

And a really impassioned defense of civil liberties, as guaranteed in the Bill of Rights, is apt to get the speaker labeled, for his pains, as a subversive.

Some years ago, when the New York Board of Education dropped Paul Gallico's *Farewell to Sport* from its lists of books approved for school libraries, I thought a storm of protest would surely follow. But it is the measure of our times and the general acceptance of thought control in this country that this action was supinely accepted by press and public.

Why was Mr. Gallico's book dropped fourteen long years after it was published? Because, said a member of the Board of Education, the book was "viciously anti-Semitic."

Since the blood, wisdom and talent of the great and ancient people of Judea flow through Mr. Gallico's veins, the charge must have come as something of a surprise to an author who has always been proud of his Jewish heritage from a maternal grandparent.

I had to read to page 325 of this 346-page book to find the one sentence which the anonymous member of the School Board and his cohorts found offensive. I read and re-read that sentence and it did not seem vicious to me.

Then I decided that I was not competent to judge. So I asked twenty of my Jewish friends to read it and give me their honest opinion of it. Not one found it either "vicious" or "anti-Semitic."

A half dozen of them came to the same conclusion: That no member of the Jewish community had complained about the book. It was the general opinion of these six that some smart politician on the board finagled the action of the Gallico book as a grandstand play to curry favor with one of the largest blocs of voters in New York City.

Without exception, they thought it odd that it had taken the Board of Education fourteen years to diagnose the book as "viciously anti-Semitic."

While the New York Board of Education was compiling its own index expurgations, a member of Congress, Representative Harold H. Velde (R., Ill.) introduced a bill which would have permitted the Librarian of Congress, the FBI, the Attorney General, or any Congressional Committee dealing with internal security to label as "subversive" any printed volume offensive to this assortment of authorities.

If this bill had ever become law, heaven would have had to help the author who had ever, in any way, offended a Congressman, any member of the FBI or anyone in the Attorney General's office! He might as well have shot his typewriter and been done with it.

However, another solution has been offered the nation. The New York Board of Education has also dropped A. Hyatt Verril's textbook *Strange Insects and Their Stories* because, a Board member said, it contained "Invidious references to the superiority of white ants over black ants."

What about red ants? Suppose they turn out to be superior to both black and white ants? Only one solution remains: Give the country back to the Indians and start all over again. It might not be a bad idea.

Three R's Favored

California, which has survived the Democratic donnybrook, is headed toward a second whose outcome may have as much significance for the nation as the Los Angeles contest.

California has been examining its public schools and their curriculum through the medium of a citizens advisory commission. One subdivision of that committee filed a powerful recommendation that both grade and high schools beef up the public school curriculum with far more concentration on the three R's, and such basic subject matter as geography and history.

The recommendations immediately had a tremendous impact in California and are bound to receive careful consideration elsewhere because of the man who wrote them: Dr. Robert G. Sproul, president emeritus of the University of California and one of the nation's most widely respected and influential educators.

Dr. Sproul and his group believe the business of primary education through the first six grades is to give school children a firm foundation in reading, writing, spelling, English and arithmetic, the basic ingredients for the American citizen no matter what his future role in life may be.

Consequently, he and his committee recommended that sixty-six per cent of the school week in the first six grades be devoted to these five fundamental subjects, instead of the fifty per cent then required in the California school system.

The educator, flying in the face of the modern educational fadists, recommended that children in the seventh and eighth grades be required to spend fifty per cent of their time on the same basic tools of education, instead of the ten hours specified in the Golden State.

Dr. Sproul further stirred up a hornet's nest by recommending that reading—which Johnny can't do, according to many critics—be taught in the old-fashioned way, with emphasis on phonetics. This is enough to madden the modern sand-box educator, who threw phonetics out the window—along with Johnny—years ago. But it will gladden the heart of many a parent who learned to read, quickly, easily and rapidly, via phonetics.

Dr. Sproul further riled the "progressives" by specifically recommending that the meaningless catch-all of "social studies" be scratched from the curriculum and girls and boys, from the fourth grade on, be solidly grounded in geography and history as separate disciplines and not a mishmash of the two.

Although some Californians fought him, I believe he will be hailed across the nation not only for these recommendations but for another —that children at the fourth-grade level begin learning a foreign language. Since we Americans are waking to the fact, in the second half of the twentieth century, that we are linguistic barbarians, many communities already are beginning foreign language instruction in the third and fourth grades.

To those of us who believe that education is to train the mind and not teach skills better learned elsewhere, Dr. Sproul's forthright recommendation that "there is no justification for driver (auto) training in the schools" is a ten-strike. Dr. Sproul and his committee believe that such a program properly belongs under the State Department of Motor Vehicles and not in the public schools.

The California educator said that he'd sweep the charm courses and the teen-age finger-painting right out of the high schools, too. Give the young minds solid stuff to chew on, he urged, in the hope that Americans with a high school education can and will speak the English language and have a solid background of history.

I rejoice that an American educator recommended four years of English and four years of history for all high school students—also a year of world geography at the high school level as well as American government.

The president emeritus of the University of California also recommended that high school students be exposed to more of the world's fine literature.

In short, Dr. Sproul recommended schooling that will turn out educated men and women. Like Dr. Arthur B. Conant, he said that public school education should educate rather than baby-sit.

Is Wizard of Oz Corny?

Some days I feel older than others, and I recall one of them: The day the head librarian of the sovereign state of Florida decided to consign to "the trash pile" the wonderful Wizard of Oz, Tom Swift, Horatio Alger, Uncle Wiggily, and the Bobbsey Twins as outmoded for small fry.

The librarian, Dorothy Dodd, said that "kids don't like that fanciful stuff." She wanted to stock the children's shelves of Florida's libraries with good, hard, eyewitness accounts of space exploration, moon landings, missile-man adventures and atomic sub stories. It's factual stuff such as this rather than the fantasy of *The Wizard of Oz* or, for that matter, Walt Disney, that children demand—she says.

Well, this is a stiff dose of medicine for us mature citizens who loved the Wizard and Uncle Wiggily. But who are we to argue with an expert? I shudder to think of the possible places to which Miss Dodd consigned *The Five Little Peppers and How They Grew* and

The Little Colonel series, which my grandmother read to me in the sweet, sweet long ago.

And lest I receive a fatal blow, I dare not inquire how the lady librarian stands on Louisa May Alcott and *Little Women, Little Men, Eight Cousins* and *Rose in Bloom.* Pretty dated stuff, too, I guess, with all that whooping and hollering when Jo—wasn't it Jo?—cut off her hair. Poo! Everyone cuts her hair nowadays.

And—do I dare ask—what now is the literary rating of Hiawatha, the noblest Iroquois of them all? What a memorable winter that was when Papa read aloud the Longfellow saga while Grandma knitted and Mama did the mending and I listened open-mouthed to the tales of derring-do among the red men.

Probably Hiawatha is pretty corny; but so is a family sitting around a black iron stove, listening enthralled while one of its members reads aloud.

And what of James Fenimore Cooper and the Leatherstocking series? I guess Natty Bumpo would cut a pretty sorry figure today, inspired frontiersman though he was, compared with any space cadet or atomic-sub sailor. So good-by, Natty, brave, resourceful Natty, based, Papa told me long ago, on the doings of a brave man close to my family, Dan'l Boone.

Daniel, too, is probably fit only for the scrap heap of today. Good-by, Dan'l. You were *great* while you had it, but you don't have it any more. Or so the authorities suspect.

What kid knows or cares about The Wilderness today? To him the wilderness is the stars or the ocean floor.

Or is it? And if today's young 'un only wants to know "factual" things about space exploration, why are the teevee moguls of the nation wasting so much money, time and film on horse opera? Why can't you pry a child loose from a teevee screen showing a Western, if all he really wants is atomic tales?

Something is wrong somewhere, and far be it from me to point to the library authorities of Florida. If Dorothy Dodd is right, then the astronauts chosen by the United States to be the first in orbit should be selected from writers of juvenile fiction. Such voyagers would come back with the facts for juvenile consumption.

Or what about putting D. Dodd in orbit? Or is she already in enough of a spin? Certainly, she got a passel of us adults off the pad and in the air, screaming like dated Comanches.

A Noble Profession

From time to time—about once a month—I am overcome with wonder that this nation can coax anyone to teach school. The fact that so many extraordinarily fine persons do dedicate their lives to teaching is a major miracle.

There are, in one woman's opinion, three noble professions—teaching, medicine and the ministry. Yet most teachers and ministers make barely enough money to keep body and soul apart. And in countless small towns and rural districts, the doctor isn't in much better financial position.

Pay (and if I were Santa I'd raise every teacher's salary five-fold) isn't the crux that would keep me out of the teaching profession. The bar, for me, would be the fact that every American community believes it has an inherent right to pry into every facet of a teacher's public and private life.

A dedicated teacher must put up with the nagging interference of the community, the school board, parents, superintendent and principals. In my day, if I got a whaling at school, I got a whaling at home, just for good measure. But your modern parent rushes to the school and whales the teacher.

Recently I read that some poor, innocent young teacher was run out of his job for trying to demonstrate the evils of tobacco to eighth graders. He let each pupil take one draw on a cigarette to show how horrid is the vile weed. Some nasty little snitch went to the principal and, before he knew it, the young man was out on his ear for debauching innocent children.

Nonsense! That teacher was doing one of the most sensible acts of his career. History will probably show that he prevented a majority of that class from succumbing to tobacco addiction.

When I was an eighth grader, I was given one puff of a cigarette, found it incredibly disgusting and have never since touched one of the things, except to empty ash trays. But a hysterical principal and indignant parents, not bothering to assay the result of the test, took it out on the hapless teacher.

In another community, a group of parents suddenly discovered that *The Scarlet Letter* is a dirty book. Nathaniel Hawthorne was incapable of writing a dirty line, much less a dirty book, and his masterpiece, *The Scarlet Letter,* is so permeated by the brooding, gloomy spirit of New England as to inflame no one, even the residents of Peyton Place.

I'll bet a nickel that the parents complaining about *The Scarlet Letter* and demanding that it be removed from the high school library, have never in their collective lives censored the sex-saturated movies or magazines to which their offspring are addicted.

Another school district has just discovered, after 300 years, that our Puritan ancestors, far from models of moral rectitude, were so naughty that some of their customs cannot be exposed to the innocent youths of 1961. Unfortunately for the teaching profession, one of its own, a chairman of Social Studies, has deemed that the old Puritan custom of "bundling" is not fit and proper for his classes to read about.

For once, high school seniors and their parents have moved in to give the professor an argument. So in this instance parents must be given an "E" for effort, and the kids an "A" for common sense.

Good grief, this would be a happier world all around if some genius would only invent a bundling board for use in a back seat.

The Unmentionable

No American could possibly be more dedicated to the complete separation of church and state than I. Yet I am sorely troubled by the modern and bitter opposition to the mere mention of God and the Ten Commandments in the public schools.

In one instance it required the action of a Supreme Court Justice of New York State to keep the words "under God" in the Pledge of Allegiance to the flag. A petition to bar those two dangerous words, brought by the Freethinkers of America, was dismissed by Justice Isador Bookstein with some wise words.

"Petitioners' right to disbelieve is guaranteed in the First Amendment," the justice pointed out. "And neither they nor their children can be compelled to recite the words 'under God' in the Pledge of Allegiance.

"But" (and here Judge Bookstein succinctly gets to the heart of the matter) "the First Amendment affords them no preference over those who do believe in God and who, in pledging their allegiance, choose to express that belief."

In that sentence, the judge upheld the will and belief of the majority which, too often in recent years, has timidly retreated before a vociferous, well-organized minority.

One would think that Americans everywhere would approve at least lip service in the public schools to basic moral values. But if he did, he'd be crazy! Throughout large sections of the United States, any attempt to speak well in the schools of ancient spiritual standards that have aided men in all ages is fought tooth and nail. The crux of the situation is that moral and spiritual values are associated with God, and God cannot be trusted in the public schools.

His influence is at once undemocratic and subversive. It would surely be undemocratic to impinge upon the right of some first- or third-grade agnostic "to be free of superstition." As for subversion— suppose the God of one sect slyly proved more compelling than the God of another!

Of course, I am not speaking of the *teaching* of religion in any form in the public schools. I am only confused that the mention of God can cause an uproar and that the moral and spiritual values of the Ten Commandments are equally suspect.

Yet the Ten Commandments proved unacceptable some years ago in Nassau County, New York, when the New Hyde Park School Board wanted to hang on classroom walls an "interdenominational" version of the Commandments as a moral and ethical guide. No one in the New Hyde Park public schools was going to teach religion via the Commandments. In an age of chilling juvenile delinquency, the Decalogue was simply to hang in classrooms where students could— or might—glance at it occasionally and, mayhap, absorb its truths.

The interdenominational interpretation of the Commandments does not copy either the Jewish, Protestant or Catholic version word for word. But they sounded, in the new version, exactly like the same old Commandments to me, with their sublime essence and eternal moral force intact.

But there was opposition to the interdenominational version. The American Jewish Congress and the New York Board of Rabbis appealed to the State Commissioner of Education to suppress the program. I must respect such opposition, but it is sad that the Ten Commandments of the Old Testament, which Jewish, Protestant and Catholic faiths alike cherish, could become a cause of dissension. This was one area in which I thought there could be easy agreement.

I would be the first to defend the right of the agnostic not to believe. But surely the rights of the vast majority of school children who come from religious homes are important, too. How tragic it is then that the great majority of Americans, Catholic, Protestants and Jews, who believe in one God, cannot agree upon a moral and ethical yardstick that would be valid for their children.

Perhaps if the Ten Commandments were given a chance, were permitted to hang on classroom walls where children from time to time might glimpse them, some of the Decalogue's moral strength and purpose would rub off. Surely, in these troubled times, that couldn't be bad.

Are There Any Questions?

Count that day lost on which the low descending sun sees no new questionnaire left at our home. I am entreated, always by total strangers, to fill out uninhibited questionnaires that will enable them to write a Ph.D. thesis, a lecture, a magazine article or a book.

At times, if the questionnaire asks date of birth and runs to twenty or thirty pages, and sometimes they do, I rebel and toss the literary Paul Pry in the wastepaper basket. To my amazement, I recently received a questionnaire from a writer of my acquaintance, the only time I have ever known the interlocutor. Mercifully, the cross-examination is a model of conciseness confined to one page.

What my friend asks me to do is to examine my television habits, a subject that can be writ on the head of a pin. The truth is that we have never acquired the television habit around our home. The set we purchased in February, 1952, to follow the Great Debate then beginning to build toward the national election in November, still is possessed of its original picture tube and other innards. Its maintenance to date has cost us $35.84, chiefly for treatment of an asthmatic condition in the upper registers.

We were warned by friend and foe alike when we purchased the set that such would be its fascinations during the first six months that, drugged and hypnotized, we would sit before it morning, noon and night. On the contrary, from the moment the set arrived, both my husband and I were repelled by its unblinking, Cyclopean eye. It so unnerved us that we moved it into the guest-room closet. There, unhonored and unsinging, it sat out its first year.

Now my writer friend wants to know if I have any favorite teevee program and if I follow any program consistently. The answer is "No."

How many hours a week do I give to teevee? The answer is sometimes one, sometimes two and sometimes none.

Next, do I prefer teevee comedy programs, drama, Westerns, soap operas, old movies, public affairs, news or news analysis? At the risk of sounding repulsively stuffy, teevee time in our home is almost always given to a program that will shed light on some local, national or international situation in which we are interested. Television often ties that kind of forum up in blue ribbons.

Occasionally we have tried to watch old movies. But we have given them up because they are ruined, for us, by interminable advertisements that kill the continuity of the story and our attention span. After the umpteenth ad, I can't tell whether the hero is supposed to get girl, cold cure, dandruff or gastric relief. God forbid he's the one who's expected to use the kissproof mascara! So I am a die-hard advocate of pay television, in hope standards will be upped and ads dropped.

Since my friend presses me for the truth, it is going to out. Any time I have a few spare moments that might be devoted to television, I automatically pick up a book, magazine or newspaper. Probably an analyst would call me a Compulsive Reader, a sweet impeachment I cannot deny. The printed word fascinates me. It has given me immense and sustained joy and enriched my life for many years.

I am reminded of a man now fading from public consciousness who was a fixture of my childhood: the late Senator William E. Borah of Idaho. The senator once said that every time a new book was published, he read an old one. I am not quite in that category. But every time I see a teevee guide, I reach for reading matter, both old and new.

My neglect of teevee has nothing to do with silly snobbism or intellectual affectation. The real truth is that television was perfected too late to woo an ingrained reader away from print. It is a simple case of an old dog's aversion to new tricks.

I can imagine a day when my great-nieces and nephews will gather at my arthritic knees and plead for stories of the Olden Days, especially about the Long Ago and what people did with their time before the advent of television.

"Well, first off, there was conversation," I shall begin as the children marvel. "People talked to and with each other. You'd be surprised how much there is to talk about, once you get the hang of it.

"Sometimes we'd sit around all evening talking about current events such as Caroline Kennedy, how Khrushchev managed to get in everybody's hair, or are there any natural blondes left, and was Judge Crater Fact or Fiction.

"But mainly," I'll explain, as the children look more and more mystified, "we read. Not only magazines and newspapers, but books, from cover to cover. Honestly, when I was your age, reading was a great national pastime, even more widespread than baseball . . ."

But now I have lost my audience. I have strained the credulity of the young. And one child, with a streak of compassion, tells the others, as they race for the teevee set, "All old people are queer. Great-Aunt Inez is just queerer than most."

Where Is the Spirit of Christ?

Home for Christmas

For a long time I dreamed of a bright Christmas in Boise, just like I used to know—when I was, well, younger. The dream came true a few years ago. I went home for the holidays for the first time since World War II. And, peace, it was truly wonderful. No matter how the world wagged time always stood still at Aunt Nell's during the Christmas holidays, and this was no exception. Generations always flowed through her big house and did then. And if there were not as many of us that Christmas as there were when I was a child, perhaps we made up for it by loving each other a little more.

That Christmas was the fifty-third that the Callaway family and its in-laws (and out-laws, as we kids used to say years ago) had gathered at Aunt Nell's for Christmas. Christmas and Aunt Nell had become synonymous to us, although only Aunt Nell and her sister, Aunt Kit (who were then proving to all of us that life begins at eighty), remembered that first Christmas at her home.

The traditions of Christmas at Aunt Nell's were as fixed as the laws of the Medes and the Persians. This was not because of her insistence or her unwillingness to experiment with new décor and new menus. If she tried to change even one loved feature of the Yule in the slightest manner, screams of anguish went up from her sons, grandchildren, nieces, nephews and finally grand-nieces and grand-nephews. We wouldn't stand for any nonsense or innovations.

Santa Claus came to Aunt Nell's on Christmas Eve and handed out presents from a tree bowed down with largesse. The idea of waiting and distributing presents on Christmas morning was barbarian and unthinkable. Ours was a family that believed unabashedly in

Santa. It was always a shattering blow to the grownups when one of the children came home from school with doubts as to the old gentleman's authenticity.

"Not believe in Santa!" I heard Aunt Kit, eighty-one, cry to her doubting great-nephew Kenton, four, two days before Christmas. And then she added, in all sincerity, "Why, I've believed in him all my life!"

The family began gathering at Aunt Nell's and Uncle Charlie's house on the day before Christmas. It was a house with five bedrooms and a broad sleeping porch across the rear. It was not unusual for twenty to twenty-four of us to spend the night there. Nor was Christmas dinner the only sumptuous meal over which Aunt Nell, having cooked it, presided as elegantly as if she had never seen the inside of a kitchen.

By Christmas Eve, every extra board had already been inserted in the big old dining room table. In a day when table mats were unknown and only spotless double- or triple-damask would do, we gathered around that big white table the night before Christmas for a traditional baked ham dinner. Naturally, everyone had to have breakfast on Christmas Day—early, if he were going to church; late, if he had attended midnight services.

From midmorning on, the glorious smells of Christmas dinner began to fill the whole house. Aunt Nell's female counterparts in the family were permitted to help in the kitchen, if they didn't get in her way. The men, knowing enough not to get underfoot, started a pinochle game in the parlor. The young ladies of the family, as we each became old enough to be entrusted with simple duties, were commissioned to set the table. There were many years when the dining room table was stretched to seat thirty-five persons, and when Uncle Charlie carved a big turkey at one end of the table and Uncle Ted tackled an equally large bird at the other.

The Christmas dinner menu didn't vary in decades. It began with crabmeat cocktail, with a special sauce whose ingredients were known only to Aunt Nell. It ended with homemade plum pudding and brandy sauce. Once, some twenty years ago, Aunt Nell, never in a rut in her eighty-seven years, decided that the family might be tired of the old menu. She started with a fruit cocktail and substituted a clear soup for her own incomparable cream of vegetable soup.

"They screamed like banshees," she said later of her family. "You would have thought I had tried to poison them. I went back to the old menu after that and never tried any more changes."

At eighty-plus, Aunt Nell on that final Christmas in the big house set before us a feast fit for Lucullus. She cooked every bit of it herself, too. She barely entrusted the menial work, such as peeling the white and the sweet potatoes, to such flighty "younger" members of the family as myself.

On that Christmas, the family had shrunk to a scanty fourteen, even with the "out-laws." We were just another typical American family with members scattered all over the world, in France and Japan and Brazil, thanks to United States obligations that were undreamed of in my childhood. But there were messages from everyone, and the tree was giddy with the ornaments, cherished through the years by Aunt Nell, that to every one of us, in Boise or half a world away, meant warmth and love and Christmas.

Christmas Carats

Even now when I go back to Idaho to visit, some member of the family invariably gets around to the story of Papa's annual martyrdom to Mama's steam pudding. For years that pudding not only delighted the inner man during the holidays, but was—and still is—the basis of one of those running jokes that make family life so warm and wonderful.

I still have the recipe, written out in Mama's beautiful script.

The recipe begins "Take one cup raw grated carrots and one cup raw grated white potatoes." That was the nub of the jest. It was Papa's plaintive contention that Mama started the steam pudding with "a nickel's worth of carrots and potatoes and then sends me to town to buy $5-worth of stuff to hide the taste of the carrots and the spuds."

On Thanksgiving, when all the family gathered at Aunt Kit's to feast, the dinner came to a climax with pumpkin pies. At Christmas, when we went to Aunt Nell's, we tapered off on plum pudding. Mama produced the steam pudding for the family gathering on New Year's Day.

(The three ladies belonged to an old-fashioned gastronomic school: Always there was a delicious, tart fruit "sorbet" served with the meat course to aid the processes of digestion. And how they needed help, after turkey or whole roast pig and trimmin's! I still think longingly of those sorbets, always homemade.)

The thousand-dollar prize for the best holiday recipe may be awarded to a better dish than Mama's steam pudding. But I doubt it. In the meantime, as an extra special attraction, I offer her recipe, although it costs more than $5 in these trying times to conceal the flavor of the basic ingredients!

Here goes: Take one cup raw grated carrots. Take one cup raw grated white potatoes, into which stir one teaspoon of soda.

One cup of sugar and one-quarter pound of butter (we churned our own) creamed together. One egg (we grew our own). One cup of raisins mixed with one cup of white flour. One-half teaspoon each of cloves, allspice, nutmeg and cinnamon.

Stir all ingredients together and stir hard. Now add one-third cup each of candied citron, candied orange peel and candied lemon peel. Pour into well-grease mold. Steam three and one-half to four hours. Serve with hard sauce laced with brandy.

And, says Mama's daughter, begin dieting next day.

Baby Doll

Anyone tried to buy a doll recently? Just an old-fashioned doll with a low IQ, a blank expression and a passive attitude toward life?

It can be done, but it takes patience, fortitude and iron character.

Because the old-fashioned doll that just opens and closes its eyes is on the way out.

Its place is being taken by a robot that walks, talks, eats, drinks, wets its unmentionables, winks, squawks, cries, burps, bites the fingers that feed it and kicks the baby sitter.

A further refinement in this mechanical brat, which requires more care than junior herself, includes hair that can not only be washed, put in pin curls and waved, just like Mummy's, but that can be dyed any color just like that peroxide blonde next door.

"Six shades of hair tint, ranging from brunette through auburn to ash blonde, come with this doll," explained the salesman.

"That ain't no doll; that's a babe!" I said. "And it wouldn't surprise me to find the hussy smoking marijuana and drinking her whisky straight by next Christmas. All I want is an old-fashioned doll; not a refugee from a reform school."

"What a girl-child seeks in a doll is companionship," said the salesman icily. "That companionship is provided by a doll that simulates life."

"I was a girl-child once and what I wanted was a doll to play with. Sack this psychological malarkey and let me see an old-fashioned doll that can't fight back," I pleaded.

But the salesman was a stubborn case. Instead, I got a demonstration of the new walking doll. It not only can walk, talk and break the sanitary code, but its head turns from side to side as it walks and its eyes roll back and forth, as if dolly were watching a tennis match.

"Jeepers! I don't want to haunt a house. I just want a doll that a little girl can enjoy without scaring the daylights out of a young father with, let us say, a slight attack of the morning-afters. All I want is an old-fashioned doll . . ."

"For a child with a parent like that we have a doll that says its prayers in French, Spanish and English," said the salesman. "It is a high-type, educational doll . . ."

"This little girl I am buying the doll for is only five years old and already in the second grade," I explained. "What she needs is a moron doll with whom she can relax between bouts with McGuffey's Reader. She doesn't need a professor, she needs a toy."

The salesman looked pained. "Not a toy," he corrected, "a playtool. Educators and child psychologists prefer the use of the word playtool to toy."

There are now on the market dolls with dolls, or a big doll with a duplicate little doll in its arms, doubtless so the big doll has a playtool and companion of its own when little Missy is at school or in bed. A sensitive mechanism that can walk, talk, eat, wet and change its hair style and color, must have companionship.

There is also a doll with no face and one with three faces. A box of crayons comes with the faceless wonder, and a girl-child can chalk on any face she fancies.

The three-faced monster is just that. This doll's head is covered with a heavy, fuzzy hood which pretty well conceals a knob atop the thing's head. A turn of the knob or dial, and the head moves, to reveal one face laughing, one crying and one pouting.

This is all very fine until little Gretchen wrests the hood off the playtool and finds the bald head surmounted by a knob, the whole resembling something really sinister from Mars. This is where little Gretchen has hysterics and ceases to believe in Santy.

Which is why I let the salesman exhaust himself and then bought an old-fashioned, housebroken doll with no bad habits.

Yule City Beautiful

On the night before Christmas you will never see a prettier sight in all your life than New York City. Those curdled persons who come to New York at other seasons of the year and say it's a fine town to visit but they wouldn't live here if you gave it to 'em (and who made the offer?) would change their tune if they could see the city at that moment, wrapped up in tinsel and bright red ribbons and millions of lights. For most of the year, it is crowded, noisy and the dirtiest city in the world. But come Christmas and somehow the dirt gets lost under the evergreens, the noise under caroling and church bells, the crowds become gay and the city is transformed.

I'll bet we New Yorkers have the most beautiful Christmas tree in the whole wide world: the enormous one put up in Rockefeller Center annually by John D. Rockefeller Jr. Long may he wave! This tree and the Channel Gardens leading to it off Fifth Avenue are so enchanting they would bring tears of joy and appreciation to the eyes of an unregenerate Scrooge.

Every year, this vista is so lovely it seems impossible that Mr. Rockefeller can top himself in the succeeding year. But he always manages to outdo himself. Who will ever forget one of the most spectacular displays of all—the year a dozen tall, ethereal, silvery angels blowing golden trumpets marched right down the gardens toward the tree, a blaze of gold and orange and chartreuse lights.

New Yorkers come by the hundreds of thousands to revel in this spectacle and innumerable families drive 200 to 300 miles for a glimpse of this Christmas fairyland—and worth every mile of it.

Park Avenue, a canyon of cold concrete, stone and glass throughout the rest of the year, is a river of light at Christmas time, like a vast, fantastic diamond necklace draped through the center of Manhattan. Big Christmas trees line the center of the avenue, their trunks wound with golden lights and their branches hung with silver. It fair turns the heart.

These are the trees bought and lighted every year by volunteer subscription in memory of American men and women killed in World War II and the Korean War. From this glowing memorial the eyes lift naturally to the great radiant cross, twelve stories high, floating above Park Avenue, a cross set in the otherwise darkened face of the New York Central Building.

East Side, West Side, up town and down, Christmas trees—both great and small—emblazon the great avenues, the little side streets, the parks, the playgrounds and any bit of space in which a neighborhood can erect and trim an evergreen.

Christmas trees, holly and evergreens are piled high in front of every neighborhood store and florist shop, forming an endless Christmas garland winding through the city.

The famous stores along Fifth Avenue offer a miracle of decorations inside and out. People stand six and eight deep in the cold outside, waiting to catch a glimpse of the fairylands into which their great show windows have been transformed. And over the whole city there flows the music of carols resounding from church carillons.

Christmas is where the heart is and the heart is where home is. To millions of us, New York is home and the bells have been crying "Merry Christmas" all day in a city as beautiful as a dream.

Only God Can Make a Christmas Tree

It is one woman's opinion that only God can make a tree, especially a Christmas tree. But it is obviously just one woman's opinion, for the so-called "homemakers' " magazines are flooded with crisp suggestions for achieving a "chic" Christmas tree.

It is apparent from these authoritative sources that nature's evergreen simply won't do any longer, except as a starting point. As is, the evergreen is merely a stodgy and tiresome "cliché" (you have to read the women's magazines to believe 'em!).

But with a little patience and imagination, backed up with silver, gilt, shocking pink, blue, mauve or buttercup yellow paint and a spray gun, even a child "can achieve a tree that is truly distinctive and compatible with modern decorator trends."

For a moment I feared that a shocking pink tree "with trim confined solely to avocado green decoration" might frighten the whiskers off Santa Claus. Since then I have taken what cold comfort there is in the belief that any household harboring a shocking pink tree with avocado green trim probably would regard Santa as a cliché, too.

Or one can be really frightfully chic and repudiate the evergreen altogether, even as a starting point. An inverted fan-shaped trellis is "a natural" for modish Christmas tree, one magazine points out. It can be masked in magnolia leaves, or ermine tails or aluminum foil to achieve a dazzling effect.

It may not be a tree, in my opinion, but no one can deny that it's "distingué." And also "frightfully right with modern décor." One of the fundamental rules is to achieve a monotone effect in tree decoration through the use of Christmas tree balls of a single color. And dye the popcorn to match, I presume.

Well, I say it's spinach! In the first place I do not want a "chic" Christmas tree. And only over my dead body will one frosted like a wedding cake and decorated in only one stylish color creep into Chez Robb.

At our house we have an aged conglomeration of unfashionable ornaments that we have hoarded from Christmas to Christmas. I grant you they may not be "chic." But to us the trees they decorate are the most joyous in the world. A handful of dowdy decorations at our house even spent Christmas in Italy in 1944! They were tucked in the Christmas packages that went to the head of the Clan Robb. I never expected to see them again.

But when the head of the Clan came home from the wars, the Christmas decorations came with him. He was quite indignant when I expressed surprise that he had bothered to bring them home. How, he snorted, could we decorate a tree in the future without Jocko, the plush monkey with the perky face, the tinkly Christmas bell or the glittering gold star?

Mrs. Scrooge

Al Smith once said no one ever shot Santa Claus. And the fact I winged him with a pot shot once is more or less accidental.

It will take a little time to explain this, as what fouled me up—and Santa along with me—is the child psychologists.

The learned Ph.D.'s with one hand in the sand box and the other on the child pulse develop new theories and lines of approach to Junior with such frequency that nothing surprises me any more. Or, not much.

One morning when I went Christmas shopping, I clawed my way through a large crowd of adults and children clustered ten deep around the biggest display window of one of New York's most imposing department stores.

Enthroned in the window, behind the shiny plate glass, was as handsome a Santa as one is apt to meet in a month of Christmases, with beaming red face and snowy beard like a silver waterfall.

In his hand, Santa clasped a microphone. From the loudspeakers above our heads he showered down his blessings.

"My, my, my!" said Santa, rocking back and forth on his throne. "I never in my life saw such nice little boys and girls. I want you to come right in the store to see me.

"Santa loves little boys and girls. I love you whether you're good or bad," he chortled, and if he had dropped a large, economy-size atom bomb on the sidewalk throng, the reaction could scarcely have been more immediate.

"Well!" snorted the mother of two moppets standing next to me, "I didn't bring Sister and Junior downtown to hear that kind of subversive talk."

"Good or bad, all you little kiddies are equally dear to me," Santa droned on, as young mothers snatched their offspring and prepared to flee before such blasphemy. "All that stuff about having to be a good little boy or girl to get a present is old stuff. Forget it!"

"Junior, come on. Do as Mama says!" ordered the mother next to me. "Junior, don't you dare kick me, or Santa won't leave a thing for you!"

"Aw, you heard what the man said!" sneered Junior, as he gave her a smart rap on the shins and took a swing at Sister.

The woman with the five-year-old twins dragged them away.

"Don't tell me that isn't the party line! There ought to be a Congressional investigation!" she said, white and shaken.

I backed out of the riot of delirious kids and distrait parents, considerably agitated by the experience myself. I was prone to dismiss it as the latest gimmick in child psychology. However, I couldn't get it out of my mind: this destruction of one more folk myth and a whip-hand over Junior.

So I called the store and got hold of the Vice-President in charge of Advertising and Promotion. Honestly, I didn't lodge any complaint: I just asked if this new Santa talk was the latest thing in child guidance, and if Santa's talk had been written by the store's copywriters with the aid of a child psychologist.

"Good heavens! It sounds insane," cried the Vice-President, obviously in great distress. "I've got a boy of four I wouldn't have hear that for the world. The only peace we get around the house is the few weeks before Christmas when we threaten him with Santa. Let me investigate and call you back."

The upshot was that Santa said he had been carried away by his own gift of gab and all those cute children looking so painfully angelic. Santa contritely promised he wouldn't do it any more, the V.P. reported, adding "And he damn well better not!"

So now you know what I felt like? I felt like a female Scrooge, that's what, and I wish I had kept my big mouth shut!

Miracle on Twelfth Avenue

"The nicest Christmas card I got this year wasn't really much to look at," said the doctor, an old friend, as we settled down to chat over a cup of office coffee. "But the hand-written message on it was appropriate to the season, since it had reference to a sort of modern miracle.

"About three years ago," the doctor continued, "a friend of mine sent a young fellow into the office to see me. Let's call the young man Tom. The first time I ever saw him, he was just coming out of a Lost

Week, or maybe a Fortnight, of Homeric proportions. He and his clothes were a mess.

"Here was a young man, a graduate engineer, who was wrecking his life because he couldn't control his drinking. He had never been able to hold a job more than a few months, or even weeks. Now, he was literally on Skid Row. He was only twenty-seven at that time, but he looked twenty years older, and skeletal.

"Obviously, the first thing to do was to rebuild him physically. Then the next step was to find psychiatric help for him. I talked an associate, one of those $50-an-hour psychiatrists, into taking Tom on. Of course, Tom had no money.

"The psychiatrist and I worked on Tom for a year. And we weren't getting to first base. Once I bought Tom a decent outfit, from the skin out, and on another occasion the psychiatrist did the same thing. Both times, Tom pawned the clothes and went on another monumental drunk.

"We even took turns taking Tom out to dinner in an effort to get a little solid food in him. It was useless to give him money, because it invariably went for drink.

"It wasn't until months later that I attached any significance to the fact that when I once spilled salt, Tom picked up a few grains and tossed them over his left shoulder. Another time, he crossed the street rather than walk under a ladder.

"But none of this seemed important in the face of the fact that Tom, was still drinking every chance he got. At the end of a year, when Tom came to my office one day, I suddenly felt that he couldn't be helped because fundamentally he didn't want help, and that the psychiatrist and I were wasting a lot of precious time on a bum.

"I don't know when I've ever been madder. I lit into Tom and dressed him down from hell to breakfast. Tom, in a rage, stalked out of the office. It wasn't until he came back eight months later—and he looked transformed—that I learned about the miracle.

"When he left my office, Tom said he was in such a fury that his only object was to get to a favorite bar on Twelfth Avenue. He walked, getting madder by the block.

"As you know that avenue is always full of big trucks carting stuff to and from the Hudson River piers. Just as Tom reached Twelfth Avenue and started south, a heavily loaded truck lumbered across the intersection in front of him. At that precise moment, a large carton tumbled off the top of the truck. By luck or fate, it landed at Tom's feet. He stared at the carton in awe. Stamped on the box was one of the oldest shipping signs. It read, 'Keep Dry!'

"When he finally came back to see me, Tom said that he knew that this was a Sign, and a Sign intended for him and him alone. St. Paul never believed more firmly in his vision on the road to Damascus. Had the carton not literally fallen out of the heavens and landed at his feet?

"In the two years since, Tom has not had a drink. What medicine and psychiatry could not do for him, a freak accident—or a miracle— has accomplished. Oh, yes, the message on his Christmas card said: 'Dear Doc. I'm still keeping dry, Tom.' "

"The Gift without the Giver"

Anyone have time to listen to a long, sad, true story about what happens to the Christmas spirit?

Scarcely a Christmas passes that I fail to receive a gift without one single, solitary clue—even a fingerprint—to identify the giver.

It would be simply dreamy if the gift was always ten dozen red, red roses from a man I could imagine as tall, dark and handsome with money. He'd have to have money to send that many roses.

But even I cannot summon up a tall, dark, handsome man loaded with lucre who would be responsible over the years for such a motley array of gifts as six cocktail napkins, a bath mat, a three-pound fruit cake, a key ring, an ash tray, four decks of monogrammed cards, a carton of avocados and, last but not least, a poinsettia plant.

No, these are merely the slips that pass in the night in New York's harassed stores at the holiday season. They forget to tuck in the identifying gift card.

The unidentified poinsettia arrived on December 24 of this last yuletide season. Despite its illegitimate status, I gave that poinsettia a mother's care. But even so, by New Year's it resembled a picked chicken more than a plant. I was thinking that soon we must part.

At that point the phone rang. A man with a voice full of melancholy asked if I were Mrs. Robb and if I had received a poinsettia plant for Christmas.

"Yes," I said bitterly, "and what's more there was no card with it and no way to identify the florist and now probably my best friend thinks I'm a heel."

"Lady, don't say nothing," the sad voice pleaded. "Already, I got two mad women on my hands. Another I can't stand. All day, yak, yak, yak until I gotta migraine aspirin won't touch.

"It's like this," the plaintive voice explained. "That poinsettia plant don't belong to you in the first place. This woman come into my store on Christmas Eve and she says she's going to send a plant to this friend she ain't spoke to in five years.

"They had a falling out, but now this woman is softened up with good will to man and she wants to make overtures to this old friend to be friends again.

"So she orders this poinsettia for a woman whose name is Hobb, and to make a long story shorter my delivery boy, who ain't got the brains to put in a thimble, makes a mistake and delivers the plant to you without any card.

"So today this woman goes to see her old friend to give her a piece of her mind account she ain't been a lady and thanked her for the poinsettia. So after they beat their gums for an hour, they decide I'm to blame. So they been in here the rest of the day beratin' me until I don't know which end I'm standin' on.

"So finally when the delivery boy comes back, I get it straightened out what he done. So what I want to know, Mrs. Robb, is can I send over the boy for the poinsettia?"

I explained to him that the poinsettia consisted of five stalks with no leaves at the moment.

"I know. Steam-heated apartments is death on poinsettias, but if I can just show these women the remains, maybe they'll go home and I can kill myself in peace."

"Sure," I said, "you send for the plant. But remember, you have been the means of uniting two old friends."

"Yeah," said the melancholy man, "over my dead body."

Where Is the Spirit of Christ?

During the weeks preceding Christmas, many stores across the land find it profitable to extend the closing hour from 6 to 9 P.M., thereby making it easier for the shopper whose money is burning holes in his head. Customers are thereby granted an extra three-hour period in which to snap up $1,000 nightgowns, $45 custom-made shirts, $495 toy automobiles for Junior, $350 cashmere sweaters heavy with white mink trim for the girls, $6,000 ermine bathrobes and glittering Christmas tree balls at $15 each.

You think there can't be a nightgown worth $1,000? My friend, you are right. But there are such nightgowns for sale in a New York Fifth Avenue emporium, and that goes for all such items as Christmas tree ornaments at $180 per dozen (just plain, ordinary five-and-dime store Christmas tree balls, tricked up with phony pearls, jewels and sequins).

I am the last person in the world opposed to luxury or the good life. If anyone can afford a chinchilla wrap, more power to her. I wish I could. But when madam orders a matching coat of the world's most expensive fur for her dog, then both my senses of value and of humor do a nose dive out the window.

If a doting husband can afford $5,000 for a leopard sports coat for his darling, hurrah! Some wife has it made. But when the order also includes $750 for a matching blanket for a police dog my reaction is one of extreme *mal de mer*.

For years, this country's Christmas binge has been about ninety per cent pagan, including the office parties. But there's inflation in the land today, and it looks as if the percentage might touch ninety-five in this year of grace.

A little useless giving won't do us any harm. But what I see on all sides today, particularly in view of the world situation, is revolting waste. I wonder how many persons fighting their way through the crowded aisles of shops ever, for even a fleeting second, think of Him whose birth we celebrate on December 25.

A few days before Christmas, '61, I was in a famous Fifth Avenue shop that had turned most of its second floor into a gift bazaar. Its tables and counters were loaded with such costly trash as jeweled beer-can openers, "feather" dusters made of mink tails, $15 Christmas tree balls and pink feather Christmas trees at $25 per.

Among the counters stalked Burns detectives, each with a loaded revolver on his hip, to prevent the theft of junk not worth carrying home. But people were fighting to buy it.

Just beyond this display, separated by a very wide arch, was the store's religious department, dominated by a twelve-foot cross on which hung the Saviour. There were two customers in this department.

I looked at Christ, surveying the scene beyond with its armed guards protecting rubbish sold, supposedly, to do Him honor on the day of His birth, and—with shame—I walked out of the store and home.

The commercialism of Christmas is one of the sickest facets of our civilization.

But the suggestion of a foremost Lutheran minister that the churches "cancel all plans for Christmas services" in protest against "the orgy of commercialism" that has not only defiled but almost totally obscured the religious meaning of the celebration is only to surrender wholly to rampant materialism.

Christ *was* long before the day of His birth became an excuse for the greediest hard-sell campaigns of the year. The indignation of the Rev. Dr. Edgar S. Brown Jr., director of the United Lutheran Church in America, is understandable at the downgrading of Christ's birthday from a joyous religious festival to a commercial carnival that would do justice to a pagan revel.

The celebration of Christmas has long since been taken out of the hands of the ministry and put in those of the merchants. But for the ministry to submit by canceling Christmas services in the churches would only be to acquiesce in the unholy transfer. It would make it complete.

Dr. Brown's anger is justified, but what he proposes is to toss out the baby with the bath water. If the church militant deserves the name, it cannot let the celebration of Christmas go by default.

If the church lays claim to militancy in the twentieth century, let it get in there and fight, toe to toe, with the forces that have turned the two principal and most solemn festivals of the Christian church— Christmas and Easter—into mercantile projects to raise dividends and the gross national product.

Who will argue with Dr. Brown when he says that "we've become so immersed in 'making Christmas pay' that we've lost its deeper significance"?

Easter is no longer a joyous celebration of the passion and resurrection of Jesus Christ, but a period of hard-sell for the whole family to buy what is ironically known as a new "Easter Outfit." It is second only to the Yuletide as a commercial gimmick.

Far from withdrawing from its own celebration of Christmas and, by inference, Easter, as Dr. Brown suggests, the church militant can no longer delay its own crusade to rescue these two great religious feasts from the money-changers. It is difficult not to believe that the church—had it been in past years as vigilant as it should have been

—could have prevented today's continuing debasement of Christmas and Easter.

Outrage at the demotion of Christmas to a secular sales competition is one point on which both Protestant and Catholic faiths agree. Even as Dr. Brown was publishing his denunciation in *The Lutheran,* the organ of his faith, the Vatican newspaper, *L'Osservatore Romano,* warned that the commercialization of Christmas was transforming "the birthday of Christ into a pagan bacchanal." It denounced wasteful spending at Christmas "as an insult to the poor."

If you are in revolt against a pagan Christmas and useless giving, sit down and make a list of the people who have everything, including the poor man's credit card—money. Then make a list of your favorite charities or good causes.

After this is done, sit down in a nice, comfortable chair at a desk or table. Put your checkbook and a pen in front of you. Now, draw a check for the cancer, heart, polio, muscular dystrophy or any other fund you favor.

Of maybe you would like to give to some fund in your own community that aids the blind, or crippled children or disabled oldsters. Probably your church or your club has a project to aid people who need help.

Anyway, the choice is up to you. Once you have made your decision and drawn the check, send it to the charitable fund or organization with a note that reads as follows:

"I am contributing this sum as my Christmas present to my friend, Josephine Blow, 419 Exeter Avenue, Truex, Anchorage, Alaska. Will you please notify her of this gift in her name?"

There is one other easy step. Next you write, "Dear Josephine, your gift this year from me (or us) is a contribution in your name to the Children's Aid Society, from which you will be hearing. Love, Mary (or Bill, or both)."

Now put air mail and special delivery stamps on the envelope and send this good deed on its way. And Josephine, who has everything including a birch-bark canoe lined in walrus skins, will be so grateful that you haven't sent her another pair of snowshoes that she'll dance with joy, even if she is wearing the ones you sent last year.

There are so many things that money can do at the holiday season in addition to buying junk. And not only will recipients of your charity gifts bless you but so will the Lord in whose name we celebrate the feast of Christmas.

Santa on the Subway

The evening subway rush had been over for more than an hour. The downtown local, headed for the lower end of Manhattan and the far, shrouded reaches of Brooklyn, was almost empty.

I settled myself with the last-minute Christmas parcels and began to unfold the evening paper before I saw the old man in the red suit slumped wearily in a corner seat. He dozed fitfully, his chin resting on the red suit trimmed with cotton ermine.

But if the ermine was false, the silvery white beard that sprayed across the red jacket was real as real. Here, I thought, is one of those rare Santas, in a city that teams with Santas at Christmas time, whose beard is authentic.

And I wondered whether he had been standing on a street corner all day, beside some Christmas kettle whose contents would feed or clothe those even poorer than he.

Or if his exhaustion stemmed from the nervous tension of playing Santa to a thousand children, pouring through some great store, and each clamorous for his moment with the Christmas saint.

The local jerked to a halt at Times Square, at seven-fifteen on a cold evening so close to Christmas, the great platforms were almost empty. The old man roused momentarily and then sank again into half-sleep.

Only three people boarded the car, a young mother and two small

children, a little boy who looked about three and a girl who seemed
scarcely a year older. Here was a trio whose poverty is always described as "genteel," whatever that may mean.

She looked tired, this young mother, and the parcels she carried
unmistakably came from the five-and-dime. But she was neat and
polished and so were the children. It seemed obvious that she had
brought the little boy and his sister uptown to behold the Christmas
glitter in the stores, so wondrously decked at this season, and to see
Santa.

Mother and children, all a little tired, settled themselves decorously
in the car. It took a moment or two for the children to spy the old
man in the red suit.

They must have seen him simultaneously, and I doubt if the Wise
Men were more astounded by the miracle as they followed the star—
or delighted. For here, right on the subway with them, riding in the
dingy old car with its litter of newspapers and candy wrappers, was
Santa Claus, real, and live, and catching forty winks.

Before his mother could catch him, the little boy was running on
unsteady legs the length of the car to the man, worn with fatigue from
a day of playing Santa. The little girl was only a foot behind him.

A Santa with reindeer who comes down chimneys is a lovely legend
for city children who have never seen a deer and whose apartment
has no chimney. But a subway Santa: he is real and true and someone
in whom a city child can place his credence.

The little boy reached the old man. He hung on his knee, and the
little girl grasped his sleeve and steadied herself in the swaying train.

And there was the awful, crucial second in which the old man
pulled himself awake and pushed back his fatigue.

Would he, old and exhausted, thrust the children away? Would
the aching back and the throbbing feet rebel at one more minute of
make-believe? Would the children, heartbroken, be harshly put off by
a tired old man?

The worn Santa gazed at the children vacantly for a moment. Then
the miracle happened. He picked up an ecstatic little boy and put him

on his knee, and he put his arm around a little girl as the anxious mother hovered over them.

As I left the subway at Fourteenth Street, a tired old man was keeping alive the miracle of Christmas for two small children on a dingy local hurtling its way toward lower Manhattan and the magic reaches of make-believe.

Nature Girl

Give Her the Sack!

A poet is a lovesome thing. But with rare exceptions poets have concentrated on spring and its insinuating fevers. Hi-ho, the merry-oh! And off to the road, a-gypsying at the first pussy willow beckoning to the open road as it leers from the window of a city florist. With modern transport what it is, from country meadow to city window is no more than a forty-eight-hour journey for any pussy willow today.

And a city father who has not forgotten his country boyhood (don't all New Yorkers come from the Midwest?) can, if his hand has not lost its cunning, contrive a willow whistle in five minutes if the pussy willow is fresh.

But there must be others than myself who are afflicted with autumn fever. Then, if ever, come perfect days in the American Northeast. Spring is apt to pass us by with scarcely a curt nod. By the time she reaches us, she has emptied her cornucopia of beauty in other regions and has scant favors left for the city.

But autumn—barring a hurricane or two—loves us. She blesses us with a long, lovely Indian summer as if to make up for our interminable winters, our chilly, wet springs and summers as hot as the hinges.

At this time, with the days still warm and long and golden, I'd tie up an extra dress in a flour sack and be on the road, if only I had a flour sack. The trouble with New York, as I discovered when I first settled there years ago, is that no one ever buys flour in fifty-pound (or were they, to be exact, forty-eight-pound?) sacks in the city.

Kitchens are compact in New York, and a ten-pound paper bag of flour is a big deal. Even a five-pound bag is boasting. The two-pounders fit more readily into a kitchen canister. And there are even one-pound bags.

When I first arrived in New York and discovered this frightful situation, I wondered where dish towels came from. I had never heard of anyone sufficiently crazy or extravagant to walk into a store and *buy* dish towels.

Dish towels in Idaho were either made from flour or sugar sacks. Sugar came by the hundredweight. Nice people didn't buy lesser quantities. I am glad that grandmother was never humiliated by the knowledge that I have bought it in a pound package!

But here I am, unable to obey that regular autumnal impulse to run away, to take to the open turnpike, toll booths and all, for lack of a decent flour or sugar sack. Agents in New England say the foliage has begun to turn. There is gold in the hills to fill the soul, and scarlet banners running through the maples.

Thomas Nashe, who loved not England's autumns, wrote an unhappy sonnet to them in the sixteenth century, and South Africa's Roy Campbell holds autumn in scarcely more esteem.

But since John Keats wrote "To Autumn," the season has needed no other celebrant. With the current revival of interest in Lord Byron, it is now respectable once again to read the lyric poets.

So, with no flour sack available, I sublimate my itch to run away along the flaming highways by reaching for Keats and "To Autumn." Whoever better described this rich, abundant harvest time?

> Season of mists and mellow fruitfulness
> Close bosom-friend of the maturing sun.

And how truly he asks:

> Where are the songs of spring? Ay, where are they?
> Think not of them, thou hast thy music, too . . .

The Truth, the Whole Truth and Nothing But—

Ever after the Robbs purchased their rural slum near Flemington, New Jersey, I looked with skeptical eye on the flamboyant illustrations in the various seed catalogs that clog the mailbox each spring and autumn. Using the mails to defraud, I figured.

I had begun to feel that only a sucker would fall repeatedly for these pictorial come-ons, the like of which I had never seen on land or sea or even in the wild blue yonder. Constant addiction to the catalogs is, like second marriage, the triumph of hope over experience.

Because experience had taught me that the roses I bought and raised were not even kissin' kin of the gorgeous roses enshrined in the catalogs; any similarity was purely accidental. The eight-foot, man-eating snapdragons illustrated in technicolor always turned out to be a spindly, Kallikak variety standing all of twelve inches with the aid of Adler elevators.

So imagine my surprise when I arrived in the Sacramento Valley and discovered that the seed catalogs were on the level—almost. Not quite, but almost. The seed and nursery boys have been sneaking out there for years, obviously, snapping pictures of the florid flora that this region produces.

Even this section of California hasn't quite managed yet to have June in January. But it does have June in April, with the result that the whole community looks as spectacular as the annual flower show in Madison Square Garden, only more so and free, to boot.

Back in New Jersey, flowers bloom in orderly succession, beginning with snowdrops, crocus, jonquils, narcissus, tulips, peonies, roses and then various annuals.

But out there, time and climate are scrambled and everything is in violent bloom at once, and I mean violent. Roses and tulips, iris and pansies all bloom in the same beds.

Calla lilies there are almost a weed that have to be kept under strict control. They must be spoken to sharply from time to time to keep them in bounds and from growing four or five feet tall. English daisies, which have sulked in the Robb rock garden, are a semi-weed in California, prone to take over lawns and almost as much of a scourge as dandelions back East (only not so good for wine).

Freesias, which grow only in florist shops in less fortunate climates, are another pest in that lush valley and have to be clubbed occasionally to keep them in hand. Ditto ranunculas. Coral bells, another item that has grown with great reluctance for me, are so prolific that California aficionados have thought of importing a Margaret Sanger to deal with the problem.

If a man stands still for ten minutes anywhere in that lush district, he is apt to be overrun by wistaria. Many Californians believe that this may account for the disappearance of Judge Crater and little Charlie Ross. Man has to carry a machete to protect himself from it. The wistaria hangs in great purple clusters all over town. Locust trees in full bloom perfume the air. And at least to this customer, it has always been a delirious experience to walk down a street overhung with orange trees in full flower.

The purely ornamental flowering peach trees are inclined to be gaudy but wonderful. The snapdragons and the stock are as big and bouncing as hollyhocks elsewhere; the iris really do look like orchids, and the broom, spilling its gold all over the countryside, is—to put it mildly—florid. The lupin and the California poppies grow in every nook and cranny.

But I have really saved the best for the last. The roses. Just as it says in the catalogs, they are as big as dinner plates. They grow like weeds; honestly, just like weeds. It's enough to drive an amateur crazy.

Give a rose an inch in the valley climate and it takes a mile. One climbing rose will cover half a house—and a big house, to boot. Every rose is a tree rose in size and absolutely, positively covered with great, big, huge, enormous blossoms.

I guess maybe it's the climbing roses that have me talking to myself. Imagine a house covered, really, truly covered with red roses the size of a salad plate; or pink roses, if you prefer. Or yellow roses, if you are a yellow rose man.

It is simply wonderful.

But I still think it's sneaky, to say the least, for the seed catalog boys to go out there and take their pictures. Honest, maybe, but sneaky and misleading.

"Free Seeds and No Weeds"

It occurs to me that the next man to attain the Presidency is probably the candidate who comes out flatly for the abolition of weeds.

I would appreciate it, also, if the gentleman in question could abolish taxes, war, communism, malfeasance in office, skulduggery at the till, Virus X and bubble gum. But as a gardener who's ranged from huge plots to window boxes, weeds have always been a pressing problem. They extend from crab grass, which we have always with us, to chickweed, which causes more city farmers to pull up stakes and go back where they came from than any other five plagues, including the mortgage.

A man who would promise to take care of Japanese beetles on the side could rest assured that I would vote for him twice for $2, standard price for a single trip to the polls. In fact, for a national savior of that caliber, I would be happy to pull the lever all day.

The optimist (that's me) says, "What buys so much beauty and joy as ten cents invested in a package of flower seeds?" The pessimist (that's the head of Clan Robb) says, "What buys so much work and weeds as ten cents worth of flower seeds?"

And the realist (that's Mr. Bib Stanley, the dairy farmer) says, *"What* ten-cent package of flower seeds?"

Inflation has hit the seed market, too, and the ten-cent package of flower seeds is now twenty-five to fifty cents, and not a fraction as many seeds as in the old days.

Howsomever, in my expanded gardening period I always had zinnias, bachelor buttons, argeratum, petunias, snapdragons, daisies and marigolds that somehow achieved parity with the weeds and bloomed their pretty heads off.

But it was nip and tuck, and I never knew from one weekend to the next whether the milkweed and the wild onions or the morning glories and cosmos would be ahead.

And if anyone is planning to write me about these marvelous new chemical compounds that kill weeds, churn the butter and turn life into one long sweet song in the hammock, he can save paper, pencil and stamps.

We counted that day lost whose low descending sun saw not one more chemical wonder-weeder at work. We had chemicals that killed the broad, the thin, the short, the fat, the tall and the recumbent varmints of the vegetable world.

But there was always one that we and the chemists missed. Or else the operation was successful but the patient—the flowers, that is— died. None of 'em (i.e., the chemical killers) gets rid of everything except the flowers.

The best way to get rid of weeds is on the hands and knees (I have also tried fasting), using the system first patented by Eve when she pulled up the burdock around the apple tree.

The first political party smart enough to write a positive no-weed plank will win not only the farm vote, hands down, but the vote of anyone who so much as messes around with a window box or a pot of geraniums.

What the winning side needs is a short and sweet platform and I have it: "Free seeds and no weeds." Grass roots without weeds? It'll set the prairies afire!

"I Think that I Shall Never See"

It was a wonderful night for walking down Fifth Avenue: warm, soft and Indian summer to the core.

I was full of good will toward man and baseball. And if my worthy spouse was less full of good will toward baseball, it was his fault for insisting on betting a champagne dinner that his favorite team would win the series.

"But it was a wonderful dinner, and what if you do have to pay for it on the installment plan? We're only middle-aged once!" I said.

So we walked another block or two and that's when we saw this big crowd on the southwest corner of Fifth Avenue and 51st Street.

It could have been an accident, an organ grinder with a monkey, an illegal street vendor with a tray of thirty-nine-cent neckties, a political rally, a street fight or a lady burglar throwing a brick through a window. Anything attracts a crowd in New York, even at 10:30 P.M.

But when we joined the mob, we discovered it was none of these everyday occurrences that fascinated the throng of sidewalk superintendents. It had gathered, instead, to superintend a rare and awesome event, one too seldom seen in this concrete city: the planting of a tree.

Only God can make a tree, but only John D. Rockefeller Jr. can afford to plant a fifty-five-foot honey locust on Fifth Avenue, and that was what he was doing. Not in person, of course. A crew of twenty was tugging and hauling, with the aid of a lot of mechanical equipment, to get the tree in place. It had been necessary to blast a hole ten feet square in the sidewalk, and now the locust was resting in the excavation. The ball of earth in which its roots were tightly wrapped in heavy canvas was eight feet in diameter and it must have weighed tons.

By the time we joined the superintendents, the tree had been inched off the heavy trailer truck that had brought it to town from the green pastures of New Jersey. The locust was leaning drunkenly out into Fifth Avenue.

"You gotta straighten her up, Joe," a dozen superintendents called to the perspiring workmen.

Sidewalk crowds in New York are used to directing bulldozers, earth-moving equipment, steam shovels, masons and all the instruments and men that go into construction of a building. But a tree! This was an unexampled opportunity.

"Gosh! Arbor Day!" said a young air force sergeant, in Midwest accents. "Don't skin the bark," he warned.

Two men pushed their way through the crowd.

"They're tearin' up the streets for a new water main," one explained knowingly as he eyed the hole in the sidewalk.

"Every time they do that, Tammany cops another billion," his companion said.

The woman in the dinner dress, the mink cape and the orchids nudged the man in dinner clothes.

"We had a tree like that in our back yard when I was a kid in Walla Walla," she said.

"Straighten her a little more," the sidewalk superintendents ordered as the men tried to get the tree in line with the aid of a huge chain attached to two trucks.

That failed to work, and a young man in the work crew suggested using an ordinary jack to move the tree slowly upright. The foreman told him to try it. In ten minutes, the tree was straight as a die.

"American ingenuity," said the man in the dinner coat. "It's what wins every time."

It was 11:30 P.M. when we resumed our walk, but the sidewalk superintendents, hundreds of them, stood glued to the pavements. It isn't every day—or night—you can see a tree planted in New York.

"And if your wife don't believe you when you get home," the cop on the corner told the superintendents, "I'll sign your excuse."

The Inside Story

Don't Work—Shirk!

The more I think of it, the more I am convinced that all the tried-and-true maxims of my childhood need overhauling and up-dating. The unprecedented strides of science and medicine in this century have invalidated most of the time-tested adages on which I cut my teeth.

Take, for example, the incontrovertible axiom that work is the curse of the drinking classes. Democracy, science and medicine between them have now broadened the base of this truism by proving that work is the curse of all classes.

It is generally agreed that all work and no play doesn't make Jack so much a dull boy as a dead Joe. In the last year, every publication in the United States has been full of grim warnings that work is a killer. It leads, as night the day, to tension, ulcers, schizophrenia and Russian roulette.

Science and medicine have been busy racking up proof that work, except in small doses, hardens the arteries, plays hob with the heart, flattens the arches and leads but to the grave. In the meantime, Horatio Alger Jr. is whirling in his.

The general theme of all such articles today is simple: Never do today what you can put off, period. If you never put off until tomorrow what you can do today, it is tension and curtains for you. Early to bed and early to rise no longer makes a man healthy, wealthy and wise. It makes him puny, looney and cuts him down to size.

Competition in the market place is as lethal to man as a jigger of cyanide. The younger generation seeking only security and not opportunity on the job has the right idea, because he who yawns and turns away will live to sleep another day.

According to the latest medical findings, the eager beaver in the gray flannel suit is really a gone goose. His frantic efforts to make good and get to the top of the ladder on a golden treadmill (there's something wrong somewhere with this metaphor!) will only get him the privilege of cutting out paper dolls with blunt scissors in a padded room.

Pluck and luck will still get you a buck. But if you're dead, says the new philosophy, are you really ahead? The latest advice is to "Go to the ant, thou sluggard, consider your ulcers and wise up."

"Get in there and pitch!" "Keep your eye on the ball" and "Do or die" were dinned into my head in my salad days. Now the grim watchward is "Do and die." The command today is relax, don't overtax!

"Sink or swim," my elders enjoined me. The best medical advice today is to float and tread water until the life raft drifts by. *"Ad astra per aspera"*—to the stars through bars—my professors cried. Now, the medics cut out everything but the bars; very relaxing, indeed.

"Moil and toil will shuffle off this mortal coil" is the present watchword, followed by "The slug-abed is full of lead; but then, again, he won't drop dead."

This is a real revolution in the folkways of the United States, the home of hustle and bustle. But since science says it is better to relax and hit the sack, as strain puts you down the drain, the new maxim, if you would live longer and be stronger, is Don't Work—Shirk!

Operation Me

"Speaking of operations," wrote the late Irwin S. Cobb in 1915, "if an operation is such a good thing to talk about, why isn't it a good thing to write about, too?"

So the late Mr. Cobb wrote a small book *Speaking of Operations,* which got him off the nut at the hospital and paid his Men in White. It has gone through dozens of editions, has sold more than 300,000 copies, sells steadily today and is still pouring money into the till of his heirs and assigns.

While I was in a hospital drydock for repairs, a friend sent me Mr.

Cobb's tome. And it is a very funny blow-by-blow description of an operation from first examination to final feather stitching. But as I read Mr. Cobb's confessions, it occurred to me that the book is at least as historic as it is hilarious.

Obviously, hospital and operative techniques have so changed that Mr. Cobb's memoirs might just as readily have been written in the Dark Ages.

I read with envy and disbelief the basis of one of Mr. Cobb's biggest beefs: That he was forced to spend ten days flat on his back following his encounter with the Men in White.

Let me tell you there is none of this leisure or self-indulgence permitted in Ye Modern Hospital! The medics and nurses can scarcely wait for a victim to come out from the anesthetic before setting-up exercises and advanced calisthenics.

I was scarcely conscious enough to ask for a martini when my nurse had me up before an open window throwing out my chest, something I am barely able to do even when in the pink. And when, four or five hours this side of the operating room, I suggested delicately that I would like to visit the bathroom, my nurse said, "Sure, why not? It's over in that corner."

I'll say this for the girl: She did stick my slippers on my feet, and when I looked at her with reproachful gaze, she had the grace to shrug and say, "Things are tough all over."

From her attitude, I gathered she deemed me lucky to have been born into a sybaritic era wherein the plumbing is indoors. Ten days in bed, indeed! I scarce had time to get my new bed jacket warm before I was back in my overalls.

Mr. Cobb objected violently to the hospital smell "compounded of iodoform, ether, gruel and something boiling." "All hospitals have it," he wrote. But not any more. The hospital in which I was stashed looks and is operated exactly like a hotel. You know—"your home away from home," including revolving bellhops and room service. It lacked only a house dick.

And as for ether: I believe that this is regarded as irrelevant, immaterial and old-fashioned. No more cone fitted over the schnozz, with the slow drip, drip, drip of ether as in Mr. Cobb's case. Now a fast jab in the arm with some new kind of anesthetic and the patient is out with the speed of light.

I came to after the operation clear of mind, bright of eye, pink of cheek and feeling like a million less the surgeon's usual ten per cent. Indeed, I thought I must be in heaven, for there were three handsome men regarding me admiringly. I took a second look and perceived that one was the sawbones, one the family physician and one my spouse.

"Unless she steps in front of a truck," the first was saying to my loved one, "you're stuck with her for another forty-fifty years."

Mr. Cobb complained bitterly that he would have starved to death if he had not surreptitiously taken to licking stamps. Apparently the practice now is to stuff the patient, as banana splits and roast beef reinforced with lamb chops were always turning up on my trays.

On the whole, I would say that hospital life today is definitely (1) more pleasant and (2) more strenuous than in Mr. Cobb's time.

However, one factor remains constant. Mr. Cobb said he wrote the book on operations because he needed money.

"Verily, one always needs money when one has but recently escaped from the ministering clutches of the modern hospital," he wrote.

Yea, verily, and Amen!

Younger Than Springtime, Anytime

Now you can whittle your age and be telling the scientific truth! Hallelujah, science has done it again!

If you shave a year or two, or even five or six off your age, you aren't kidding anyone, not even yourself. You really *are* younger and that's a fact.

A wonderful, brainy physiologist at the University of California stuck his head out of his laboratory long enough to announce that we Americans in our middle years are physiologically four years younger than our father and grandfathers at the dawn of this century.

We are getting younger all the time. This sweet man also figures that five to twenty years have been added to the active, productive early middle age of all of us. So, even if you have been whittling a decade or a mite more off your chronological age, you haven't been lying. You have just been a prophet without honor in your own back yard.

This scientist has made honest men and women of millions of us, and saved a whole nation from premature old age. I guess this announcement will silence a critic or two around Chez Robb who have been caustic because I am still thirty-five.

Naturally, I have always looked younger than I am, and I know you do, too. It just takes me a little longer to look that way, that's all. Say an extra hour a day. So by dawn's early light, who looks good? But by dinner time and candlelight, with a little extra eye shadow and a teensy-weensy bit of this and that, honestly, I'm a living doll. Well, all right, I'm living. At a permanent thirty-five, who can ask for anything more?

Let me tell you what takes the heart out of persons such as you and me who don't look our age: It's our contemporaries who do! Is there anything more disturbing than to go to a party, looking a dead ringer for your daughter's sister or your son's brother and be greeted by a one-time school friend who has lost his/her waistline and/or hair? If only such squares would get lost along with their hair!

A pox on any boor who can tell another's age at a glance and does!

It's one thing to feel one's age, or even to act it. The unforgivable sin is to look it. That's why Elizabeth Arden, Helena Rubinstein, Alexandra de Markoff, Charles Revson—and Vic Tanny—were born. Time and tide may wait for no man. But both will know they've been in a fight when the above mentioned get through with 'em.

Man is growing younger, says my favorite physiologist, because he is healthier. The body's internal chemical processes do not age as rapidly as in the past, since they are freer from infectious diseases and injury. This, in time, can be bigger than a fountain of youth.

Who's for laughing at Jack Benny now?

Rallying Cries

Nothing Risked, Nothing Gained

Right on schedule, the frost is on the pumpkin and the corn is in the shock. But corn isn't the only thing in a state of shock today.

Potential voters are dropping like flies and that ominous sound swelling up over the horizon is the piteous keening of voters of all political faiths crying: "Hit me again! I can still hear him."

However, there is hope: If October is here, can November be far behind? And the consensus is "No," although in an election year October is the longest and windiest month of the annum.

I have a hint for the politicians who are beating the hustings in search of votes. I will vote for any candidate who quits bleating about security and comes out four-square for opportunity.

It will require a courageous candidate, for this will be regarded in many quarters as a dangerous and revolutionary philosophy. But the questing candidates can always anchor this doctrine in the Founding Fathers.

Some of the Fathers even confused opportunity with the pursuit of happiness. The welfare state, preaching the gospel of security from conception to cremation, has, however, done its best to give opportunity a bad odor and correct this error.

Grandma used to say, "Nothing risked, nothing gained," and backed it up by adding, "God helps those who help themselves."

Undoubtedly, Grandma's view was prejudiced. Security is not uppermost in the mind of a woman who crosses the prairies in a covered wagon, sets up housekeeping in the wilderness, bears her children without benefit of doctors and takes those children to the fort when her husband has to go off occasionally to tend to an Indian raid.

Grandma was prejudiced in favor of opportunity. She always said it knocked at least once at every door. Today opportunity would have to knock the door down before it made any impression on the average householder, preoccupied with filling out his social security dossier.

Social security is a very fine item, indeed, and I am not giving it the back of my hand. I am merely contending that it has been oversold to a generation convinced that the only goal in life is security from birth to burial, and on the government, at that.

Once upon a time an umbrella sufficed for a rainy day. Now, a potential voter wants a written guarantee for a nine-room, water-repellent ranch-type house, with self-drying windows, built-in copper gutters, flood control and a blanket insurance policy covering fire, theft and acts of God.

Grandma used to say that the world didn't owe anyone a living. Today she would be regarded as a dangerous subversive and burned as a heretic. It isn't enough for candidates to promise two cars in every garage. The voter feels himself equally entitled to free oil, gas and repairs until he turns this year's candidate in on a new model that will also promise white-walled tires, uniformed chauffeur and no cross traffic.

Former Judge Harold R. Medina put the bee on security. The judge said he was shocked that boys out of college, instead of looking for opportunity, were squinting around for security, asking "personnel directors what the pension rights are and at what age they will be allowed to retire."

The judge shed another nugget, one every candidate would do well to put in his pipe and smoke, when he said, "The truth is that this do-nothing policy of playing everything safe is just about the worst thing that a person can do."

Amen!

And furthermore, no one can deny that the safest man in the world is the one in Alcatraz for life. Social security is what he ain't got nothing else but.

Don't Sell Us Short

Life is real, life is earnest, in this mid-twentieth century, and the grave may well be its goal. Nonetheless, I am not yet ready to toss in my hand to an eminent British medico. This doctor maintains that modern man, without the chicken solace of alcohol and the craven easement of tranquilizers, is unable to face the complexities, the uncertainties and the general temper of the times.

"Modern man cannot do without drink and drugs to survive. He takes drugs to overcome his mind and problems," Dr. B.G.B. Lucas told the Royal Institute of Public Health and Hygiene.

"The use of these drugs," said the doctor in a subsequent statement in reference to alcohol and tranquilizers, "is necessary for man's continued existence in our so-called civilized world. If he did not take them, he would commit suicide when things got too bad for him."

Oh, nuts, say I.

Granted that life in the sixties is no bowl of cherries, neither is it a punch bowl to be spiked with 100-proof Old Woodbine Twineth. There are days when I feel I should have stood in bed, such as those when the Reds are first to orbit a spaceman, the Congo acts up more than usual and Southeast Asia is so far out it's a puzzlement to understand what's really going on there.

Still, I believe Dr. Lucas is barking up the wrong juniper tree. Far from soothing the savage modern breast, alcoholic plenty simply drives man farther off his rocker. The Atomic Age is no bed of roses. But I doubt that we who are trying to make do in it feel any more terrified or overwhelmed by its problems than did our predecessors.

Times have been tough all over history, East or West, North or South. Somehow, man has stood up to them. I refuse to believe that my generation has to resort to the false courage of an alcoholic haze or a tranquilized daze to get through his three score and ten, plus.

Only one hundred years ago our ancestors, sober as judges, were settling the great West in the known face of Indian tortures and death on the trail. I question whether the threat of nuclear annihilation is any more nerve-wracking to me than the sight of an Indian war party, heading toward a wagon train, was to my great-grandmother and her sisters and brothers-in-law when they crossed the endless plains in a covered wagon.

I should hate to feel that I didn't have the "gumption," one of Great-Grandma's favorite words, to face up to the problems of my world as bravely as she faced up to the trials of hers. She did it on H_2O neat and without so much as an aspirin in the medical kit. Great-Grandmother Fulton would have advised a little git-up-and-go in meeting one's challenges rather than a martini with a Miltown float.

I doubt that gin is any substitute for intestinal fortitude or tranquilizers for patience and courage. I enjoy a cocktail before dinner, just a soupçon to disqualify me for the WCTU. But I reject it as a crutch.

Please Pass the Gravy

I'll never forget the fine, indignant article that Peter Edson, the Washington columnist, wrote a while back, asking the American citizen if and when he is finally going to get sufficiently angry about corruption in politics, in public life, and in the unions, to demand action and real reform.

In the last half dozen years this continuing corruption has been aired daily, in the press via the medium of crusading newspapers, in legislative committees on the state level and by Congressional investigative bodies on the national scene.

But very little has been done to correct the flagrant abuses. Certainly, the present Congress shows small intent to clean up its own premises or to risk even one gangster vote by forcing reform on some of the hoodlum-ridden unions.

In the United States, the living is easy all year round. It could be that we are so sunk in our own fat and good living that our anger or indignation quotient has dribbled away.

Perhaps I ought to do something about my tensions, for at the moment I am not only hopping mad about our laissez-faire attitude on corruption I am boiling over about the wastage of my tax or blood money on the city, state and national level.

In my present charitable mood I would like to give the Senate a wall-to-wall hiding instead of carpeting. The municipality, the state and the nation have the right to levy taxes on me to the extent necessary to enable them to function efficiently. But in return, I have the right to expect and demand that tax money be spent carefully and intelligently and not tossed around like ticker tape at a Broadway parade.

Everyone has his hands in the till except the taxpayer who doesn't belong to a bloc. In one way or another, millions of citizens are subsidized today. Grow wheat, join the armed forces for ninety-one days, drill for oil, build warehouses to store wheat, get your name on a union card and you have it made. Otherwise, you're dead at the tax office.

I guess I'm mad because I am a boob taxpayer who doesn't get a subsidy for anything.

In my lifetime I have heard so much favorable discussion of free enterprise that I would dearly love to see the United States give it an experimental try.

It is not a return to laissez-faire economics I crave, but a halt to leaping socialism. And just to prove that Fearless Fosdick is a quaking coward compared with me, I would, if I had the power, end any and all government subsidies at once.

That would send the whole nation, both the "haves" and "have-nots" into a tailspin. The "haves" who wouldn't have it (a subsidy) any more would be screaming like banshees until their voices gave out. And the "have-nots" who have been giving the "haves" a free ride for years, would be numb with joy.

I would un-subsidize everyone—and give the law of the market place, good old supply and demand, a chance to operate. Surely we couldn't be any worse off under free enterprise than under subsidy socialism, with which the nation runs up annual national deficits as high as $12 billion.

Under the subsidy system, we are certainly going for broke. Congress, which gives all these lovely, fat subsidies to the powerful minorities of which it lives in terror, goes on voting increases in the national debt ceiling. That ceiling is now so far up above the cloud line that I can't see it with a telescopic lens. But I think it is $285 billion. Next year, "East Lynne" and $300 billion. Mark my words, it will have to be raised to $300 billion to enable us to pay interest on the debt. This is known as a vicious circle in cold cash.

Oh, I'm a hardhearted Hannah, all right. I would cut everyone loose from his subsidy to sink or swim, survive or perish, in true Horatio Alger fashion. Maybe that would help dry up the river of surplus wheat and end the racket in storage facilities for the nation's surplus commodities. (There's even more money to be made now in storage or warehouse facilities than in agricultural surpluses.)

Maybe if subsidies ceased so would the American miracle of constantly decreasing farm population and constantly increasing farm surpluses. I would chop off airline and shipping subsidies before the railroads cut themselves in on this melon, as they are now threatening. And the oil and mineral depletion tax would be out the window.

Only veterans with service-connected disabilities, plus the widows and orphans of men who have died in the military service of the nation, would be generously cared for by the government. There would be no blanket subsidies in the way of free-for-all hospitalization and pensions. As for subsidization of repeated illegitimate motherhood, a subsidy of which taxpayers in every section of the country have complained, that would be out, too. These mothers-for-profit would go off the relief rolls, pronto, and their helpless children put in good homes to be reared in decency.

Unless this country is willing to give free enterprise a chance by abolishing subsidies and making everyone stand on his own two feet, we unsubsidized taxpayers will be supporting politically powerful

minorities the rest of our lives. It's obvious that we have no recourse
but to lick 'em or join 'em.

Alive and Kicking

In the past decade it has been increasingly difficult, on the eve of
December 31, to decide whether to wish everyone "Happy New
Year" or just sit down and wail.

Usually, it's been a lousy year and a lousy world. But I've got to be
honest about it: When faced with another December 31, there's never
been a minute when I haven't been glad to be alive and kicking. Perhaps one of the reasons I've been glad to be alive is that I can kick.
Kicking prerogatives have been receding in large segments of the
world for a long time. It's a privilege to be an American and able to
kick, complain and jay walk to one's heart's content.

There are times when it is most gratifying to be able to swing a cat,
even a dead one. We can still do that in the U.S.A., let the deceased
feline fall where it may. And the same goes with flowers. This is one
of the few countries left where bouquets and brickbats are still privileged matters.

No one has ever confused me with either Einstein or Pollyanna. But
I figure that as long as I'm alive, I might as well get a little pleasure out
of my predicament. Even a little fun. I can't see that a long face and
a sour one is going to improve my lot or solve the international situation. As long as I've got to put up with the world, it might as well be
mutual.

Common sense tells me it may be a little harder to make a home in
the coming year than in the last year. I wouldn't be surprised if most
of us eat chuck a bit oftener. And if we are reduced to chittlin's, why,
during World War II the majority of us—who weren't on C-rations
anyway—learned to cook just any cut we could get our hands on, so
a gourmet could hardly tell it from T-bone—much.

So if I am full of frustrations, it is not because I don't have a new fur coat or Cadillac, but because my government hasn't told me what vital duties I must perform, what small—by any measure—sacrifices I must make to see this New Year through the way I began it—as an American. At the moment I think American citizens are several light years ahead of their government, prepared to make ten times the sacrifices that the men in office are loath, or afraid, to ask of this great people.

And it is my conviction that the general frustrations we feel are the forcing ground of the Radical Right. Let the government set the American people a task or tasks commensurate with their power, their pride, their willingness, their great abilities and their deep love of their country, and the Radical Right will fade simultaneously as the frustrations disappear before a dedicated mission.

As the years pass, I become more and more understanding and tolerant of Abbé Sieyes. When asked at the close of the French Revolution what he had done during that cataclysmic event, the Abbé said "I lived."

When as a school girl I first read the Abbé's famous words, I felt he wasn't such-a-much, even though I knew he had played an active part in the Revolution up to the time of the Terror. After all the preliminary spade work he did for the Revolution, it seemed shameful, once the Terror began, that he faded into the woodwork in order to survive.

The heroes and villains then, as now, were larger than life size. It, too, was an age for greatness. So when I first made the Abbé's acquaintance, I felt he ought to have rushed about saving innocents, given Madame Lafayette a hand, and done something about that poor child, the Dauphin. But as the years go by and each one brings new complications that seem both menacing and insoluble, my feeling for the Abbé Sieyes grows more kindly. Perhaps he wasn't so much ignoble as unable to grapple with the magnitude of forces he helped unleash.

It is said that survival is an art consisting chiefly of not sticking the neck out. This may not be an admirable solution of the times, but it has the mark of sensibility. Who can say the Abbé wasn't sensible in his will to survive? I would still like him better if he had organized an underground to help the Sydney Cartons. But at least I don't despise him any longer, because I have a hunch that when I am ninety and my great-niece yells into my ear "What did *you* do during the Time of Troubles?" truth will force me to answer:

"I trod water."

Yet who does not long to be heroic, who does not dream of slaying the dragons of the twentieth century, who does not eagerly wait the clarion call to work that would restore law, order and peace of mind? We Americans look with eagerness to our leaders for the word that will inform us of the way to set all men on fire for the freedom we cherish.

There have been times, in the past, when I haven't been in love with officialdom, but I have never fallen out of love with my countrymen. Americans are dandy, and anyone may quote me. I wouldn't be surprised if conditions get worse for all of us before they get better. But we'll manage, given even a hint or a clue.

It is something to tread water, to keep the head above the flood. But for an American, that is not enough.

America the Beautiful

For some strange reason—perhaps because as a nation we are so young—we Americans share a wistful itch for international approval. We have a deep-seated yen to be elected Miss Universe by the world's other sovereign states.

Since the last war we have been told so often by our cosmic thinkers that no one likes a rich relative, particularly a global one, that we have developed a complex as big as a barrel.

"Does everyone overseas really hate us?" is a plaintive query put to me in a dozen different forms every time I fly home from Europe.

If everyone hates Americans, I am, happily, oblivious of the fact. And if anyone wants to slit my throat, he manfully refrains even from hinting at the project.

Perhaps this widespread belief at home that we are polecat-popular overseas stems from the fact that even our best friends abroad from time to time get sore as a boil over some United States policy or are deeply offended by some local blowhard, probably the very policy or blowhard that has caused half the American electorate to scream bloody murder over the morning coffee and vow to throw the rascals out.

But I do not and cannot believe that as man to man, our European allies hate our tripes and find us revolting in all things.

And one of the reasons I believe this is because of a Columbus, Ohio, schoolteacher who happily elected to tour Chartres the day I made a pilgrimage to its noble cathedral.

Let's call her Miss Smith, because she would be terribly embarrassed to have her good works made public. She was in her early sixties, was Miss Smith, and a blind man would have known that she was a schoolteacher. He would also have guessed instantly that here was a woman of greatness and shining character.

This was her first trip to Europe, for the Miss Smiths of America must save a lifetime for such a journey.

We lunched together at Chartres and, to make conversation, I asked Miss Smith where she planned to go after she had "done" France. England, she said, and added in a shy, excited rush of confidence, "I am going to see my adopted son for the first time!"

Her foster son, she explained under my prodding, was placed by his Warsaw family on one of the last planes to leave Poland as the Germans began their blitzkreig in 1939. Eventually he got to England, alone, friendless and penniless.

The Foster Parents Plan, then swinging into action, took charge of the boy (all his family eventually perished in the German furnaces and the Russian graveyards). Miss Smith wrote the group as soon as war was under way and asked to adopt a child, just any child in need.

And that is how she came to adopt a European boy, and to feed, clothe and see him through school.

Now the boy is a young man with a good job. All through the years, he has begged his "mother" to come visit him. Now she was on her way.

I have thought about Miss Smith and her adopted son ever since that sunny day at Chartres. And I thought of all the American Miss Smiths, and the Mr. and Mrs. Smiths, too, who adopted European and Asian orphans, or families, or whole villages, if they happened to be rich Smiths.

There are hundreds of thousands of Europeans who may not always love us as a nation, but who will never feel anything but love and gratitude for some Americans who, out of basic humanity and in disinterested kindness, have helped bind up war wounds with food, money, clothing and sympathy.

People around the world may get mad at Uncle Sam from time to time. But hate Americans? Not really. Not really; there are too many Miss Smiths.